KNOWING THE DOCTRINES
OF THE BIBLE

KNOWING THE DOCTRINES
OF THE BIBLE

By
MYER PEARLMAN

GOSPEL PUBLISHING HOUSE

Springfield, Missouri 65802

02-0534

22nd Printing 2002

International Standard Book Number 0-88243-534-5

Printed in the United States of America

CONTENTS

INTRODUCTION

We confidently expect that theology or doctrine will find its deserved place in religious thought and education. Whatever has been said, in recent years, derogatory to this branch of study, has been ill-timed in view of the world's great need of sober and satisfying truth. The truth about God and destiny and the way to eternal life can never be unimportant to an immortal being. If men think at all these are things that must press for consideration. They are age-long and race-old questions and can be forgotten only when the race has sunk into idiocy or lost the image of God.

"As a man thinketh in his heart so is he." All a man's life turns on what he thinks; and most of all on what he thinks of God.—David S. Clarke.

I. THE NATURE OF DOCTRINE

Christian doctrine (the word "doctrine" means literally "teaching" or "instruction") may be defined as the fundamental truths of the Bible arranged in systematic form. This study is also commonly called theology, which means literally "a treatise or reasoned discourse about God." (The two terms will be used interchangeably in this section.) Theology or doctrine may be described as the science which deals with our knowledge of God and His relations to man. It treats of all things in so far as they are related to God and the Divine purposes.

Why do we describe theology or doctrine as a "science"? Science is the systematic and logical arrangement of certified facts. Theology is called a science because it consists of facts relating to God and Divine things, presented in an orderly and logical manner.

What is the connection between theology and religion? Religion comes from a Latin word meaning "to bind"; religion represents those activities which bind man to God in a certain relationship. Theology is knowledge about God. Thus religion is practice, while theology is knowledge. Religion and theology should go together in the balanced experience; but in practice they are sometimes separated so that one may be a theologian without being truly religious and on the other hand one may be truly religious without possessing a systematic knowledge of doctrinal truth. "If ye know these things, happy are ye if ye do them," is God's message to the theologian. "Study to shew thyself approved unto God, a workman that needeth not to be ashamed, rightly dividing the word of truth" (2 Tim. 2:15), is God's message for the spiritual man.

What is the difference between a doctrine and a dogma? A doctrine is God's revelation of a truth as found in the Scriptures; dogma is man's statement of that truth as set forth in a creed.

II. THE VALUE OF DOCTRINE

1. Doctrinal knowledge supplies the need for an authoritative and systematic statement of truth.

There is a tendency in some quarters not only to minimize the value of doctrine but to dismiss it as outgrown and useless. However, as long as men think about the problems of existence they will feel the need of an authoritative and systematically arranged answer to these problems. Doctrine will always be necessary as long as men ask, Where did I come from, what am I, and whither am I going?

It is often said, "It does not matter what a man believes so long as he does right." This is one way of dismissing doctrine as having no importance in relation to life. But every person has a theology whether he knows it or not; man's actions are influenced by what he believes. For example, there would be a wide difference between the conduct of a ship's crew who knew that they were headed for a definite destination, and a crew who realized that they were drifting aimlessly without a definite course or destination.

Human life is a journey from time to eternity, and it matters much whether one believes that it is an aimless, meaningless journey, or one planned by man's Maker, and directed to a heavenly destiny.

2. Doctrinal knowledge is essential to the full development of Christian character.

Strong beliefs make for strong character; clear-cut beliefs make for clear-cut convictions. Of course, a person's doctrinal belief is not his religion any more than the backbone is the man's personality. But as good backbone is an essential part of a man's body, so a definite system of belief is an essential part of a man's religion. It has been well said that "a man does not need to wear his backbone in front of him, but he must have a backbone and a straight one or he will be a flexible if not a humpbacked Christian."

A French Unitarian preacher once made the statement: "Purity of heart and life is more important than correctness of opinion." To which another French preacher answered: "Healing is more important than the remedy; but without the remedy there would be no healing." Certainly it is more important to live the Christian life than to merely know Christian doctrine, but there would be no Christian experience if there were no Christian doctrine.

3. Doctrinal knowledge is a safeguard against error. Matt. 22:29; Gal. 1:6-9; 2 Tim. 4:2-4.

It is often said that the stars came before the science of astronomy, and that flowers existed before botany, and that life existed before biology, and that God existed before theology.

That is true. But men in their ignorance conceived superstitious notions about the stars, and the result was the false science of astrology. Men conceived false ideas about the plants, attributing virtues which they did not possess; and the result was witchcraft. Man in his blindness formed wrong conceptions of God, and the result was paganism with its superstitions and corruption.

But astronomy came with true principles about heavenly bodies and so exposed the errors of astrology; botany came with the truth about plants and so banished the errors of witchcraft. In like manner, Bible doctrine exposes false notions about God and His ways.

"Let no man think error in doctrine a slight practical evil," declared D. C. Hodge, the noted theologian. "No road to perdition has ever been more thronged than that of false doctrine. Error is a shield over the conscience, and a bandage over the eyes."

10

4. Doctrinal knowledge is a necessary part of the Christian teacher's equipment.

When a consignment of goods reaches a store the goods are unpacked and placed in their proper compartments and receptacles, so that they may be handled in an orderly manner. This is a rather homely illustration of one purpose of systematic study. The Bible indeed follows a central theme. But the various truths relating to its great theme are scattered throughout the various books. In order therefore to gain a comprehensive view of each doctrine, and impart it to others, one must gather the references relating to it and place them in compartments (topics) and in smaller receptacles (sub-topics).

III. THE CLASSIFICATION OF DOCTRINE

Theology includes many departments.

1. Exegetical theology (exegetical comes from a Greek word meaning to "draw out" the truth) seeks to ascertain the true meaning of the Scriptures. A knowledge of the original languages in which the Scriptures were written is involved in this department of theology.

2. Historical theology traces the history of the development of doctrinal interpretation. It involves the study of church history.

3. Dogmatic theology is the study of fundamentals of the faith as set forth in church creeds.

4. Biblical theology traces the progress of truth through the several books of the Bible, and describes the manner in which each writer presents the important doctrines.

For example: in studying the doctrine of the atonement according to this method one would study how the subject was dealt with in the various sections of the Bible—the Acts, Epistles, and Revelation. Or one would find out what Christ, Paul, Peter, James or John said about the

11

subject. Or one could ascertain what each book or section of the Scriptures taught concerning such doctrines as God, Christ, atonement, salvation and others.

5. Systematic theology. In this branch of study the Biblical teachings concerning God and man are arranged in topics, according to a definite system; for example, scriptures relating to the nature and work of Christ are classified under the heading, Doctrine of Christ.

The material contained in this book is a combination of Biblical and systematic theology. It is Biblical in that the truths are taken from the Scriptures and the study is guided by the questions: What do the Scriptures say (exposition), and what do the Scriptures mean (interpretation)? It is systematic in that the material is arranged according to a definite order.

IV. A SYSTEM OF DOCTRINE

According to what order shall the topics be arranged? No hard and fast rules may be laid down. There are many arrangements, each having its value. We shall try to follow an order based on God's redemptive dealings with man.

1. The Doctrine of the Scriptures. From what source shall we derive inerrant truth about God? Nature indeed reveals His existence, power and wisdom, but it tells of no way of pardon, provides no escape from sin and its consequences, supplies no incentive to holiness and contains no revelation of the future. We leave God's first book— Nature—and go to God's other Book—the Bible, where we find God's revelation concerning these matters.

On what grounds do we accept the Biblical view as being the right one? The answer to this question leads to the study of the nature, inspiration, accuracy and reliability of the Scriptures.

12

2. The Doctrine of God. We then seek to ascertain what the Scriptures teach about the greatest of all facts—the fact of God, His nature and existence.

3. The Doctrine of Angels. From the Creator we naturally pass to a study of His creatures, and so we consider the highest of His creatures, angels. This topic takes in also wicked angels, Satan and demons.

4. The Doctrine of Man. We do not dwell long on the subject of good and wicked spirits but come quickly to consider the Biblical view of man, for all truths in the Scriptures cluster round two focal points—God and man. Next in importance to the study of God is the study of man.

5. The Doctrine of Sin. The most tragic fact connected with man is sin and its consequences. The Scriptures tell us of its origin, nature, consequences and cure.

6. The Doctrine of Christ. The study of man's sin is followed by a study of the Person and Work of Christ, man's Saviour.

7. The Doctrine of the Atonement. Under this head we consider the facts which throw light on the meaning of Christ's supreme work on man's behalf.

8. The Doctrine of Salvation. How is the atonement applied to man's needs and made real in his experience? The facts supplying the answer are grouped under the doctrine of Salvation.

9. The Doctrine of the Holy Spirit. How is Christ's work for man made real in man? This is discussed in the doctrine of the nature and work of the Holy Spirit.

10. The Doctrine of the Church. Christ's disciples obviously need some kind of organization for the purposes of worship, instruction, fellowship and the propagation of the gospel. The New Testament tells us about the nature and work of this organization.

11. The Doctrine of the Last Things. It is natural to direct one's gaze into the future and ask how everything—life, history, the world—will end. All that has been revealed concerning the future is grouped under the heading of "The Last Things."

1

THE SCRIPTURES

"Heaven and earth shall pass away: but my words shall not pass away." "The grass withereth, and the flower fadeth: but the word of our Lord shall stand for ever." Matt. 24:35; Isa. 40:8.

"Destroy this volume, as the enemies of human happiness have vainly endeavored to do, and you render us profoundly ignorant of our Creator, of the formation of the world which we inhabit, of the origin and progenitors of our race, of our future destination, and consign us through life to the dominion of fancy, doubt, and conjecture. Destroy this volume, and you deprive us of the Christian religion, with all the animating consolations, hopes, and prospects which it affords, and leave us nothing but the choosing (miserable alternative!) between the cheerless gloom of infidelity and the monstrous shadows of paganism. Destroy this volume, and you unpeople heaven, bar forever its doors against the wretched posterity of Adam, restore to the king of terrors his fatal sting, bury hope in the same grave which receives our bodies, consign all who have died before us to eternal sleep or endless misery, and allow us to expect nothing at death but a similar fate. In a word, destroy this volume, and you take from us at once everything which prevents existence becoming of all curses the greatest; you blot out the sun, dry up the ocean, and take away the atmosphere of the moral world, and degrade man to a situation from which he may look up with envy to that of the brutes that perish."—Dr. Payson.

OUTLINE

I. THE NEED FOR THE SCRIPTURES.

1. Such a Revelation Is to Be Desired.
2. Such a Revelation Is to Be Expected.
3. Such a Revelation Would Be in Written Form.

II. THE INSPIRATION OF THE SCRIPTURES.

1. Divine and Not Merely Human.
2. Unique and Not Common.
3. Living and Not Mechanical.
4. Complete and Not Merely Partial.
5. Verbal and Not Merely Conceptual.

III. THE VERIFICATION OF THE SCRIPTURES.

1. They Claim to Be Inspired.
2. They Appear to Be Inspired.
3. They Are Felt to Be Inspired.
4. They Prove to Be Inspired.

I. THE NEED FOR THE SCRIPTURES

"What is truth?" asked Pilate, and his tone inferred that the search for it was vain and hopeless. If there be no authoritative guide to knowledge about God, man and the world, then Pilate was right.

But there is no need to grope in doubt and skepticism, for there is a Book—"the holy scriptures, which are able to make thee wise unto salvation through faith which is in Christ Jesus." 2. Tim. 3:15.

1. Such a Revelation Is to Be Desired.

The God who created the universe must be a God of wisdom, and a God of wisdom will certainly have a purpose for His creatures. To neglect this purpose would be folly and to defy it would be sin. But how may the Divine purpose be certainly known? History proves that mankind arrives at very different conclusions, and many people come to none. Experience shows that the problem cannot be solved by study alone. Some do not have the time, others, even if they have the desire, do not possess the ability: and even if successful their conclusion would be reached slowly and doubtfully. Wise men may build ladders of thought in the attempt to attain to heavenly truth, but the tallest ladder will always prove to be too short. "The world by wisdom (philosophy) knew not God." Truths that tell man how to pass from earth to heaven, must be sent down from heaven to earth. In other words, man needs a revelation.

2. Such a Revelation Is to Be Expected.

In Nature we have a revelation of God that may be grasped by reason. But when man is bound by sins and burdened in soul, Nature and reason are powerless to give light and relief. Let the men of Reason testify. Said Kant, one of the greatest thinkers of all times, "You do well to base your peace and piety on the Gospels, for in the Gospels alone is the source of deep spiritual truths, after reason has measured out its territory in vain." Another able philosopher, Hegel, when on his death bed would have no book read to him but his Bible. He said that if he were to prolong his life he would make this book his study, for in it he found what reason could not discover.

If, as we believe, there be a good God, it is reasonable to expect that He will grant a personal revelation of Himself to His creatures. Writes David S. Clarke:

> We cannot conceive that a natural father should forever conceal himself from his son, and never have communication with him. No more can we conceive of a good God who would withhold knowledge of His being and His will from creatures created in His own image. God has made man capable and desirous of knowing the reality of things, and will He withhold a revelation capable of satisfying that desire? Ancient Egyptian mythology tells of the fabled Sphinx who asked riddles of passers-by and killed them if they failed to answer. Surely a loving and wise God would not permit man to perish for lack of knowledge, baffled at the Riddle of the Universe.

And Dr. Hodges writes:

> The intelligence of God leads us to hope that He has adapted the means to the end, and that He will crown a religious nature with a supernatural religion. The benevolence of God leads us to hope that He will relieve the grievous bewilderment and avert the danger of His creatures. The righteousness of God leads us to hope that He will speak in distinct and authoritative tones to the conscience.

3. Such a Revelation Would Be Written.

It is reasonable that God should embody His message to man in a book. As Dr. Keyser says, "Books are the best method of preserving truth in its integrity and transmitting it from generation to generation. Memory and tradition are very untrustworthy. Therefore God acted with the greatest wisdom and also in the normal way in giving His revelation to men in book form. In no other way, so far as we can see, could He have imparted to mankind an infallible standard that would be available to all mankind and that would continue intact throughout the ages and from which all people could procure the same standard of faith and practice."

It is reasonable to expect that God would inspire His servants to record truths which could not have been discovered by human reason. And finally, it is reasonable to believe that God has providentially preserved the manuscripts of the Bible Scriptures and led His church to include in the canon only those books that had their origin in Divine inspiration.

II. THE INSPIRATION OF THE SCRIPTURES

That a religion without inspired writings could be Divine is a conceivable possibilty. As Professor Francis L. Patton observes:

If on simple historical testimony it can be proved that Jesus wrought miracles, uttered prophecies and proclaimed His divinity—if it can be shown that He was crucified to redeem sinners, that He rose again from the dead and that He made the destiny of men to hinge on their acceptance of Him as their Saviour—then whether the records be inspired or no, woe unto him who neglects so great salvation.

We need not, however, discuss further this possibility, for we are not left in any doubt concerning the matter. "All scripture is given by inspiration of God (literally, 'is God-breathed')," declares Paul. 2 Tim. 3:16. "For the prophecy came not in old time by the will of man," Peter writes, "but holy men of God spake as they were moved by the Holy Ghost." 2 Pet. 1:21.

Inspiration is defined by Webster as "the supernatural influence of the Spirit of God on the human mind, by which prophets and apostles and sacred writers were qualified to set forth Divine truth without any mixture of error."

According to Dr. Gaussen, it is the "inexplicable power which the Divine Spirit exercised over the authors of the Scriptures, to guide them even in the employment of the words they were to use, and to preserve them from all error as well as from every omission."

"Inspiration, as defined by Paul in this passage (2 Tim. 3:16) is the strong, conscious inbreathing of God into men, qualifying them to give utterance to truth," writes Dr. William Evans. "It is God speaking through men, and the Old Testament is therefore as much the Word of God as though God spoke every word of it. The Scriptures are the result of Divine inbreathing, just as human speech is uttered by breathing through man's mouth." Peter's declaration "may be said to intimate that the Holy Ghost was especially and miraculously present with and in the writers of Scriptures, revealing to them truths which they did not know before, and guiding them alike in their recording of these truths, and of the transactions of which they were eye and ear witnesses, so that they were enabled to present them with substantial accuracy to the minds of others."

One might gather from the reading of various creeds of Christendom that Christianity is a rather complicated affair, bristling with theological puzzles and cumbered with abstruse definitions. Such is not the case. The doctrines of the New Testament as originally set forth, are simple, and may be simply defined. But as time passed the church was confronted with erroneous and defective views of doctrines and was therefore obliged to hedge and protect them with definitions. From this process of exact and detailed definition arose the creeds. The doctrinal statements played an important and necessary part in the life of the church, and became a hindrance only when assent to them was substituted for a living faith.

The doctrine of inspiration as set forth in the Word is quite simple, but the advancing of erroneous and defective views has made it necessary to "fence" the doctrine with full and detailed definitions. Against certain theories, it is necessary to contend that inspiration of the Scriptures is:

1. Divine and Not Merely Human.

The modernist identifies the inspiration of the sacred writers with that spiritual insight and wisdom which is possessed by such men as Plato, Socrates, Browning, Shakespeare and other geniuses in the literary, philosophical and religious world. Inspiration is thus considered purely natural. This theory empties the word inspiration of all meaning, and is inconsistent with the unique and supernatural character of the Bible.

2. Unique and Not Common.

Some confuse inspiration with illumination. Illumination refers to the influence of the Holy Spirit, common to all Christians, which influence helps them to grasp the things of God. 1 Cor. 2:4; Matt. 16:17. They hold that such illumination is an adequate explanation of the origin of the Bible. There is a faculty in man, so they teach, by which man can know God—a kind of eye of the soul. As the godly men of old meditated upon God, the Divine Spirit quickened this faculty, giving it insight into the Divine mysteries.

Such illumination is promised to believers and has been experienced by them. But it is not the same as inspiration. We are told (1 Pet. 1:10-12) that at times the prophets received truths by inspiration and were denied illumination for the comprehension of those same truths. The Holy Spirit inspired their words, but did not see fit to grant the knowledge of the meaning of those words. Caiaphas is described as being a vehicle for an inspired message (howbeit unconsciously), while as yet his mind was not on God. At the moment he was inspired, but not illumined. John 11:49-52.

Note two specific differences between illumination and inspiration. (1) As to duration, illumination is, or can be, permanent. "The path of the just is as the shining light, that shineth more and more unto the perfect day." The anointing that the believer has received of the Holy One abides in him, says John. 1 John 2:20-27. On the other hand, inspiration was intermittent; the prophet could not prophesy at will, but was subject to the will of the Spirit. "For the prophecy came not in old time by the will of man," declares Peter, "but holy men of God spake as they were moved by the Holy Ghost." The suddenness of prophetic inspiration is implied by the common expression, "The word of the Lord came to such an one." A clear distinction is drawn between the true prophets who speak only as the word of the Lord comes to them and the false prophets who speak a message of their own devising. Jer. 14:14; 23:11, 16; Ezek. 13:2, 3. (2) Illumination admits of degrees, inspiration admits of none. People vary as to the degree of their illumination, some possessing a greater degree of insight than others. But in the case of inspiration, in the Bible sense, a person is either inspired or he is not.

3. Living and Not Mechanical.

Inspiration does not mean dictation, in the sense that the writers were passive, their faculties having no part whatsoever in the recording of the material; although it is true that some portions of the Scriptures were dictated, for example, the Ten Commandments and the Lord's Prayer. The very word inspiration excludes mere mechanical action, and mechanical action excludes inspiration. For example, a business man does not inspire a stenographer when he dictates letters to her. God did not speak through man as one would speak through a megaphone; His Divine Spirit used their faculties, so producing a perfectly Divine message which bore the marks of their individuality. It is the word of the Lord and yet in a sense, the word of Moses, or of Isaiah, or of Paul. "God has done nothing but by man; man has done nothing but by God. It is God speaking in man, God speaking by man, God speaking as man, God speaking for man."

The fact of Divine and human co-operation in the producing of an inspired message, is clear enough; but the "how" of the matter is beyond our observation. The interaction of even mind and body is a mystery to the wisest man; how much more the interaction of the Spirit of God and the spirit of man!

4. Complete and Not Merely Partial.

According to the theory of partial inspiration, the writers were preserved from error in matters necessary to salvation, but not in subjects like history, science, chronology and others. Therefore, according to this theory it would be more correct to say that "the Bible **contains** the word of God, rather than that it **is** the word of God."

This theory plunges us into a morass of uncertainty, for who can unerringly judge of what is and what is not essential to salvation? Where is the infallible authority to decide as to which part is the Word of God and which is not? And if the history of the Bible be false then the doctrine cannot be true, for Biblical doctrine is founded upon Biblical history. Finally, the Scriptures themselves claim full or plenary inspiration. Christ and His apostles apply the term "word of God" to the entire Old Testament.

5. Verbal and Not Merely Conceptual.

According to another view, God inspired the **thoughts** but not the words of the writers. That is, God inspired the **men,** and left them to their own judgment in the selection of words and expressions. But the Scriptural emphasis is not upon inspired **men** but on inspired **words.** "God . . . spake in time past unto the fathers by the prophets." Heb. 1:1. "Holy men of God spake as they were moved by the Holy Ghost." 2 Peter 1:21. Moreover, it is difficult to separate word and thought; a thought is an internal word ("Begin not to say within yourselves"; "The fool hath said in his heart") ; a word is a thought expressed. Divinely inspired thoughts would naturally be expressed in divinely inspired words. Paul tells us of "words . . . which the Holy Ghost teacheth." 1 Cor. 2:13. Finally, single words are cited as the basis of weighty doctrines. John 10:35; Matt. 22:42-45; Gal. 3:16; Heb. 12:26, 27.

Distinguish between revelation and inspiration. By revelation we mean that act of God by which He discloses what man could not find out for himself; by inspiration we mean that the writer is preserved from error in **recording** that revelation. For example, the Ten Commandments were **revealed** and Moses was inspired to record them in the Pentateuch.

Inspiration does not always imply revelation; for example, Moses was inspired to record events which he himself had witnessed and which were therefore within the scope of his own knowledge. Distinguish also between uninspired **words** and the inspired **record.** For example, many sayings of Satan are recorded in the Scriptures and we know that the devil was not God-inspired when he said them; but the **record** of those Satanic utterances is inspired.

III. THE VERIFICATION OF THE SCRIPTURES
1. They Claim to Be Inspired.

The Old Testament claims to have been written under special inspiration of God. The term "and God said," or its equivalent, is used over 2,600 times. The history, law, psalms, and prophecies, are said to have been written by men under special inspiration from God. See for example: Ex. 24:4; 34:28; Josh. 3:9; 2 Kings 17:13; Isa. 34:16; 59:21; Zech. 7:12; Psalm 78:1; Prov. 6:23. Christ Himself endorsed the Old Testament, quoted it and lived in harmony with its teachings. He endorsed its truth and authority (Matt. 5:18; John 10:35; Luke 18:31-33; 24:25, 44; Matt. 23:1, 2; 26:54), and so did the apostles. Luke 3:4; Rom. 3:2; 2 Tim. 3:16; Heb. 1:1; 2 Pet. 1:21; 3:2; Acts 1:16; 3:18; 1 Cor. 2:9-16.

Does the New Testament claim for itself a similar inspiration? In particular, the inspiration of the Gospels is guaranteed by the promise of Christ that the Spirit should bring to the minds of the apostles all things which He had taught them, and that the same Spirit should lead them into all truth. Everywhere the New Testament claims to give a fuller and clearer revelation of God than that given in the Old Testament, and authoritatively declares the abrogation of the old laws. Therefore, if the Old Testament is inspired so must be the New. Peter seems to place the writings of Paul on a level with those of the Old Testament (2 Pet. 3:15, 16), and Paul and the other apostles claim to speak with a Divine authority. 1 Cor. 2:13; 1 Cor. 14:31; 1 Thess. 2:13; 1 Thess. 4:2; 2 Pet. 3:2; 1 John 1:5; Rev. 1:1.

2. They Appear to Be Inspired.

The Scriptures claim to be inspired, and an examination of them reveals the fact that their character supports their claim. The Bible comes into court with a good record. As to authorship, it was written by men whose honesty and integrity cannot be questioned; as to contents, it contains the most sublime revelation of God that the world knows; as to influence, it has brought saving light to nations and individuals, and it possesses a never-failing power to lead men to God and to transfigure their characters; as to authority, it meets the need of a final court of appeal in religion, so that false cults find it necessary to quote its words in order to make an impression on the public.

To be specific, note: (1) Its accuracy. One finds a total absence of the absurdities found in other sacred books. We do not read, for example, of the earth hatched out of an egg with a given number of years for incubation, resting on a tortoise, the land surrounded by seven seas of salt water, juice of sugar cane, spiritous liquors, clarified butter, sour milk, etc. Writes Dr. D. S. Clarke, "There is a difference between the Bible and any other book that no man can fathom. The difference is caused by its origin." (2) Its unity. Consisting of sixty-six books, written by about forty different authors, over a period of about sixteen hundred years, and covering a variety of topics, it nevertheless carries a unity of theme and purpose that can be explained only by one superintending Mind. (3) How many books can stand even two readings? But the Bible can be read hundreds of times without its depths being fathomed or its losing its interest for the reader. (4) Its remarkable circulation, being translated into hundreds of languages, and read in most countries of the world. (5) Its timelessness. It is one of the most ancient of books, and yet the most modern. The human soul can never out·grow it. Bread is one of the most ancient of foods, and yet the most modern. As long as men are hungry they will want bread for the body; and as long as men yearn for God and things eternal they will want the Bible. (6) Its re·markable preservation in the face of persecution, and the opposition of science. "The hammers break, the anvil remains." (7) Its many fulfilled prophecies.

3. They Are Felt to Be Inspired.

"But you don't believe that book, do you?" said a professor of a New York college to a Christian lady who had been attending Bible classes. "Oh, yes," she answered, "I happen to have a personal acquaintance with the Author." She had stated a most weighty reason for believing the Bible to be the Word of God, namely, its appeal to our personal consciousness, speaking a tone which makes us feel that it comes from God.

The Roman church asserts that the Divine origin of the Scriptures depends, in the final analysis, on the testimony of the Church, which is considered an infallible guide in all matters of faith and practice. "As if the eternal and inviolable truth of God depended on the judgment of man!" declared John Calvin, the great Reformer. He declared further:

It is asserted that the church decides what reverence is due to Scripture, and what books are to be included in the sacred canon. . . . The question, "How shall we know that they came from God, unless we are assured thereof by the decision of the church?" is as foolish as the question, "How shall we discern light from darkness, white from black, bitter from sweet?"

The witness of the Spirit is superior to all arguments. God in His Word is the only adequate witness concerning Himself: and in like manner His Word will not find true credence in the hearts of men until it is sealed by the witness of the Spirit. The same Spirit that spoke by the Prophets must enter our heart to convince us that they faithfully delivered the message which He gave to them. Isa. 59:21.

Let this then be a settled point, that those who are inwardly taught by the Holy Spirit place firm reliance on Scripture; and that Scripture is its own evidence, and may not lawfully be subjected to proofs and arguments, but obtains by the testimony of the Spirit that confidence which it deserves.

Since this is the case why adduce external evidence of the accuracy of the Scriptures and of their general reliability? We do this first, **not in order** to believe that they are true, but **because** we feel that they **are** true; in the second place, it is natural and inspiring to be able to point to outward evidence of what we inwardly believe; finally, these proofs supply vehicles and containers, so to speak, wherewith we may convey our heart conviction in words, and so "be ready always to give an answer to every man that asketh you a reason of the hope that is in you." 1 Peter 3:15.

4. They Prove to Be Inspired.

Dr. Eugene Stock has said:

When I was a boy, I read a story which showed me the different ways in which we can be sure that this great library of Sacred Books, which we call the Bible, is really the Word of God, His Revelation to mankind. The writer of the story had been explaining three different kinds of evidence— the Historical, the Internal, and the Experimental. Then he told how he once sent a boy to the chemist's to get some phosphorus. The boy brought back a little packet; was it phosphorus? The boy reported that he went to the shop and asked for phosphorus; that the chemist went to his shelves, took some kind of stuff from a jar, put it in the little packet, and gave it to him, and that he had brought it straight back. That was the historical evidence that the packet had phosphorus in it. Then the gentleman opened the packet. The substance inside looked like phosphorus and smelled like phosphorus. That was the internal evidence. Then he put a light to it—"See how it burns!" that was the experimental evidence.

Intellectual defenses of the Bible have their place; but after all, the best argument is the practical one. The Bible has worked. It has influenced civilization, transformed lives, brought light, inspiration and comfort to millions. And its work continues.

2

GOD

We live in a universe whose immensity presupposes a mighty Maker and whose beauty, design and order point to a wise Lawgiver. But who made the Maker? We can keep going back from cause to effect, but we cannot keep going back forever without admitting a "Forever" being. That Forever Being is God, the Eternal One, the Cause and Source of every good thing which exists.

OUTLINE

I. THE EXISTENCE OF GOD.
1. His Existence Affirmed.
2. His Existence Proven.
   a. The argument from creation.
   b. The argument from design.
   c. The argument from man's nature.
   d. The argument from history.
   e. The argument from universal belief.
3. His Existence Denied.

II. THE NATURE OF GOD.
1. The Biblical View (The Names of God).
   a. Elohim.
   b. Jehovah.
   c. El.
   d. Adonai.
   e. Father.
2. Erroneous Beliefs.
   a. Agnosticism.
   b. Polytheism.
   c. Pantheism.
   d. Materialism.
   e. Deism.

III. THE ATTRIBUTES OF GOD.
1. Unrelated Attributes (God's Inner Nature).
   a. Spirituality.
   b. Infinity.
   c. Unity.
2. Active Attributes (God and the Universe).
   a. Omnipotence.
   b. Omnipresence.
   c. Omniscience.
   d. Wisdom.
   e. Sovereignty.
3. Moral Attributes (God and Moral Creatures).
   a. Holiness.
   b. Righteousness.
   c. Faithfulness.
   d. Mercy.
   e. Love.
   f. Goodness.

IV. THE TRINITY OF GOD.
1. The Doctrine Stated.
2. The Doctrine Defined.
3. The Doctrine Proven.
4. The Doctrine Illustrated.

I. THE EXISTENCE OF GOD
1. His Existence Affirmed.

The Scriptures nowhere attempt to prove the existence of God by formal proofs. It is assumed as an evident fact, and as a belief natural to man. The Scriptures nowhere set forth a series of proofs of His existence as a preliminary to faith; they declare the fact and call upon man to make the venture of faith. "He that cometh to God must believe that he is," is the Bible's starting point for man's dealing with God.

The Bible indeed speaks of men who say in their heart that there is no God, but these are "fools," that is, the practically ungodly, who would put God out of their thinking because they would put Him out of their lives. They belong to the large number of **practical** atheists, that is, those who live and speak as if there were no God; they far outnumber the **theoretical** atheists, that is, those who claim to hold to the intellectual belief that God does not exist. It has been pointed out that the statement, "There is no God," does not imply that God does not exist, but that He does not interfere in the affairs of the world: counting on His absence, men become "corrupt" and do abominably. Psalm 14. Writes Dr. A. B. Davidson:

No attempt is made to demonstrate God's existence because everywhere in the Bible God is set forth as known. There appears to be no passage in the Old Testament which represents men as reaching the knowledge of the existence of God through nature or the events of providence, although there are some passages which imply that false ideas of what God is may be corrected by the observation of nature and life. . . . The Old Testament as little thinks of arguing or proving that God may be known as it thinks of arguing that He exists. How should men think of arguing that God could be known when they were persuaded that they knew Him, when they knew that they were in fellowship with Him, when their consciousness and whole mind were filled and aglow with the thought of Him, and when they knew His Spirit moved them, enlightened them, and guided their whole history?

The idea of man reaching to a knowledge or fellowship of God through his own efforts is wholly foreign to the Old Testament. God speaks, He appears; man listens and beholds. God brings Himself nigh to men; He enters into a covenant or special relation with them; He lays commands upon them. They receive Him when He approaches: they accept His will and obey His behests. Moses and the prophets are nowhere represented as thoughtful minds reflecting on the Unseen and forming conclusions regarding it, or ascending to elevated conceptions of the Godhead. The Unseen manifests Himself before them, and they know it.

When a man says, "I know the President," he does not mean, "I know that the President exists," for that is assumed in his statement. In like manner the Biblical writers tell us that they know God, and that statement assumes His existence.

2. His Existence Proven.

If the Scriptures offer no reasoned demonstration of God's existence, why do we make the attempt? For the following reasons:

First, to convince genuine seekers after God, that is, people whose faith has been obscured by some difficulty, and who say, "I wish to believe in God; show me that it is reasonable to do so." But no amount of evidence will convince that person, who desiring to live in sin and selfishness, says, "I defy you to prove to me that God exists." After all, faith is a moral rather than an intellectual matter; if a person is not willing to pay the price he will sidestep any kind of evidence. Luke 16:31.

Second, to strengthen the faith of those who already believe. They study the proofs not in order to believe but because they believe. This faith is so precious to them that they welcome anything that increases and enriches it.

Finally, in order to enrich our knowledge of the nature of God, for what greater object of thought and study exists than He?

Where shall we find evidences of God's existence? In creation, human nature and human history. From these three spheres we deduce the following five evidences of God's existence:

The universe must have a First Cause or a Creator. (Cosmological argument, from the Greek word "cosmos," meaning "world.")

The design evident in the universe points to a Supreme Mind. (Teleological argument, from "teleos," meaning "design or purpose.")

Man's nature, with its urges and aspirations points to a personal Ruler. (Anthropological argument, from the Greek word "anthropos," meaning "man.")

Human history gives evidences of an overruling Providence. (Historical argument.)

The belief is universal. ("Common consent" argument.)

(a) The Argument from Creation. Reason tells us that the universe must have had a beginning. Every effect must have an adequate cause. The universe is an effect and therefore must have a cause. Consider the size of the universe. In the words of George W. Grey: "The universe as we picture it is a system of thousands and millions of galaxies. Each galaxy is a swarm of thousands and millions of stars. Toward the outer rim of one of these galaxies—the Milky Way—is a star of medium size and moderate temperature, already yellowing into old age—our sun." And to think that the sun is more than a million times larger than our little earth! Continues the same writer, "The sun is spinning a dizzy course toward the outer rim of the Milky Way at 12 miles per second, trailing the earth and all the other planets with it, and at the same time the solar system is being swung in a gigantic arc at 200 miles a second as the galaxy itself rotates like some colossal stellar pinwheel. . . . By photographing sections of the sky it is possible to take a census of the stars. At the Harvard College observatory I saw one photograph which includes the images of more than 200 Milky Ways—all recorded on a photographic plate of 14 by 17 inches. It is estimated that the number of galaxies composing the universe is of the order of 500 million million."

Consider our own little planet with its teeming forms of life revealing intelligence and design. The question naturally arises, How did it all begin? The question is natural, for our minds are so constituted as to expect that every effect must have a cause. We conclude then that the universe must have had a first Cause, or a Creator. "In the beginning—God." Gen. 1:1.

This argument is set forth in a homely way in the following incident:

Said a young skeptic to an elderly lady, "I once believed in God, but now, since studying philosophy and mathematics, I am convinced that God is but an empty word."

"Well," said the lady, "it is true that I have not learned these things, but since you have, can you tell me from whence this egg comes?"

"Why, of course, from a hen," was the reply.

"And where does the hen come from?"

"Why, from an egg."

Then the lady inquired, "May I ask which existed first, the hen or the egg?"

"The hen, of course," rejoined the young man.

"Oh, then, a hen must have existed without having come from an egg?"

"Oh, no, I should have said the egg was first."

"Then I suppose you mean that one egg existed without having come from a hen?"

The young man hesitated: "Well, you see—that is—of course, well, the hen was first!"

"Very well," said she. "Who made the first hen from which all succeeding eggs and hens have come?"

"What do you mean by all this?" he asked.

"Simply this," she replied, "I say that He who created the first egg or hen is the One who created the world. You can't explain the existence even of a hen or an egg without God, and yet you wish me to believe that you can explain the existence of the whole world without Him!"

(b) The Argument from Design. Design and beauty are evident in the universe; but design and beauty imply a designer; therefore the universe is the work of a Designer of sufficient intelligence and wisdom to account for them. The great clock at Strasbourg, has, in addition to the regular features of a clock, a combination of moons and planets moving through the days and months with the accuracy of the heavenly bodies, with its groups of figures that appear and disappear with equal regularity as the great clock strikes the hours. To suggest that there was no designer and that this "just happened," is to insult intelligence and reason. It is just as foolish to assume that the universe "just happened," or, in scientific language, that it was due "to the fortuitous concourse of atoms."

Supposing the composition of Pilgrim's Progress were to be described as follows: the author took a carload of printer's type and with a shovel threw it into the air. When it fell to the ground it naturally and gradually resolved itself into Bunyan's famous story. The most pronounced unbeliever would say, "Ridiculous!" And so say we to the assumptions of atheism.

Examination of a watch reveals that it bears the marks of design because the several parts are put together for a **purpose.** They are so arranged as to produce motion and this motion is so regulated as to tell the time of day. From this we infer two things: first, that the watch had a **maker,** and second, that this maker understood its construction, and **designed** it for the purpose of telling time. In like manner, we observe design and adaptation in the world and naturally conclude that it had a Maker who wisely designed it for the purposes it fulfills.

These conclusions would not be affected by the fact that we never saw a watch made; never saw a watchmaker; and had no idea how the work could be done. In similar manner, our conviction that the universe had a Designer is in nowise affected by the fact that we did not observe its construction, or that we never saw the Designer.

Again, our conclusion would not be altered should someone observe that "the watch is a result of the working of mechanical laws and is accounted for by the properties of matter." We should still consider it to be the work of a skillful watchmaker who made use of these laws and properties in order to enable the watch to run. In like manner, when we are told that the universe is simply due to the operation of the laws of nature, we are constrained to inquire, "Who designed and imposed and used these laws?" for a law implies a lawgiver.

Take an illustration from insect life. There is a particular type of beetle called the staghorn, of which there are two kinds, male and female. The male has magnificent horns twice as long as his body; the female has none. In the larva state they have to bury themselves in the earth and wait in silence and darkness for their transformation. They are of course mere grubs with no apparent difference, and yet one of them digs for itself a hole twice as deep as does the other. Why? In order that his horns may have room to grow and that he may come out with them unbroken and unimpaired. Now why should these apparently similar grubs act so differently? Who taught the

male staghorn to dig twice as deep as the female?
Did he reason it out for himself? No; God the
Creator implanted within that creature the in-
stinctive perception of what was for its highest
good.

Whence did the little grub get its wisdom?
It may be suggested that it inherited the wisdom
from its parent. But does a trained dog, for
example, pass on its tricks to its offspring? Even
if we admit that the instinct was inherited, it
would still remain true that someone must have
instructed the first staghorn. The explanation
of the wonderful instinct of creatures is found in
the words of the first chapter of Genesis, "And
God said,"—that is, the will of God. Our observation of the working of a watch convinces us that
the intelligence lies not in the watch but in the
maker. And, as we observe the remarkable instinct in the smallest of creatures, we conclude
that the intelligence is not in them primarily but
in their Maker, and that there is a Mind which
controls the smallest details of life.

Dr. Whitney, former president of the American Society and Fellow of the American Academy
of Arts and Sciences, once stated that "the magnet
repels another by the will of God, and no man
today can give a more precise answer." "What do
you mean by the will of God?" he was asked. Dr.
Whitney replied, "What do you mean by light?
. . . We have our corpuscular theory, and our wave
theory, and now our quantum theory; and they
are all just educated guesses. About as good an
explanation as any is to say that light travels by
the will of God. . . . The will of God, the law
which we discover, but cannot explain—that alone
is final."

Mr. A. J. Pace, cartoonist of the Sunday
School Times, tells of an interview with the late
Wilson J. Bentley, who was an expert in photo-
micrography (photographing what is seen through

a microscope). For over a third of a century this man had been photographing snow crystals, and after photographing thousands he noted three outstanding facts: first, that no two were alike; second, that each was a beautiful pattern; third, that invariably each was six-pointed. When asked how he accounted for this six-pointed symmetry, he answered:

"Of course, no one knows but God, but here is my own theory. As you know, snow crystals are formed from water-vapor at temperatures below freezing, and water is composed of three molecules, two of hydrogen combining with one of oxygen. Each molecule is charged with positive and negative electricity, the tendency of which is to polarize at opposite sides. The number three, you see, enters the business at the start."

"How may we account for all these curious dots and loops, and graceful curves, these delicately chiseled, beveled edges, all of them arranged about the center in perfect symmetry?" asked Pace.

He shrugged his shoulders and said, "Only the Artist who designed and fashioned them knows how it is done."

His remark about the "three at the start of the business" set me to thinking. May it not be that the triune God who fashions all the loveliness of creation has signed His "threeness" in these fragile stars of ice crystals as an artist signs his name to his masterpiece? On examination one instantly sees that the prevailing principle underlying the structure of the snowflake is that of the hexagon or six-sided figure, unique in all the realm of geometry in this respect, that the radius of the circumscribing circle is exactly the same length as each of the six sides of the hexagon. Thus we have six perfectly equilateral triangles gathered into a central nucleus, and all the angles are sixty degress, one third of all the area on one side of a straight line. What a fitting symbol of the triune God the triangle is! Here we have unity, one triangle but three lines each essential to the integrity of the whole.

Curiosity now impelled me to examine the references in the Bible containing the word "snow," and I found to my delight this same "threeness" inhering there. For example, there are 21 (3x7) references containing the noun "snow" in the Old Testament, and 3 in the New Testament, 24 in all. Then I found 3 references speaking of "leprosy white as snow." Three times cleansing from sin is likened to snow. I found 3 more speaking of raiment being of the "whiteness of snow." Three times the Son of God in appearance is likened to snow, but what was my amazement to find the Hebrew word for "snow" is made up of **threes** entirely! It is a fact, even though not generally known, that having no numerals both Hebrews and Greeks used the letters of their alphabet as numbers. Only the casual glance of a Hebrew at the word **sheleg** (Hebrew for "snow") would be needed to see that it reads 333 as well as "snow." The Hebrew for the first letter answering to our "SH" is 300, the second consonant "L" is 30, and the final one is our "G"—3. Add them and we have 333, three digits of three! Curious, isn't it? But why should we not expect mathematical exactness in a book plenarily inspired, and fully as wonderful as the world God has made?

Of God it is said: "Great things doeth He, which we cannot comprehend. For He saith to the snow, Fall thou on the earth." Job 37:5, 6, R. V. Here I have been two whole days trying to draw after His pattern six snow crystals with pen and ink, and I am dreadfully fatigued. How easily He does it all! "He **saith** to the snow"—He speaks and it is done. Try to imagine how many millions of billions of snow crystals can fall upon an acre of ground in an hour's time and imagine if you can the staggering fact that each crystal bears an individuality all its own, a design and a pattern without a duplicate in this or any other storm. "Such knowledge is too wonderful for me; it is high, I cannot attain unto it." Psalm 139:6. How can any thoughtful person in the presence of such evidence of design, multiplied by countless variations, doubt the existence, and the handiwork of a Designer, whose capabilities are measured only by infinity? A God who can do this, can do anything, even fashion and mold our lives into creations of beauty and symmetry.

(c) The Argument from Man's Nature. Man has a moral nature, that is, his life is regulated by conceptions of right and wrong. He knows there is a right course of action to be followed and a wrong course to be avoided. That knowledge is called "conscience." When he does right, conscience approves; when he does wrong, conscience condemns. Whether obeyed or not, conscience speaks with authority. Said Butler of the conscience: "Had it power as it has manifest authority it would govern the world; that is, if conscience had the power to enforce what it commands it would revolutionize the world." But alas! man has free will and therefore the power to disobey the inner voice. Even when misguided and unenlightened, conscience nevertheless speaks with authority, and makes man feel that he is a responsible being. "Two things fill my soul with awe," declared Kant the great German philosopher. "The starry heavens above me, and the moral law within me."

What conclusion is drawn from this universal consciousness of right and wrong? That there is a Lawgiver who has designed a standard of conduct for man and has made man's nature capable of understanding that standard. Conscience does not create the standard; it simply testifies to it, and registers either conformity or non-conformity. Who originally created those two mighty conceptions of Right and Wrong? God the Righteous Lawgiver! Sin has darkened the conscience and well nigh obliterated the law of man's being, but at Sinai God engraved that law in stone that man might have a perfect law wherewith to direct his life. The fact that man understands this law and feels a responsibility, argues the existence of a Lawgiver who created him that way.

And what conclusion may be drawn from the feeling of responsibility? That the Lawgiver is also a Judge who will reward the good and punish the wicked. He who imposed the law will finally vindicate that law.

Not only man's moral nature but his entire nature testifies to God's existence. Even the most

degraded of religions are but man's blind striving and groping after a something that his soul
craves. When a person is physically hungry we
know that the hunger argues for something that
can satisfy it; and when man hungers after God
that hunger argues for Someone or Something
that can satisfy it. The cry, "My soul thirsteth
for God" (Psalm 42:2) is an argument for God's
existence, for the soul would not deceive man by
thirsting for something that did not exist. As a
scholar of the ancient church once said: "Thou
hast made us for Thyself, and our heart is restless till it find rest in Thee."

(d) **The Argument from History.** The march
of events in the world's history gives evidence of
an overruling Power and Providence. All the
history of the Bible was written to reveal God in
history, that is, to illustrate God's workings in
human affairs. "The principles of God's moral
government are exhibited in the history of nations
as well as in the experience of men," writes D. S.
Clarke. (Psalm 75:7; Dan. 2:21; 5:21.) "English
Protestantism looks upon the defeat of the Span-
ish Armada as a Divine intervention. The settle-
ment of America by Protestant immigrants saved
it from the fate of South America and thereby
saved the world for democracy. Who will deny
that God's hand is in all this?" "The history of
mankind, the rise and fall of nations, like Babylon
and Rome, show that progress accompanies the
use of God-given faculties and obedience to God's
law, and that national decline and decay follow
disobedience." (D. L. Pierson.) A. T. Pierson, in
his book, the New Acts of the Apostles, sets forth
evidences of God's overruling providence in
modern missions.

Especially do God's dealings with individuals
evidence His active presence in the affairs of men.
Charles Bradlaugh, at one time England's outstanding atheist, challenged a Christian minister,

Charles Hugh Price, to a debate. It was accepted and the preacher added a challenge of his own.

"Since we know, Mr. Bradlaugh, that 'a man convinced against his will is of the same opinion still,' and since the debate as a matter of mental gymnastics will not likely convert any one, I propose to you that we bring some concrete evidences of the validity of the claims of Christianity in the form of men and women who have been redeemed from lives of sin and shame by the influence of Christianity and by atheism. I will bring one hundred such men and women, and I challenge you to do the same.

"If you cannot bring one hundred, Mr. Bradlaugh, to match my hundred, I will be satisfied if you will bring fifty men and women who will stand and testify that they have been lifted up from lives of shame by the influence of your atheistic teachings. If you cannot bring fifty, I challenge you to bring twenty people who will testify with shining faces, as my one hundred will, that they have a great new joy in a life of self-respect as a result of your atheistic teachings. If you cannot bring twenty, I will be satisfied if you bring ten. Nay, Mr. Bradlaugh, I challenge you to bring one, just one man or woman who will make such a testimony regarding the uplifting influence of your atheistic teachings. My redeemed men and women will bring an unanswerable proof to the saving power of Jesus Christ in the lives of those who have been redeemed from the slaveries of sin and shame. Perhaps, Mr. Bradlaugh, this will be the real demonstration of the validity of the claims of Christianity."

Mr. Bradlaugh withdrew his challenge!

(e) The Argument from Universal Belief. Belief in the existence of God is practically as widespread as the race, although it is often found in perverted and grotesque form and overlaid with superstitious ideas. This position has been challenged by some who contend that there are some races absolutely devoid of the idea of God. But Jevons, an expert on the subject of races and comparative religions, says that this view, "as every anthropologist knows, has gone to the limbo of dead controversies . . . all agree that there are no races however crude, which are destitute of all idea of religion." Even if the exceptions could be proven we know that the exception does not disprove the rule. For example, if there could be produced some human beings entirely destitute of all feelings of humanity and compassion, that would not prove that man was essentially an un-feeling creature. The presence of blind men in the world does not prove that man is not a see-ing creature. In the words of William Evans, "the fact that some nations do not have the multi-plication table does not do violence to arithmetic."

How did this universal belief originate? Most atheists seem to imagine that a group of clever theologians met in secret session, invented the idea of God and then presented it to the people. But the theologians did not invent God any more than the astronomers invented stars, or the botan-ists flowers. To be sure, the ancients had wrong ideas about the heavenly bodies, but that did not disprove the existence of heavenly bodies. And if mankind has held distorted ideas about God, it implies that there was a God about whom they could have wrong ideas.

This universal knowledge did not necessarily come through reasoning for there are reasoning men who deny God's existence. But it is evident that the same God who made Nature with its beauties and wonders made man capable of look-ing **through** Nature and seeing its Creator. "Be-cause that which may be known of God is mani-fest in them; for God hath shewed it unto them. For the invisible things of him from the creation of the world are clearly seen, being understood by the things that are made, even his eternal power and Godhead." Rom. 1:19, 20. God did not make the world without leaving hints, suggestions and tell-tale evidence of His handiwork. But "when they knew God, they glorified him not as God, neither were thankful; but became vain in their imaginations, and their foolish heart was darkened." Sin marred their vision, they lost sight of God, and instead of seeing God through the creature they ignored Him and worshiped the creature; and so began idolatry. But even this proved that man was a worshiping creature who must have some object to worship.

What does the universal belief in God prove? That man's nature is so constituted as to understand and appreciate that idea. As one writer has expressed it: "Man is incurably religious." This deep-seated belief has produced "religion," which in its broadest meaning includes: (1) The acceptance of the fact of the existence of a Being over and above the forces of nature. (2) A feeling of dependence upon God as controlling man's destiny, this feeling of dependence being awakened by the thought of his own weakness and littleness and the mightiness of the universe. (3) The conviction that friendly intercourse can be effected and that in this union he will find security and happiness. Thus we see that man is naturally constituted to believe in God's existence, to trust in His goodness and to worship in His presence.

This "religious sense" is not found in the lower creatures. For example, it would be vain to attempt to teach religion to the highest type of ape. But the lowest type of man may be taught about God. And why? The animal lacks a religious nature—is not made in God's image; man has a religious nature and must have some object to worship.

3. His Existence Denied.

Atheism consists in the absolute denial of God's existence. Some question whether there be real atheists, but if there are such, it cannot be shown that they are earnestly seeking God or that they are logically consistent.

Since atheists are opposed to the deepest and most fundamental convictions of the race, the burden of proof rests upon them. They cannot sincerely and logically claim to be atheists unless they can establish proof that God does not exist. Now it is undeniable that the evidence for the existence of God far outweighs the evidence against His existence. In this connection, Mr. D. S. Clarke writes:

> A little proof may show that there is a God, while no amount of proof that man can gather can ever prove that there is no God. The imprint of a bird's foot on a rock would prove that sometime a bird had visited the Atlantic seaboard. But before anyone can say that no bird has ever been there, he must know the whole history of the coast since life began on the globe. A little evidence may show that there is a God; before any man can say that there is no God he must analyze all the matter in the universe, he must track down all forces, mechanical, electrical, vital, mental and spiritual—he must hold converse with all spirits and understand them thoroughly; he must be in all points of space at every moment lest God somewhere and somehow elude his notice. He must be omnipotent, omnipresent and eternal, in fact he must himself be God before he can dogmatically afirm that there is no God.

Strange as it may sound, only God, whose existence the atheist denies, could have the ability to prove that there was no God!

Moreover, even the bare possibility that a moral Sovereign exists places a heavy responsibility upon man, and the atheistic conclusion should not be accepted until the non-existence of God has been demonstrated beyond a doubt.

The inconsistency of the atheistic position is seen in the fact that many atheists, when in danger or trouble, have prayed. The storm and stress of life have swept away their refuge of theories and revealed the foundations of their souls—and they have acted human. We say "human" because he who denies God's existence thwarts and suppresses the deepest instincts and finest impulses of the soul. As Pascal has said, "Atheism is a disease." When a man loses faith in God it is not due to any argument (no matter how logically his denial may be stated) but "to some inner disaster, betrayal, or neglect, or else some acid distilled in the soul has dissolved the pearl of great price."

The following incident, told by a Russian nobleman, will illustrate our point.

It was in November 1917, when the Bolsheviks overthrew the government of Kerensky and began a reign of terror. The nobleman was staying at his mother's home, in constant fear of arrest. The door-bell rang, and the servant who answered brought back a card bearing the name of Prince Kropotkin—the father of anarchism. He entered and asked permission to examine their apartment. There was nothing to do but to comply, for he evidently had authority to make the search and even to requisition the house.

"My mother let him pass ahead," says the narrator. "He entered one room and then another without stopping, as if he had lived there before or knew the arrangement of the lodgings. He entered the dining room, looked around and suddenly wended his way to the room that was occupied by my mother.

"'Oh, pardon me,' my mother said when the Prince was going to open the door, 'It is my sleeping room.'

"He stopped for a moment before the door, looked at my mother and then, as if embarrassed, with some vibration in his voice said quickly:

"'Yes, yes—I know. Excuse me—but I must enter this room.'

"He put his right hand on the door-knob and began to open the door slowly, then suddenly pulled the door and disappeared into the room.

"I was so excited by the Prince's behavior that I was tempted to reprimand him. I approached the room, flung open the door—and suddenly stood rooted to the spot. Prince Kropotkin was kneeling before the image-case in the room of my mother and was praying. I saw him making the sign of the cross, doing the genuflection. I did not see his face, nor his eyes, as I looked at him from behind. His kneeling figure, his ardent prayer, made him appear so humble as he whispered slowly the words of the prayer. He was so absorbed that he did not notice that he was not alone.

"Suddenly all my rage, my hatred toward this man had evaporated as a fog under the rays of the sun. I was so moved that I gently closed the door.

"Prince Kropotkin stayed in my mother's room about twenty minutes. At last he came out. He came out as a child who had fallen into error, not raising his eyes as if acknowledging his fault—but smiling. He came near my mother, took her hand, kissed it and then said in a very low voice·

" 'I thank you very much for allowing me to visit your house. Don't be angry with me. . . . You see—in that room my mother died. . . . It was a great solace to me, being in her room again. . . . Thank you—thank you very much.'

"His voice trembled, his eyes were damp. Quickly he took his leave and disappeared."

He was an anarchist, revolutionary, and atheist—but he prayed! Was it not evident that he had become an atheist only by crushing some of the deepest impulses of the soul?

Atheism is a crime against society, for it destroys the only adequate foundation for morality and righteousness—a personal God who holds man responsible for keeping His laws. If there be no God, there is no Divine law and all law is of man. But why should one live right because a mere man, or body of men, say so? There may be lofty souls who would do and be right without belief in God, but for the mass of mankind there is only one sanction for doing right and that is— "Thus saith the Lord," the Judge of the living and the dead, the mighty Ruler of our eternal destiny. To remove that is to tear up the foundations of human society. Remarks James M. Gillis:

The atheist is like some drunken lout who stumbles into a laboratory and starts fumbling with chemicals that may blow him and all about him into atoms . Indeed, the atheist is fooling with a force more mysterious and more powerful than anything that can be contained in a test-tube; more mysterious than the death-ray of science. What would ensue if the atheist really did extinguish belief in God cannot be imagined; in all the tragic history of this planet there has been no event that could serve as a symbol of that universal cataclysm

Atheism is a crime against man. It attempts to tear out of the heart of man his craving for the spiritual, his hunger and thirst for the infinite. Atheists protest against the crimes of religion, and we acknowledge that religion has been perverted by priestcraft and ecclesiasticism. But to attempt to blot out the idea of God because it has been abused is just as logical as attempting to root out love from man's heart because in some cases it has become perverted and debased.

II. THE NATURE OF GOD
1. The Biblical View.

Who and what is God? The best definition ever given is the one found in the Westminster Catechism: "God is a Spirit, infinite, eternal, and unchangeable in His being, wisdom, power, holiness, justice, goodness and truth." The Scriptural definition may be formulated from a study of the names of God. God's "name," in Scripture, means more than a combination of sounds; it stands for His revealed character. God reveals Himself by making known or proclaiming His name. Ex. 6:3; 33:19; 34:5, 6. To worship God is to call upon His name (Gen. 12:8), to fear it (Deut. 28:58), to praise it (2 Sam. 22:50), to glorify it. Psalm 86:9. It is wickedness to take His name in vain (Ex. 20:7) or to profane or blaspheme it. Lev. 18:21; 24:16. To reverence God is to sanctify or hallow His name. Matt. 6:9. God's name defends His people (Psalm 20:1), and for His name's sake He will not forsake them. 1 Sam. 12:22.

The following are the most common Scriptural names of God.

(a) Elohim (translated "God"). This word is employed wherever the creative power and omnipotence of God are described or implied. Elohim is the Creator-God. The plural form signifies fullness of power and foreshadows the Trinity.

(b) Jehovah (translated "Lord" in our version.) Elohim, the Creator-God, does not stand aloof from His creatures. Seeing their need He came down to help and save them; in assuming this relationship He reveals Himself as Jehovah, the covenant God. The name JEHOVAH comes from the verb TO BE and includes the three tenses of that verb—past, present, and future. The name therefore means: He who was, is, and is to come; in other words, the Eternal One. Since Jehovah is the God who reveals Himself to man the name means: I have manifested, do manifest, and will yet manifest Myself.

What God does for His people is expressed by His names, and when His people experience His grace then it is said that they "know His name." Jehovah's relationship to Israel is summed up in Jehovah's covenant names. To those upon beds of sickness He is known as JEHOVAH-RAPHA, "the Lord that healeth." Ex. 15:26. Pressed by the enemy they call upon JEHOVAH-NISSI, "the Lord our banner." Ex. 17:8-15. Cumbered with care, they learn that He is JEHOVAH-SHALOM, "the Lord our peace." Judg. 6:24. As pilgrims in the earth they feel the need of JEHOVAH RA'AH, "the Lord my shepherd." Psalm 23:1. Conscious of condemnation and needing justification they hopefully call upon JEHOVAH-TSIDKENU, "the Lord our right-

eousness." Jer. 23:6. When in need they learn that
he is JEHOVAH-JIREH, "the Lord who provides." Gen. 22:14. And when the kingdom of
God shall have come upon earth He shall be known
as JEHOVAH-SHAMMAH, "the Lord is there."
Ezek. 48:35.

(c) El ("God") is used in combinations: EL-
ELYON (Gen. 14:18-20), "the most high God," the
God who is exalted above that which is called god
or gods, EL-SHADDAI, "the God who is sufficient
for the needs of His people." Ex. 6:3. EL-OLAM,
"the everlasting God." Gen. 21:33.

(d) **Adonai** means literally "Lord" or "Master," and conveys the idea of rulership and dominion. Ex. 23:17; Isa. 10:16, 33. Because of
what He is and what He has done, He claims the
service and allegiance of His people. The name
is applied in the New Testament to the glorified
Christ.

(e) **Father** is employed in both the Old and
the New Testament. In its widest meaning it describes God as the Producer of all things and
Creator of man; so that, in the creative sense, all
may be called God's offspring. Acts 17:28. However, this relationship does not guarantee salvation. Only those who have been quickened into
new life by His Spirit are His children in the intimate and saving sense. John 1:12, 13.

2. Erroneous Views.

There are other views of God apart from the
Scriptures. Of these, some are overemphasized
truths; some, inadequate; others, perverted or
distorted. Why take time to consider such? Because it is very difficult perfectly to describe the
being of God, and by seeing what He is **not** we
shall be helped to a better understanding of what
He **is**.

(a) **Agnosticism** (from two Greek words

meaning "not knowing") denies the human ability to know God. "The finite mind cannot grasp the infinite," declares the agnostic. But he fails to see that there is a difference between knowing God absolutely and knowing some things about God. We cannot **comprehend** God, that is, know Him perfectly; but we can **apprehend** Him, that is, know **of** Him.

"We can know that God is, without knowing **all** that He is," writes D. S. Clarke. "We can touch the earth while not able to embrace it in our arms. The child can know God while the philosopher cannot find out the Almighty unto perfection."

The Scriptures are based upon the thought that God is knowable; on the other hand, they warn us that as yet "we know in part." Compare Ex. 33:20; Job 11:7; Rom. 11:33, 34; 1 Cor. 13:9-12.

(b) Polytheism (the worship of many gods) was characteristic of the ancient religions and is still practiced in many heathen lands. It is based on the idea that the universe is governed not by one force but by many, so that there is a god of water, a god of fire, a god of the mountains, a god of war, and so forth. This was the natural consequence of paganism, which made gods of finite objects and natural forces "and worshiped and served the creature more than the Creator." Rom. 1:25.

Abraham was called to separate himself from heathenism and become a witness to the one true God; and his call was the beginning of the mission of Israel, which was to preach monotheism (worship of one God) as opposed to the polytheism of the surrounding nations.

(c) Pantheism (from two Greek words meaning "all is God") is that system of thought which identifies God with the universe. Trees and stones, birds and animals, land and water, reptiles and man—all are declared parts of God, and God lives and expresses Himself through these substances and forces as the soul expresses itself through the body.

How did this system originate? Rom. 1:20-23 supplies a clue. It may be that in the dim past, pagan philosophers, having lost sight of God and having dismissed Him from their hearts, saw that it was necessary to find something to take His place. For man must worship something. To take the place of God, there must be something **as big** as God. God being gone from the world, why not let the **world** be God? So they reasoned, and so began the worship of mountains and trees, men and beasts, and all the forces of nature.

At first sight this nature worship may seem beautiful, but it involves an absurd conclusion. For if the tree and the flower and the star be God, then so also must be the worm, the microbe, the tiger, and the vilest sinner—an unthinkable conclusion!

Pantheism confounds God with nature. But the poem is not the poet, the art is not the artist, the music is not the musician, and the creation is not God. A beautiful Jewish tradition tells how Abraham saw the distinction.

When Abraham began to reflect on the nature of God, he at first took the stars for deities because of their luster and beauty. But when he realized that they were outshone by the moon he thought of the moon as Deity. The moon's light, however, faded before the light of the sun and made him think of the latter as Deity. Yet at night the sun also disappeared. "There must be something in the world greater than these constellations," mused Abraham. Thus from the worship of nature he rose to the worship of the God of nature.

The Scriptures correct the perverted view of pantheism. While teaching that God is revealed through nature, they distinguish God from nature.

Pantheists say that God is the universe; the Bible states that God made the universe.

Where is pantheism professed today? First, among some poets who speak of nature as Divine. Second, it underlies most of India's religions and is their justification for worshiping idols. "Is not the tree of the image part of God?" they argue. Third, Christian Science is a form of pantheism, for one of its fundamentals is, "God is all and all is God." Technically, it is "idealistic" pantheism, because it teaches that all is mind or "idea," and that matter is therefore unreal.

(d) Materialism denies any distinction between mind and matter and affirms that all manifestations of life and mind, and all forces, are simply properties of matter. "The brain secretes thought as the liver secretes bile"; "man is a machine," are some of the favorite sayings of materialists. "Man is simply an animal," they declare, in order to sweep aside the thought of man's higher nature and Divine destiny.

This theory seems so crude and absurd as hardly to deserve refutation. Yet, in scores of universities, in hundreds of novels, and in many other ways, the idea is being discussed and believed, that man is either a brute or a machine; that he is not responsible for his actions, and that there is neither good nor bad.

By way of refuting this error let us observe: (1) Our own consciousness tells us that we are more than matter and that we are different from a tree or a stone. An ounce of common sense is worth more than a load of philosophy. We are told that Daniel O'Connell, the Irish orator, once encountered an old Irish woman, who was feared because of her sharp tongue and blistering vocabulary. But the orator, in an encounter with her, overwhelmed the lady with a volley of trigonometrical terms: "You miserable rhomboid," he shouted, "you shameless hypotenuse! Every one knows that you keep a parallelogram in your house," and so he continued, until the poor woman became confused and bewildered. In like manner modern philosophers would attempt to terrify us with high-sounding words. But error does not become truth by being stated in five-syllable words. (2) Experience and observation show that life can come only from existing life and that therefore the life of this world had a living cause. No instance has been demonstrated of life coming from dead matter. Some years ago some scientific investigators thought that they had made this discovery, but when the presence of microbes in the air was discovered, their theory was spoiled! (3) The evidence of intelligence and design in the universe contradicts a blind materialism. (4) Granting that man is a machine, we know that a machine does not make itself. The machine did not produce the inventor, but the inventor created the machine.

The evil of materialism is seen in the fact that it destroys the foundation of morality. For if man be only a machine, he is not responsible for his actions. Consequently we cannot call the hero noble and the villain bad, for they cannot help acting as they do. Therefore one man cannot condemn another, for shall the buzz-saw say to the guillotine, "How can you be so cruel?"

What is the antidote for materialism? The gospel preached in the demonstration of the Spirit and with signs following!

(e) Deism admits that there is a personal God, who created the world; but insists that after Creation He left it to be governed by natural law. In other words, He wound the world up like a clock and then left it to run without further interference on His part. Hence no revelation or miracle is possible. This system is sometimes called Rationalism because it makes reason the supreme guide in religion; it is also described as Natural Religion, as opposed to Revealed Religion. This system is contradicted by the evidences of the inspiration of the Bible and the evidences of God's working in history.

The deist's view of God is one-sided. The Scriptures teach two important truths concerning God's relation to the world: First, His **transcendence,** meaning His separation from and exaltation above the world and man (Isa. 6:1); second, His **immanence,** meaning His presence in the world and nearness to man. Acts 17:28; Eph. 4:6. Deism overemphasizes the first truth, while pantheism overemphasizes the second. The Scriptures give the true and balanced view: God is indeed separate from and above the world; but on the other hand, He is in the world. He sent the Son to be **with** us, and the Son sent the Holy Spirit to be **in** us. Thus the doctrine of the Trinity avoids those two extremes. To the question, Is God out of the world or in the world? the Bible answers, Both.

III. THE ATTRIBUTES OF GOD

As God is infinite in His being, it is impossible for any creature to know Him exactly as He is. Yet He has graciously willed to reveal Himself in language that we can understand, and that revelation is contained in the Scriptures. For example, God says of Himself, "I am holy"; therefore we can say, God is holy. Holiness, then, is an attribute of God, because holiness is a quality that we may attribute or apply to Him. Thus we may regulate our thoughts about God with the help of the revelation God has given of Himself.

What is the difference between the names of God and the attributes of God? The names of God express His whole being, while His attributes indicate various sides of His character.

There are many things which may be said

of so great a Being as God, and our task will be made easier if we classify His attributes. To comprehend God fully would be like trying to carry the Atlantic Ocean in a teacup; but He has revealed Himself sufficiently to fill our capacity. The following classification may be found helpful:

1. Unrelated attributes, or what God is in Himself, apart from creation. They answer the question, What qualities characterized God before anything came into existence?

2. Active attributes, or what God is in relation to the universe.

3. Moral attributes, or what God is in relation to His moral beings.

1. God's Inner Nature (Unrelated Attributes).

(a) **God Is a Spirit.** John 4:24. God is a Spirit with personality; He thinks, feels, speaks, and therefore can have direct communion with His creatures made in His image. As a Spirit, God is not subject to the limitations to which possession of a body subjects human beings. He does not possess bodily parts or passions, is composed of no material elements, and is not subject to the conditions of natural existence. Hence He cannot be seen with natural eyes or apprehended by the natural senses.

This does not imply that God lives a shadowy, unsubstantial existence, for Jesus refers to God's "shape." John 5:37; compare Phil. 2:6. God is a real Person, but of so infinite a nature, that He cannot be fully apprehended by the human mind or adequately described by human language.

"No man hath seen God at any time," declares John (John 1:18; compare Ex. 33:20); yet in Ex. 24:9, 10 we read that Moses and certain elders "saw God." There is no contradiction; John means that no man has ever seen God **as He is.** But we know that spirit may be manifested in bodily form (Matt. 3:16); therefore God can manifest Himself in a way that can be apprehended by man. God also describes His infinite personality in language understood by finite minds; therefore the Bible speaks of God's having hand, arm, eyes and ears, and describes Him as seeing, feeling, hearing, repenting and so forth.

But God is unsearchable and inscrutible. "Canst thou find out the Almighty unto perfection?" (Job 11:7)—and our answer must be, "We have nothing to draw with, and the well is deep." John 4:11.

(b) God Is Infinite, that is, not subject to natural and human limitations. God's infinity may be viewed in two ways: (1) In relation to **space.** God is characterized by immensity (1 Kings 8:27); that is, the nature of the Godhead is equally present to the whole of infinite space and to every part of it. No part of existence is untouched by His presence and energy, and no point of space escapes His influence. "His center is everywhere, His circumference nowhere." Yet we must not forget that in one particular place His presence and glory are revealed in extraordinary manner; that place is heaven. (2) In relation to **time** God is eternal. Ex. 15:18; Deut. 33:27; Neh. 9:5; Psalm 90:2; Jer. 10:10; Rev. 4:8-10. He has existed from eternity and will exist to eternity. Past, present and future are present to His mind. Being eternal He is unchangeable—"the same yesterday, and to day, and for ever." This is a comforting truth to the believer, who may rest in the confidence that "The eternal God is thy refuge, and underneath are the everlasting arms." Deut. 33:27.

(c) God Is One. Ex. 20:3; Deut. 4:35, 39; 6:4; 1 Sam. 2:2; 2 Sam. 7:22; 1 Kings 8:60; 2 Kings 19:15; Neh. 9:6; Isa. 44:6-8; 1 Tim. 1:17. "Hear, O Israel: the Lord our God is one Lord," was a fundamental of Old Testament religion and was Israel's distinctive message to a world that worshiped many false gods.

Does this teaching of the unity of God conflict with the New Testament teaching of the Trinity? We must distinguish between two kinds of unity—**absolute** unity and **compound** unity. The expression "one man," conveys the thought of absolute unity, because we refer to one person. But when we read that man and wife shall be "one flesh" (Gen. 2:24), that is a compound unity, because a union of two persons is meant. Compare also Ezra 3:1; Ezek. 37:17; which scriptures employ the same word for "one" (echad) as used in Deut. 6:4. A different word (yachidh) is used to convey the idea of absolute oneness. Gen. 22:2, 12; Amos 8:10; Jer. 6:26; Zech. 12:10; Prov. 4:3; Judges 11:34.

What kind of unity is referred to in Deut. 6:4? From the fact that the word "our God" is in the plural (Elohim), we conclude that a compound unity may be inferred. The doctrine of the Trinity teaches the unity of God as a compound unity, including three Divine Persons united in eternal and essential unity.

2. God in Relation to the Universe (Active Attributes).

(a) God Is Omnipotent. Gen. 1:1; 17:1; 18:14; Ex. 15:7; Deut. 3:24; 32:39; 1 Chron. 16:25; Job 40:2; Isa. 40:12-15; Jer. 32:17; Ezek. 10:5; Dan. 3:17; 4:35; Amos 4:13; 5:8; Zech. 12:1; Matt. 19:26; Rev. 15:3; 19:6. God's omnipotence signifies two things: (1) His freedom and power to do all that is consistent with His nature. "For with God nothing shall be impossible." Of course this does not mean that He can or would do anything contrary to His own nature—for example, lie or steal; or that He would do anything absurd or self-contradictory, such as to make a triangular circle, or make dry water. (2) His control and sovereignty over all that is or can be done. But if this is so, why is evil practiced in the world? Because God has endowed man with a free will, which He will not violate; He therefore permits evil acts, but for a wise purpose, and with the prospect of ultimately overruling evil. Only God is Almighty and even Satan can do nothing without His permission. See Job, chapters 1 and 2.

All life is sustained by God' (Heb. 1:3; Acts 17:25, 28; Dan. 5:23); man's existence is like the note of an organ, lasting as long as God's fingers are on the keys. Therefore, every time a person sins he is using the Creator's own power to outrage Him.

(b) God Is Omnipresent, that is, unlimited by space. Gen. 28:15, 16; Deut. 4:39; Josh. 2:11; Psalm 139:7-10; Prov. 15:3, 11; Isa. 66:1; Jer. 23:23, 24; Amos 9:2-4, 6; Acts 7:48, 49; Eph. 1:23. What is the difference between immensity and omnipresence? Immensity is God's presence in relation to **space,** while omnipresence is His presence viewed in relation to **creatures.** He is present to His creatures in the following ways: (1) In glory, to the adoring hosts of heaven. Isa. 6:1-3; (2) Effectively, in the natural order. Nahum 1:3. (3) Providentially, in the affairs of men. Psalm 68:7-8. (4) Attentively, to those who seek Him. Matt. 18:19, 20; Acts 17:27. (5) Judicially, to the consciences of the wicked. Gen. 3:8; Psalm 68:1, 2. Man cannot hope to find a corner in the universe where he may escape the law of his Maker. "If your God is everywhere, then He must be in hell," said a Chinese to a native Christian. "His wrath is in hell," was the quick reply. We are told of an atheist who wrote, "God is nowhere." But his little daughter read it, "God is now here." It convicted him. (6) Bodily, in the Son. Col. 2:9. "God with us." (7) Mystically, in the church. Eph. 2:12-22. (8) Officially, with His workers. Matt. 28:19, 20.

While God **is** everywhere, He does not **dwell** everywhere. Only when He enters into **personal relationship** with a group or an individual is He said to **dwell** with them.

(c) God Is Omniscient, knowing all things. Gen. 18:18, 19; 2 Kings 8:10, 13; 1 Chron. 28:9; Psalm 94:9; 139:1-16; 147:4, 5; Prov. 15:3; Isa. 29:15, 16; 40:28; Jer. 1:4, 5; Ezek. 11:5; Dan. 2:22, 28; Amos 4:13; Luke 16:15; Acts 15:8, 18; Rom. 8:27, 29; 1 Cor. 3:20; 2 Tim. 2:19; Heb. 4:13; 1 Pet. 1:2; 1 John 3:20. God's knowledge is perfect, He does not have to reason, or find out things, or learn gradually—His knowledge of past, present and future is instantaneous.

There is great comfort in the consideration of this attribute. In all tests of life the believer may be sure that —"your Father knoweth." Matt. 6:8.

The following difficulty presents itself to some: since God knows all things, He knows who will be lost; therefore, how can a person help being lost? But God's knowledge of how an individual will use his free will does not force that person's choice. God foresees but does not fix.

(d) God Is Wise. Psalm 104:24; Prov. 3:19; Jer. 10:12; Dan. 2:20, 21; Rom. 11:33; 1 Cor. 1:24, 25, 30; 2:6, 7; Eph. 3:10; Col. 2:2, 3. God's wisdom is a combination of His omniscience and omnipotence. He has power to so apply His knowledge that the best possible purposes are realized by the best possible means. God always does the right thing, in the right way, and at the right time. "He hath done all things well."

When God designs all things and overrules the course of events for His own good purpose, this action is called Providence. God's **general** providence has to do with the government of the universe as a whole; His **particular** providence, with the details of man's life.

(e) God Is Sovereign; that is, He has an absolute right to govern and dispose of His creatures as He pleases. Dan. 4:35; Matt. 20:15; Rom. 9:21. He possesses this right by virtue of His infinite superiority, His absolute ownership of all, and the absolute dependence of all things on Him for their continuance. Therefore it is both foolish and wicked to criticize His ways. Observes D. S. Clarke:

> The doctrine of God's sovereignty is a most helpful and encouraging doctrine. If we had our choice, which should we choose—to be governed by blind fate, or capricious chance, or irrevocable natural law, or shortsighted and perverted self, or a God infinitely wise, holy, loving and powerful? He who rejects God's sovereignty may take his choice of what is left.

3. God in Relation to Moral Creatures (Moral Attributes).

Reviewing the record of God's dealings with mankind we learn that:

(a) God Is Holy. Ex. 15:11; Lev. 11:44, 45; 20:26; Josh. 24:19; 1 Sam. 2:2; Psalm 5:4; 111:9; 145:17; Isa. 6:3; 43:14, 15; Jer. 23:9; Luke 1:49; James 1:13; 1 Pet. 1:15, 16; Rev. 4:8; 15:3, 4. The holiness of God means His absolute moral purity; He can neither sin nor tolerate sin. The root meaning of "holy" is "separated." In what sense is God separated? He is separated from man in **space**—He is in heaven, man is on earth. He is separated from man in **nature and character** —He is perfect, man is imperfect; He is Divine, man is human; He is morally perfect, man is sinful. We see then that holiness is the attribute which guards the distinction between God and the creature. It denotes not merely an attribute of God, but the Divine nature itself. Therefore, when God reveals Himself in a way that impresses man with His Godhead, He is said to sanctify Himself (Ezek. 36:23; 38:23); that is, He reveals Himself as the Holy One. When the seraphim describe the Divine radiance emanating from Him that sits on the throne, they cry "Holy, holy, holy, is the Lord of hosts." Isa. 6:3.

Men are said to sanctify God when they honor and reverence Him as Divine. Num. 20:12; Lev. 10:3; Isa. 8:13. When they dishonor Him by the violation of His commandments they are said to "profane" His name—which is the opposite of sanctifying or hallowing (Matt. 6:9) His name.

Only God is holy in Himself. Holy people, buildings and objects are so described because God has **made** them holy, or sanctified them. The word "holy" applied to persons or objects is a term expressing a **relationship** to Jehovah—the fact of being set apart for His service. Having been thus set apart, articles must be clean; and persons must consecrate themselves to live according to the Law of Holiness. These facts constitute the basis of the doctrine of sanctification.

(b) God Is Righteous. What is the difference between holiness and righteousness? "Righteousness is holiness in action," is one answer. Righteousness is God's holiness manifested in right dealing with His creatures. "Shall not the Judge of all the earth do right?" Gen. 18:25. Righteousness is conformity to a right standard; it is right conduct in relation to others. When does God manifest this attribute? (1) When He clears the innocent and condemns the wicked and sees that justice is done. God judges, not as modern judges do, on evidence set before them by others; He discovers the evidence for Himself. Thus the Messiah, filled with the Divine Spirit, does not judge "after the sight of his eyes, neither reprove after the hearing of his ears," but judges with righteousness. Isa. 11:3. (2) When He pardons the penitent. Psalm 51:14; 1 John 1:9; Heb. 6:10. (3) When He chastises and judges His people. Isa. 8:17; Amos 3:2. (4) When He saves

His people. God's interposition on behalf of His people is called His righteousness. Isa. 46:13; 45:24, 25. Salvation is the negative side, righteousness is the positive. He delivers His people from their sins and their enemies, and the result is righteousness of heart. Isa. 60:21; 54:13; 61:10; 51:6. (5) When He gives victory to the cause of His faithful servants. Isa. 50:4-9. After God has delivered His people and judged the wicked we shall have "new heavens and a new earth, wherein dwelleth righteousness." 2 Pet. 3:13.

God not only deals righteously but He **requires** righteousness. But what if the man has sinned? Then He graciously imparts righteousness to (or justifies) the penitent. Rom. 4:5. This is the basis of the doctrine of justification.

It will be noted that the Divine nature is the basis of God's dealings with men. As He is, so He acts. The holy One sanctifies, the righteous One justifies.

(c) God Is Faithful. He is absolutely trustworthy, His words will not fail. Therefore His people may stand on His promises. Ex. 34:6; Num. 23:19; Deut. 4:31; Josh. 21:43-45; 23:14; 1 Sam. 15:29; Jer. 4:28; Isa. 25:1; Ezek. 12:25; Dan. 9:4; Mic. 7:20; Luke 18:7, 8; Rom. 3:4; 15:8; 1 Cor. 1:9; 10:13; 2 Cor. 1:20; 1 Thess. 5:24; 2 Thess. 3:3; 2 Tim. 2:13; Heb. 6:18; 10:23; 1 Pet. 4:19; Rev. 15:3.

(d) God Is Merciful. "God's mercy is the divine goodness exercised with respect to the miseries of His creatures, feeling for them, and making provision for their relief, and in the case of impenitent sinners, leading to long-suffering patience." (Hodges.) Tit. 3:5; Lam. 3:22; Dan. 9:9; Jer. 3:12; Psalm 32:5; Isa. 49:13; 54:7. For one of the most beautiful descriptions of the mercy of God see Psalm 103:8-18. The knowledge of His mercy becomes a ground of hope (Psalm

130:7) and a ground of trust. Psalm 52:8. God's mercy was pre-eminently manifested in sending Christ into the world. Luke 1:78.

(e) God Is Love. Love is the attribute of God by reason of which He desires a personal relation with those who bear His image, and especially with those who have been made holy and are like Him in character. Notice how God's love is described (Deut. 7:8; Eph. 2:4; Zeph. 3:17; Isa. 49:15, 16; Rom. 8:39; Hos. 11:4; Jer. 31:3); notice to whom it is manifested (John 3:16; 16:27; 17:23; Deut. 10:18); notice how it was exhibited. John 3:16; 1 John 4:9, 10; Rom. 9:11-13; 1 John 3:1; Isa. 43:3, 4; Isa. 63:9; Tit. 3:4-7; Isa. 38:17; Eph. 2:4, 5; Hos. 11:4; Deut. 7:13; Rom. 5:5.

(f) God Is Good. The goodness of God is that attribute by reason of which He imparts life and other blessings to His creatures. Psalm 25:8; Nahum 1:7; Psalm 145:9; Rom. 2:4; Matt. 5:45; Psalm 31:19; Acts 14:17; Psalm 68:10; 85:5. Writes Dr. Howard Agnew Johnson:

Some years ago I was invited to a home for dinner. The host asked me to say grace. After the blessing was asked and our thanks expressed for the gifts of God spread before us, he said rather bluntly: "Really now, I don't see much point to that: for I provided this meal myself." For reply we asked: "Had you ever stopped to think that if seedtime and harvest should fail once on the whole earth, half of the people would be dead before another harvest? And had it occurred to you that if seedtime and harvest should fail two years in succession over the entire planet, every one living would be dead before another harvest?" Evidently astonished, he admitted that he had never thought of such a possibility. Then we suggested that he was very much mistaken in saying that he had furnished the meal set before us. God had given him his own life and his power to get gain. God had put life into grain and animal which we were using for food, which he could never do.

We suggested that he had been a laborer together with God, by entering into God's laws for the provision of our needs. Then we said: "If any one should give you something, you would say 'Thank you!' and if the gifts should be repeated two or three times a day, you would say 'Thank you' each time." He quickly agreed. "Now, you understand why we say 'Thank you' to God each time we receive His blessings." To this he exclaimed: "Why, that is just being decent, to say nothing of being intelligently thankful!"

To some the existence of evil and suffering presents an obstacle to belief in the goodness of God. "Why did a God of love create a world with so much suffering?" they ask. The following considerations may cast some light on the problem: (1) God is not responsible for evil. If the careless workman throws sand into a delicate machine should the manufacturer be held responsible? God made everything good but man marred His work. Subtract from the suffering of the world all that is due to man's wilful sin, and there would not be so much left. (2) God being almighty, evil exists by His permission. We cannot, in every instance, understand why He permits evil, for "His ways are past finding out." To the overspeculative He would say, "What is that to thee? follow thou Me." Yet we can understand a part of His ways—sufficient to know that He makes no mistakes. Wrote Stevenson, the noted author, "If I from my spy-hole, looking with purblind eyes upon a least part of a fraction of the universe, yet perceive in my own destiny some broken evidences of a plan, and some signals of an overruling goodness; shall I then be so mad as to complain that all cannot be deciphered? Shall I not rather wonder with infinite and grateful surprise, that in so vast a scheme I seem to have been able to read, however little, and that little was encouraging to faith?" (3) God is so great that He can overrule evil for good. Remember how He overruled the wickedness of Joseph's brethren, Pharaoh, Herod, and those who rejected and crucified Christ. An ancient scholar has well said that "God Almighty would in no way permit evil in His works were He not so omnipotent and good that even out of evil He could work good." Many a Christian has come out of the fires of suffering with character purified and faith strengthened. Suffering has pressed them into the bosom of God. Suffering has been the coin wherewith they have bought character tried in the fire. (4) God has arranged the universe according to natural laws, and these laws imply the possibility of accidents. For example, if a person carelessly or deliberately steps off a precipice, he suffers the consequence of violating the law of gravity. Yet we are glad for these laws, for otherwise the world would be in a state of confusion. (5) It should always be remembered that this is not the perfect order of things. God has another life and a future age in which to vindicate all His dealings. Because He works according to "Heavenly Standard Time," we may think that He delays; yet He avenges His elect "speedily." Luke 18:7, 8. God must not be judged until the curtain has fallen on the last scene of the Drama of Ages. Then we shall see that "He hath done all things well."

IV. THE TRINITY OF GOD

1. The Doctrine Stated.

The Scriptures teach that God is One, and that beside Him there is no God. The question might arise, "How could God have any fellowship before finite creatures came into existence?" The answer is that the Divine Unity is a compound unity, and that in this unity there are really Three distinct Persons, every One of whom is the Godhead, and yet is supremely conscious of the other Two. So we see that there was an Eternal

Fellowship before any finite creatures were created; therefore, God was never alone.

Not that there are three Gods, all of whom are
independent and self-existing. The three co-
operate with one mind and purpose, so that in the
truest sense of the word they are "one." The
Father creates; the Son redeems, and the Holy
Spirit sanctifies; and yet in each operation the
Three are present. The Father is pre-eminently
Creator, yet the Son and the Spirit are described
as co-operating in that work. The Son is pre-
eminently the Redeemer, yet God the Father and
the Spirit are described as sending the Son to redeem. The Holy Spirit is the Sanctifier, yet the
Father and the Son co-operate in that work.

The Trinity is an eternal fellowship, but the
work of man's redemption called forth its historical manifestation. The Son entered the world
in a new way when He took to Himself human
nature, and He was given a new name, Jesus.
The Holy Spirit entered the world in a new way,
that is, as the Spirit of Christ, embodied in the
church. And yet all three worked together. The
Father testified of the Son (Matt. 3:17); and the
Son testified of the Father. John 5:19. The
Son testified of the Spirit (John 14:26), and later
the Spirit testified of the Son. John 15:26.

Does all this seem difficult of comprehension?
How could it be otherwise, since we are attempting to describe the inner life of Almighty God!
The doctrine of the Trinity is clearly a revealed
doctrine, and not one conceived by the human
reason. How else could we learn of the inner
nature of the Godhead except by revelation?
1 Cor. 2:16. It is true that the word "Trinity"
does not appear in the New Testament; it is a
theological expression, invented during the second
century to describe the Godhead. But the planet
Jupiter existed before it was so named; and the

doctrine of the Trinity was in the Bible before it was technically called the Trinity.

2. The Doctrine Defined.

We can quite understand why the doctrine of the Trinity was sometimes misunderstood and misstated. It was very difficult to find human terms in which to express the unity of the Godhead and at the same time the reality and distinctness of the Persons. In laying stress upon the reality of Christ's Deity and the personality of the Holy Spirit some writers seemed to be in danger of falling into Tritheism, or belief in three Gods. Other writers, laying stress on the unity of God, seemed in danger of forgetting the distinction of Persons. This last error is commonly known as Sabellianism, from Bishop Sabellius who taught that Father, Son, and Holy Spirit are simply three aspects or manifestations of God. This error has appeared many times in the history of the church and is current even today.

The doctrine is clearly unscriptural and is excluded by the sharp distinctions drawn in Scripture between the Father, Son, and Spirit. The Father loves and sends the Son; the Son leaves and returns to the Father. The Father and the Son send the Spirit; the Spirit intercedes with the Father. If, then, the Father, Son and Spirit are only God under different aspects or names, then the New Testament is a mass of confusion. For example, a reading of the intercessory prayer (John 17) with the thought in mind that Father, Son and Spirit are one Person, will reveal the absurdity of the doctrine: "As I have given myself power over all flesh, that I should give eternal life to as many as I have given myself . . . I have glorified myself on earth; I have finished the work which I gave myself to do. And now I glorify myself with my own self with the glory which I had with me before the world was."

How was the doctrine of the Trinity preserved from becoming overbalanced either on the side of Unity (Sabellianism) or on the side of Tri-unity (Tritheism)? By the formulation of **dogmas,** that is, interpretations which define the doctrine and "fence" it against error. The following example of dogma is found in the Athanasian Creed, formulated during the fifth century.

We worship one God in trinity, and trinity in unity. Neither confounding the persons, nor separating the substance. For the person of the Father is one, of the Son another, and of the Holy Ghost another. But of the Father, of the Son, and of the Holy Ghost there is one divinity, equal glory and coeternal majesty. What the Father is, the same is the Son, and the Holy Ghost. The Father is uncreated, the Son uncreated, the Holy Ghost uncreated. The Father is immense, the Son immense, the Holy Ghost immense. The Father is eternal, the Son eternal, the Holy Ghost eternal. And yet there are not three eternals, but one eternal. So there are not three (beings) uncreated, nor three immenses, but one uncreated, and one immense. In like manner the Father is omnipotent, the Son is omnipotent, the Holy Ghost is omnipotent. And yet there are not three omnipotents, but one omnipotent. Thus the Father is God, the Son is God, the Holy Ghost is God. And yet there are not three Gods, but one God. Thus the Father is Lord, the Son is Lord, and the Holy Ghost is Lord. Yet there are not three Lords, but one Lord. Because we are thus compelled by Christian verity to confess each person severally to be God and Lord; so we are prohibited from saying that there are three Gods or Lords. The Father was made from none, nor created, nor begotten. The Son is from the Father alone, neither made, nor created, but begotten. The Holy Ghost is from the Father and the Son, neither made, nor created, nor begotten, but proceeding. Therefore there is one Father, not three Fathers, one Son, not three Sons, one Holy Ghost, not three Holy Ghosts. And in this trinity there is nothing first or last; nothing greater or less. But all the three coeternal persons are coequal among themselves; so that through all, as is above said, both unity in trinity, and trinity in unity, is to be worshiped.

This statement may appear dry, involved and hair-splitting to us, but in the early days, it proved an effective means of preserving the correct statement of truths that were precious and vital to the church.

3. The Doctrine Proven.

Inasmuch as the doctrine of the Trinity concerns the inner nature of the Trinity, it could not be known except by revelation. That revelation is found in the Scriptures.

(a) The Old Testament. The Old Testament does not plainly and directly teach the Trinity, and the reason is evident. In a world where the worship of many gods was common, it was necessary to impress upon Israel the truth that God was One, and that there was none beside Him. Had the Trinity been directly taught in the beginning, it might have been misunderstood and misinterpreted.

But though not explicitly mentioned, the germ of the doctrine may be detected in the Old Testament. Every time a Hebrew uttered the name of God (Elohim) he was really saying "Gods," for the word is in the plural, and is sometimes used in the Hebrew with a plural adjective (Josh. 24:18, 19) and with a plural verb. Gen. 35:7. Let us imagine a devout and enlightened Hebrew pondering the fact that Jehovah is One, and yet He is Elohim—"Gods." He could conceivably be imagined as concluding that there was a plurality of persons within the one God. Paul the Apostle never ceased to believe in the unity of God as he had been taught it from his youth (1 Tim. 2:5; 1 Cor. 8:4); indeed, he insisted that he taught no other things but which were found in the Law and the Prophets. His God was the God of Abraham, Isaac, and Jacob. Yet he preaches the Deity of Christ (Phil. 2:6-8; 1 Tim. 3:16) and the personality of the Holy Spirit (Eph. 4:30), and puts three Persons together in the apostolic benediction. 2 Cor. 13:14.

Each member of the Trinity is mentioned in the Old Testament: (1) Father. Isa. 63:16; Mal. 2:10. (2) The Son of Jehovah. Psalm 45:6, 7; 2:6, 7, 12; Prov. 30:4. The Messiah is described with Divine titles. Jer. 23:5, 6; Isa. 9:6. Mention is made of the mysterious Angel of Jehovah who bears God's name and has power to either forgive or retain sins. Ex. 23:20, 21. (3) The Holy Spirit Gen. 1:2; Isa. 11:2, 3; 48:16; 61:1; 63:10.

Foreshadowings of the Trinity have been seen in the triple benediction of Num. 6:24-26 and the triple Doxology, Isa. 6:3.

(b) The New Testament. The early Christians held as a fundamental of their faith the fact of the unity of God. To both Jew and heathen they could testify, "We believe in one God." But at the same time they had the plain words of Jesus to prove that He claimed a position and an authority which it would have been blasphemy for Him to have claimed if He were not God, and the New Testament writers in referring to Jesus, used language which indicated that they recognized Jesus as "over all, God blessed for ever." Rom. 9:5. And the spiritual experience of Christians bore out and supported these claims. When they knew Jesus, they knew Him as God.

The same is true of God the Holy Ghost. The early Christians could not but believe that the Holy Ghost who dwelt in them, teaching them, guiding them, and inspiring them to newness of life, was no mere influence or feeling, but a Being whom they could know and between whom and their souls there could be real communion. And when they turned to the New Testament they found He was described as possessing the attributes of personality.

So the early church was confronted with two facts, that God is One, and that the Father is God, the Son is God, and the Holy Ghost is God. And these two great facts concerning God constitute the doctrine of the Trinity. God the Father was a reality to them; the Son was a reality to them, and so was the Holy Spirit. And the only conclusion that could be reached from these facts was that in the Godhead there was a real but mysterious distinction of personality, which distinction became manifest in the Divine work for man's redemption.

Several New Testament passages mention the three Divine Persons. Compare Matt. 3:16, 17; 28:19; John 14:16, 17, 26; 15:26; 2 Cor. 13:14; Gal. 4:6; Eph. 2:18; 2 Thess. 3:5; 1 Pet. 1:2; Eph. 1:3, 13; Heb. 9:14.

A comparison of texts taken from all parts of Scripture shows that: (1) Each of the three Persons is Creator, although it is stated that there is but one Creator. Job 33:4 and Isa. 44:24. (2) Each is called Jehovah (Deut. 6:4; Jer. 23:6; Ezek. 8:1, 3), the Lord (Rom. 10:12; Luke 2:11; 2 Cor. 3:18), the God of Israel (Matt. 15:31; Luke 1:16, 17; 2 Sam. 23:2, 3), the Lawgiver (Rom. 7:25; Gal. 6:2; Rom. 8:2; James 4:12), omnipresent (Jer. 23:24; Eph. 1:22; Psalm 139:7, 8), and the Source of Life (Deut. 30:20; Col. 3:4; Rom. 8:10). Yet it is affirmed that there is only one Being who may be thus described. (3) Each made mankind (Psalm 100:3; John 1:3; Job 33:4), quickens the dead (John 5:21; 6:33), raised Christ (1 Cor. 6:14; John 2:19; 1 Pet. 3:18), commissions the ministry (2 Cor. 3:5; 1 Tim. 1:12; Acts 20:28), sanctifies God's people (Jude 1; Heb. 2:11; Rom. 15:16), and performs all spiritual operations (1 Cor. 12:6;

Col. 3:11; 1 Cor. 12:11). Yet it is clear that but one God is capable of these things.

4. The Doctrine Illustrated.

How can three Persons be one God? is a question which puzzles many people. We do not wonder at their perplexity, for in considering the inner nature of the eternal God we are dealing with a form of existence much different from our own. Writes Dr. Peter Green:

Let us suppose that there was a being, some kind of an angel, or visitor from the planet Mars, who had never seen anything alive. How difficult he would find it to understand the fact of growth. He would easily understand how a thing can increase, so to speak, from outside, as a pile of stones becomes larger and larger as more stones are thrown on to it. But he would find it hard to understand how anything could grow, so to speak, from inside and by itself. The idea of growth would be to him a thing very hard to grasp. And if he were conceited, impatient, and unteachable, he would almost certainly fail to understand it.

Now let us suppose that this same strange being, having learned something about life and growth, as displayed in trees and plants, were introduced to a new fact, namely, that of intelligence, as displayed in the higher animals. How difficult he would find it to understand what is meant by liking and disliking, choosing and refusing, knowing or being ignorant. If life is hard to understand, how much more difficult is mind. Here, too, he would need to be humble, patient and teachable if he were to grasp these ideas. But as soon as he began to understand what is meant by mind and how it works, he would have to try to understand something higher than mind, as we find it in human beings. Here, again, he would be confronted with something new, strange, and not to be explained by reference to anything with which he had hitherto met. He would have to be careful, humble, and teachable.

He then, our angel or visitor from Mars, will expect, and we too shall do well to expect, that when we pass from considering the nature of man to considering the nature of God we shall find something new.

But there is a method whereby truths far above human reason may yet, in a measure, be made intelligible to the reason. We refer to the use of illustration or analogy. But these should be used with caution, and not pressed too far. "Every comparison limps," said a wise man of ancient Greece. At best they are imperfect and inadequate. They may be compared to tiny flashlights that help us glimpse the reasonableness of truths too vast for perfect comprehension.

Illustrations may be drawn from three sources: Nature; human personality; human relations.

(a) Nature furnishes many analogies. (1) Water is one, yet it is known in three forms— water, ice, and steam. (2) There is one electricity, yet in a street-car it works as motion, light, and heat. (3) The sun is one, yet is manifest as light, heat, and fire. (4) When St. Patrick was evangelizing the Irish he explained the doctrine of the Trinity with a three-leafed shamrock. (5) It has been pointed out that every beam of light has three rays: first, the actinic, which is invisible; second, the luminiferous, which is visible; third, the calorific, which gives heat, and is felt but not seen. Where these three are, there is light; where there is light, we have these three. John the Apostle said, "God is light." God the Father is invisible: He became visible in His Son; and He is operative in the world through the Spirit, who is invisible yet effective. (6) Three candles in one room will give but one light. (7) A triangle has three sides and three angles; take away one side and it is no longer a triangle Where there are three angles there is one triangle.

(b) Human Personality. (1) God said, "Let us make man in our image, after our likeness." Man is one, yet tripartite, consisting of spirit, soul, and body. (2) Human consciousness points to divisions in personality. Have we not at times become conscious of reasoning with ourselves and of ourselves listening to the conversation? I talk to myself, and I listen to myself talking to myself!

(c) Relationship. (1) God is love. He was eternally a Lóver. But love requires an object of love; and being eternal He must have had an eternal object of love, namely His Son. The eternal Lover and the eternal Beloved! And the eternal Bond and outflowing of that love is the Holy Spirit. (2) Our government is one, yet it has three branches: legislative, judicial, and executive.

3

ANGELS

Surrounding us is a spirit world, far more populous, powerful, and resourceful than our own visible world of human beings. Spirits, good and evil, wend their way in our midst. With lightning speed and noiseless movement they pass from place to place. They inhabit the spaces of the air about us. Some we know to be concerned for our welfare, others are set on our harm. The inspired writers draw aside the curtain and give us a glimpse of this invisible world, in order that we may be both encouraged and warned.

OUTLINE

I. **ANGELS.**

    1. **Their Nature.**
        a. **Creatures.**
        b. **Spirits.**
        c. **Immortal.**
        d. **Numerous.**
        e. **Sexless.**

    2. **Their Classification.**
        a. **The angel of the Lord.**
        b. **The archangel.**
        c. **Elect angels.**
        d. **Angels of the nations.**
        e. **Cherubim.**
        f. **Seraphim.**

    3. **Their Character.**
        a. **Obedient.**
        b. **Reverent.**
        c. **Wise.**
        d. **Meek.**
        e. **Mighty.**
        f. **Holy.**

    4. **Their Work.**
        a. **God's agents.**
        b. **God's messengers.**
        c. **God's servants.**

II. **SATAN.**

    1. **His Origin.**
    2. **His Character.**
    3. **His Activities.**
    4. **His Destiny.**

III. **WICKED SPIRITS.**

    1. **Fallen Angels.**
    2. **Demons.**

I. ANGELS

1. Their Nature.

The angels are—

(a) Creatures, that is, created beings. They were called forth out of nothing by the almighty power of God. We are not told the exact time of their creation, but we know that before man appeared, they had been long in existence, and that the rebellion of those under Satan had already taken place, leaving two classes—the good and evil angels. Being creatures, they refuse worship (Rev. 19:10; 22:8, 9), and man, on his part, is forbidden to worship them. Col. 2:18.

(b) Spirits. The angels are described as spirits, because unlike man, they are not limited by physical and natural conditions. They appear and disappear at will, and travel with unimagined rapidity without the use of natural means. Though purely spirits, they have the power to assume the form of human bodies in order to make their presence visible to the senses of men. Gen. 19:1-3.

(c) Immortal, that is, not subject to death. In Luke 20:34, 35, Jesus explains to the Sadducees that the resurrected saints will be like the angels in the sense that they cannot die any more.

(d) Numerous. The Scriptures teach that their number is very great. "Thousand thousands . . . and ten thousand times ten thousand." Dan. 7:10. "More than twelve legions of angels." Matt. 26:53. "Multitude of the heavenly host." Luke 2:13. "An innumerable company of angels." Heb. 12:22. Their Creator and Master is therefore described as the "Lord of hosts."

(e) Sexless. Angels are always described as male, but in reality they are sexless; they do not propagate their kind. Luke 20:34, 35.

2. Their Classification.

Since "order is the first law of heaven," it is to be expected that angels be classified according to rank and activity. Such classification is implied in 1 Peter 3:22, where we read of "angels and authorities and powers." Compare Col. 1:16; Eph. 1:20, 21.

(a) **The Angel of the Lord.** The manner in which "the Angel of the Lord" is described distinguishes him from any other angel. The power of pardoning or retaining transgressions is attributed to him, and the name of God is in him. Ex. 23:20-23. In Ex. 32:34 it is said: "Mine Angel shall go before thee"; which in Ex. 33:14 is varied: "My presence (literally, "my face") shall go with thee, and I will give thee rest." The two are combined in Isa. 63:9: "In all their affliction he was afflicted, and the angel of his presence saved them." Two important things are said concerning this angel: first, that Jehovah's name, that is, His revealed character, is in him; and that he is Jehovah's face, that is, the face of Jehovah may be seen in him. Hence he saves, and will not pardon transgression, though he has the power. Compare also Jacob's identification of the angel with God Himself. Gen. 32:30; 48:16. One cannot avoid the conclusion that this mysterious Angel is none other than the Son of God, the Messiah, the Deliverer of Israel and Saviour-to-be of the world. Therefore, the Angel of the Lord is really an uncreated being.

(b) **The Archangel.** Michael is mentioned as the archangel, or chief angel. Jude 9; Rev. 12:7; compare 1 Thess. 4:16. He appears as the guardian angel of the Israelitish nation. Dan. 12:1. The manner in which Gabriel is mentioned would also indicate that he also was of very high rank. He stands in the presence of God (Luke 1:19) and to him are committed messages of the highest import in relation to the kingdom of God. Dan. 8:16; 9:21.

(c) **"Elect Angels"** are probably those angels

who stood true to God during Satan's rebellion.
1 Tim. 5:21; Matt. 25:41.

(d) Angels of the Nations. Dan. 10:13, 20
seems to teach that every race has its guardian
angel, which is concerned with the welfare of that
nation. It was time for the Jews to return from
captivity (Dan. 9:1, 2), and Daniel set himself to
prayer and fasting for their return. After three
weeks an angel appeared and gave as a reason
for the delay the fact that the prince, or angel,
of Persia had opposed the return of the Jews, perhaps being reluctant to lose their influence for the
land of Persia. The angel tells him that in his
petition for the return of the Jews he had no sup-
porter except Michael the prince of the Hebrew
nation. 10:21. The prince of the Greeks was no
more inclined than the prince of the Persians to
favor the departure of the Jews. 10:20. The New
Testament word "principalities" may refer to
these angelic princes of the nations; it is used of
both good and bad angels. Eph. 3:10; Col. 2:15;
Eph. 6:12.

(e) The Cherubim appear to be a high rank
of angels connected with God's retributive (Gen.
3:24) and redemptive purposes (Ex. 25:22) concerning man. They are described as having the
face of a lion, man, ox and eagle, and this suggests that they represent creaturely perfection—
lion-like strength, man-like intelligence, eagle-like
speed, and ox-like service. Their composite form
and their nearness to God carry the assurance that
"the creature itself also shall be delivered from
the bondage of corruption." Rom. 8:21.

(f) The Seraphim are mentioned in Isaiah 6.
We know little about them. One writer thinks
that they constitute the very highest order of
angels, and that their distinguishing characteristic
is a most burning love for God (the word Seraphim means literally "burning ones").

3. Their Character.

(a) Obedient. They fulfill their commissions without question or hesitancy. Therefore we pray, "Thy will be done in earth, as it is in heaven." Matt. 6:10; compare Psalm 103:20; Jude 6; 1 Peter 3:22.

(b) Reverent. Their highest activity is the worship of God. Neh. 9:6; Phil. 2:9-11; Heb. 1:6.

(c) Wise. "As an angel . . . to discern good and bad," was a proverbial expression in Israel. 2 Sam. 14:17. Angelic intelligence exceeds that of men in this life, but is necessarily finite. Angels cannot directly discern our thoughts (1 Kings 8:39) and their knowledge of the mysteries of grace is limited. 1 Peter 1:12. Speculates one writer: "It is held that their intellectual images are so far more comprehensive than our own that a single image in the angelic mind may comprise more details than a lifetime of study might reveal to us here."

(d) Meek. They do not harbor personal resentments, neither do they rail against their opponents. 2 Peter 2:11; Jude 9.

(e) Mighty. They "excel in strength." Psalm 103:20.

(f) Holy. Being set apart by and for God, they are "holy angels." Rev. 14:10.

4. Their Work.

Angels are—

(a) God's Agents. They are mentioned as the executors of God's decrees of judgment. Gen. 3:24; Num. 22:22-27; Matt. 13:39, 41, 49; 16:27; 24:31; Mark 13:27; Gen. 19:1; 2 Sam. 24:16; 2 Kings 19:35; Acts 12:23.

(b) God's Messengers. (Angel means literally "messenger.") Through angels God sends: (1) Annunciations. Luke 1:11-20; Matt. 1:20, 21. (2) Warnings. Matt. 2:13; Heb. 2:2. (3) Instruction. Matt. 28:2-6; Acts 10:3; Dan. 4:13-17; (4)

Encouragement. Acts 27:23; Gen. 28:12. (5) Revelation. Acts 7:53; Gal. 3:19; Heb. 2:2; Dan. 9:21-27; Rev. 1:1.

(c) God's Servants. "Are they not all ministering spirits, sent forth to minister for them who shall be heirs of salvation?" Heb. 1:14. Angels are sent to sustain (Matt. 4:11; Luke 22:43; 1 Kings 19:5), to preserve (Gen. 16:7; 24:7; Ex. 23:20; Rev. 7:1), to deliver (Num. 20:16; Psalm 34:7; 91:11; Isa. 63:9; Dan. 6:22; Gen. 48:16; Matt. 26:53), to intercede (Zech. 1:12; Rev. 8:3, 4), to minister to the righteous after death. Luke 16:22.

Reading the above scriptures in the light of our Lord's words in Matt. 18:10, some have formulated the doctrine of "Guardian Angels," which teaches that each believer has a special angel assigned to guide and protect him through life. They contend that the words in Acts 12:15 imply that the first Christians so understood His words. We cannot be dogmatic about the matter; however, the promises of angelic help are sufficiently numerous and plain to prove a source of encouragement to every Christian.

II. SATAN.

Some people assure us that there is no such being as the devil; but after viewing the evil that is present in the world, simple folk will be excused for asking who is carrying on his business during his absence.

The Scriptures tell us of—

1. His Origin.

Read Isa. 14:12-15; Ezek. 28:12-19.

The popular conception of a horned, cloven-footed, hideous-looking devil is taken from pagan mythology and not from the Bible. According to the Scriptures, Satan was originally Lucifer (literally, "the light-bearer"), the most glorious of the angels. But he proudly aspired to be "like the most high," and fell into "the condemnation of the devil." 1 Tim. 3:6.

Notice the background of the accounts in Isaiah 14 and Ezekiel 28. People have wondered why the kings of Babylon and Tyre are first addressed, before the account of Satan's fall. One answer is that the prophet described Satan's fall for a practical purpose. Certain of the kings of Babylon and Tyre blasphemously claimed worship as Divine beings (compare Dan. 3:1-12; Rev. 13:15; Ezek. 28:2; and Acts 12:20-23), and made their subjects the playthings of their ruthless ambition. In order to warn such, God's inspired prophets drew the veil from the dim past and depicted the fall of the rebel angel, who said, "I will be like God." The lesson was: if God punished the blasphemous pride of this high angel, He will not fail to judge any king who dares to usurp the place of God. Notice how Satan tried to infect the first parents with his spirit. Compare Gen. 3:5 and Isa. 14:14. Note how disappointed pride and ambition still consume him, so that he desires to be worshiped (Matt. 4:9) as "god of this world" (2 Cor. 4:4), an ambition which will be temporarily satisfied when he becomes incarnate in Antichrist. Rev. 13:4.

As a penalty for his wickedness, Satan was cast out of heaven, together with a group of angels whom he had enlisted in his rebellion. Matt. 25:41; Rev. 12:7; Eph. 2:2; Matt. 12:24. He attempted to gain Eve as an ally, but God thwarted the plot and said, "I will put enmity between thee and the woman." Gen. 3:15.

2. His Character.

The quality of Satan's character is indicated by the names and titles by which he is known.

(a) **Satan** means literally "adversary," and pictures his malicious and persistent attempts to hinder God's purposes.

This opposition was especially manifest in his attemps to thwart God's plan by destroying the chosen line from which the Messiah was to come —an activity predicted in Gen. 3:15. And from the very beginning he has persisted in this effort. Cain, Eve's first son, "was of that wicked one and slew his brother." 1 John 3:12. God gave Eve another son, Seth, who became the appointed seed through whom earth's Deliverer should come. But the serpent's venom was still working in the race, and in the course of time the line of Seth yielded to evil influences and deteriorated. The result was that condition of universal wickedness which brought on the Flood. God's plan was not thwarted, however, for there was at least one righteous person, Noah, whose family became the fathers of a new race. Thus failed Satan's attempt to destroy mankind and so defeat God's purpose.

From Shem, Noah's son, was descended Abraham, the progenitor of a chosen people, through whom God should save the world. Naturally the Enemy's efforts would be directed against this particular family. One writer traces Satan's hidden opposition in the following incidents: Ishmael's opposition to Isaac; Esau's attempt to kill Jacob; Pharaoh's oppression of the Israelites.

Satan is described as seeking to destroy the church, in two ways: first, from within by the introduction of false teaching (1 Tim. 4:1; compare Matt. 13:38, 39) and from without by persecution (Rev. 2:10). The same was true of Israel, God's Old Testament church. The worship of the golden calf at the beginning of their national life is typical of what occurred constantly throughout their history; and in the book of Esther we have the example of an attempt to destroy the chosen people. But God's chosen people have survived both the taint of idolatry and the fury of the persecutor, because of the Divine grace which has always preserved a faithful remnant.

When, in the fullness of time, the Redeemer was born into the world, His death was planned by the wicked Herod. But once again God prevailed and Satan was frustrated. In the wilderness Satan attempted to hinder God's Anointed and to divert Him from His saving mission. But he was defeated; and his Conqueror "went about doing good, and healing all who were oppressed of the devil."

This great age-long conflict will reach its climax when Satan, incarnate in Antichrist, will be destroyed at the coming of Christ.

(b) Devil means literally "slanderer." Satan is so called because he slanders both God (Gen. 3:2, 4, 5) and man. Rev. 12:10; Job 1:9; Zech. 3:1, 2; Luke 22:31.

(c) Destroyer is the thought conveyed by "Apollyon" (Greek) and "Abaddon" (Hebrew). Rev. 9:11. Filled with hatred against the Creator and His works, the devil would set himself up as the Destroyer-god.

(d) Serpent. "That old serpent, called the Devil" (Rev. 12:9) recalls to our minds the one who, of old, used a serpent as the agent to bring about man's downfall.

(e) Tempter. Matt. 4:3. To "tempt" means literally to try or test, and the term is used also in connection with God's dealings (Gen. 22:1). But whereas God tests men for their good—to purify and develop character—Satan tempts them with the malicious design of destroying them.

(f) Prince and god of this world. John 12:31; 2 Cor. 4:4. These titles suggest his influences over society as organized apart from God's will ("the world"). "The whole world lieth in wickedness (in the power of the evil one)" (1 John 5:19), and is animated by his spirit. 1 John 2:16. The world, in the sense in which it is denounced in the Scriptures, "is that vast assemblage of human activities, whose triune god is honor, pleasure, profit. To these three it subordinates everything; the pursuit of these it endeavors by clever arguments to exalt and ennoble. It has at its back for this purpose the vast machinery of literature, business, commerce, government, which are constantly insinuating reverence for these three, holding them up as the object of honorable desire, and continually lauding those who attain them. It judges all things by exterior position and success, by false maxims of honor, by false ideas of the purpose of pleasure; and by false estimates of the value and dignity of wealth. It appeals to the lower part of our nature, investing itself with a false and materialistic refinement."

3. His Activities.

(a) **Their Nature.** Satan opposes God's work (1 Thess. 2:18), hinders the gospel (Matt. 13:19; 2 Cor. 4:4), possesses, blinds, deceives, and snares the wicked. Luke 22:3; 2 Cor. 4:4; Rev. 20:7, 8; 1 Tim. 3:7. He afflicts (Job 1:12) and tempts (1 Thess. 3:5) the saints of God.

He is described as being presumptuous (Matt. 4:4, 5), proud (1 Tim. 3:6), powerful (Eph. 2:2), malignant (Job 2:4), subtle (Gen. 3:1 and 2 Cor. 11:3), deceitful (Eph. 6:11), fierce and cruel. 1 Peter 5:8.

(b) **Their Sphere.** He does not confine his operations to the wicked and depraved. He often moves in the highest circles as an "angel of light." 2 Cor. 11:14. Indeed, that he attends religious gatherings is indicated by his presence at the angelic convention (Job, chapter 1), and by such terms as "doctrines of devils" (1 Tim. 4:1) and "the synagogue of Satan." Rev. 2:9. His agents often pose as "ministers of righteousness." 2 Cor. 11:15.

The reason for his frequenting religious meetings is his malicious determination to destroy the church, for he knows that once the salt of the earth has been robbed of its savor, mankind becomes an easier prey to his lawless spirit.

(c) Their Motive. Why is Satan so intent on our ruin? Answers Joseph Husslein: "He hates the image of God in us. He hates the very human nature we bear, which has been assumed by the Son of God. He hates the external glory of God, which we have been created to promote and thereby to attain our own unending happiness. He hates the happiness itself to which we are destined, because he himself has forfeited it forever. He hates us for a thousand reasons and envies us." As an ancient Jewish scribe has said, "But by the envy of the devil, death came into the world: and they that follow him are on his side."

(d) Their Limitation. While recognizing that Satan is strong, we should be careful not to exaggerate his power. For those who believe in Christ he is already a defeated foe (John 12:31), and he is strong only to those who yield to him. In spite of his blustering rage he is a coward, for James says, "Resist the devil, and he will flee from you." James 4:7. Power he has, but it is limited. He can neither tempt (Matt. 4:1), afflict (Job 1:16), kill (Job 2:6; Heb. 2:14), nor touch a believer without God's permission.

4. His Destiny.

In the very beginning God predicted and decreed the downfall of the power that had caused man's fall (Gen. 3:15), and the humbling of the serpent to the dust was a prophetic picture of the final degradation and defeat of "that old serpent the devil." Satan's career has indeed been downward. He was cast out of heaven in the beginning; during the Tribulation he will be cast from the heavenlies to the earth (Rev. 12:9); during the Millennium he will be imprisoned in the bottomless pit, and after a thousand years he will be cast into the lake of fire. Rev. 20:10. Thus God's Word assures us of the ultimate defeat of evil.

III. WICKED SPIRITS.

1. Fallen Angels.

The angels were created perfect and blameless, and like man, were endowed with power of choice. Under the leadership of Satan many of them sinned and were cast out of heaven. John 8:44; 2 Peter 2:4; Jude 6. The sin by which they and their leader fell was pride. Some have thought that the occasion of their rebellion was a revelation of the coming incarnation of the Son of God and of their obligation to worship Him.

The present abode of evil angels is described in Scripture as partly in hell (2 Peter 2:4) and partly in the world, especially in the air around us. John 12:31; 14:30; 2 Cor. 4:4; Rev 12:4, 7-9. By ensnaring men in sin they have acquired great power over them (2 Cor. 4:3, 4; Eph. 2:2; 6:11, 12); this power has been broken for those who are faithful to Christ, by the redemption which He has achieved. Rev. 5:9; 7:13, 14. Angels have never come under the provision for redemption (1 Peter 1:12), but hell has been prepared for their everlasting punishment. Matt. 25:41.

2. Demons.

The Scriptures do not describe the origin of demons; that question seems to be part of the mystery surrounding the origin of evil. But they testify very clearly to their real existence and activity. Matt. 12:26, 27. In the Gospels we see them as wicked disembodied spirits, which enter people who are thereupon said to have a demon. In some cases more than one demon takes up his abode in the same victim. Mark 16:9; Luke 8:2. The effects of their indwelling are madness, epilepsy, and other diseases, chiefly connected with the mental and nervous system. Matt. 9:33; 12:22; Mark 5:4, 5. The person who is under the influence of a demon is not master of himself; the evil spirit speaks through his lips or makes him dumb at his pleasure, drives him whither he wills and generally uses him as a tool, sometimes imparting for this a supernatural strength.

Writes Dr. Nevius, a missionary to China who has made a thorough study of demon-possession:

We notice in cases of demon-possession in China and those given in the Scripture, in some instances a kind of double consciousness, or actions and impulses directly opposite and contrary. A woman in Fuchow, though under the influence of a demon whose instinct was to shun the presence of Christ, was moved by an opposite influence to leave her home and come to Fuchow to seek help from Jesus.

The following are some conclusions of the same writer, based upon a study of demon-possession among the Chinese.

The most striking characteristic of these cases is that the subject evidences another personality, and the normal personality for the time being is partially or wholly dormant. The new personality presents traits of character utterly different from those which really belong to the subject in the normal state, and this change of character is with rare exceptions in the direction of moral perverseness and impurity. . . . Many persons while demon-possessed give evidence of knowledge which cannot be accounted for in ordinary ways. They often appear to know the Lord Jesus Christ as a divine person, and show an aversion to and a fear of Him.

Mark especially this good news:

Many cases of demon-possession have been cured by prayer to Christ, or in His name; some very readily, some with difficulty. So far as we have been able to discover, this method of cure has not failed in any case, however stubborn and long continued, in which it has been tried.

And in no instance, so far as appears, has the malady returned, if the subject has become a Christian and continued to lead a Christian life. . . . As a result of the comparison which has been made we see that the correspondence between the cases met with in China and those recorded in Scripture is complete and circumstantial, covering almost every point presented in the Scripture narrative.

What is the motive which influences demons to possess themselves of the bodies of men? Answers Dr. Nevius:

The Bible teaches clearly that in all Satan's dealings with our race his object is to deceive and ruin us by drawing our minds from God and inducing us to break God's laws and bring upon ourselves His displeasure. These objects are secured by demon-possession. Superhuman effects are produced, which to the ignorant and uninstructed seem divine. Divine worship and implicit obedience are demanded, and are enforced by the inflictions of physical distress and by false promises and fearful threats. In this way idolatrous rites and superstitions, interwoven with social and political customs, have usurped the place in almost every nation in history of the pure worship of God. (See 1 Cor. 10:20, 21; Rev. 9:20; Deut. 32:16; Isa. 65:3.) As regards the demons themselves it appears that they have additional personal reasons. The possession of human bodies seems to afford them a much desired place of rest and physical gratification. Our Saviour speaks of evil spirits walking through dry places and seeking rest, and especially desirous of finding rest in the bodies of the victims. When deprived of a place of rest in the bodies of human beings, they are represented as seeking it in the bodies of inferior animals. Matt. 12:43-45.

Said Martin Luther, "The devil is the ape of God." In other words, the Enemy is ever counterfeiting God's works. And surely demon-possession is a devilish travesty of that sublimest of experiences—the indwelling of the Holy Spirit in man. Notice some parallels: (1) Demon-possession means the introduction of a new personality into the victim's being, making him in a sense a new creature. Notice how the Gadarene demoniac (Matt. 8:29) acted and spoke as one controlled by another personality. He who is controlled by God has a Divine personality indwelling him. John 14:23. (2) Demon-inspired utterances are a satanic travesty on Spirit-inspired utterances. (3) It has been observed that when a person has consciously yielded himself to demon-power he often receives some gift such as fortune-telling, mediumship, etc. Writes Dr. Nevius, "In this stage the demonized subject has developed capacities for use, and is willing to be used. He is the trained, accustomed, voluntary slave of the demon." A satanic imitation of the gifts of the Holy Spirit! (4) Demoniacs often manifest extraordinary and superhuman strength—a satanic imitation of the power of the Holy Spirit.

Thus we see that the demonstrated possibility of demon-possession argues for the possibility of possession by the Divine Spirit. The Lord Jesus came into the world to deliver people from the power of evil spirits and put them under the control of God's Spirit.

4

MAN

Only God can truly reveal God. This self-revelation, so necessary for salvation, has been given through the Scriptures. From the same source we derive God's view of man, which is the true view, for who can know man like his Maker? In these days, when false philosophies are misrepresenting the nature of man, it is important that we be grounded in the true representation. Also, we shall be better able to understand the doctrines of sin, judgment, and salvation, which are based upon the Biblical view of man's nature.

OUTLINE

I. **THE ORIGIN OF MAN.**
1. Special Creation
   Versus
2. Evolution.

II. **THE NATURE OF MAN.**
1. The Human Tri-unity.
2. The Human Spirit.
3. The Human Soul.
   a. The nature of the soul.
   b. The origin of the soul.
   c. Soul and body.
   d. The soul and sin.
   e. The soul and the heart.
   f. The soul and blood.
4. The Human Body.
   a. A house.
   b. A sheath.
   c. A temple.

III. **GOD'S IMAGE IN MAN.**
1. Kinship with God.
2. Moral Character.
3. Reason.
4. Capacity for immortality.
5. Dominion over the Earth.

I. THE ORIGIN OF MAN

The Bible teaches plainly the doctrine of special creation, which means that God made every creature "after his kind." He created the various species and then left them to develop and progress according to the laws of their being. The distinction between man and the lower creatures is implied in the statement that "God created man in his own image."

Opposed to special creation is the theory of evolution which teaches that all forms of life developed from one form and that higher species developed from a lower, so that, for example, what was once a snail became a fish; what was once a fish became a reptile; what was once a reptile became a bird, and (passing on quickly) what was once an ape became a human being. The theory is as follows: Far back in the remote past there appeared matter and force—how and when science does not know. Within matter and force there appeared a life-cell—whence, no one knows. In this cell was a spark of life, and from this original cell all living things, from the vegetable to man, have originated, this development being controlled by inherent laws. These laws, in connection with environment, account for and explain the various species that have existed and that now exist, man included. So then, according to this theory, there has been a gradual and steady ascent from lower to higher forms of life until man was reached.

What is a species? A class of plants or animals which have characteristic properties in common and can be indefinitely propagated without changing those characteristics. A species may produce a **variety,** that is, one or more individual plants or animals possessing a striking peculiarity not common to the species generally. For example, a special type of race horse may be produced by skillful breeding; but it always remains a horse.

When a variety is produced and perpetuated through many generations we have a **race.** Thus in the canine (dog) species we have many breeds that differ considerably from one another; still, they retain certain characteristics that mark them as belonging to the dog family. Now when we read that God made every creature after his kind, we do not assert that God made them incapable of developing into new varieties; we mean that He made each species distinct and separate and placed a barrier between them, so that, for example, a horse should not so develop as to produce a race of creatures that could no longer be called horses.

What is the test by which the distinction of species is known? This: if animals can be paired together and so propagate indefinitely a fertile off-spring, they are of the same species; else, they are not. For example, horses and asses are known to be different species, because, although by crossing they generate the mule, the mule is incapable of generating another mule, and so producing the mule species. This fact runs counter to the evolutionary theory, for it shows plainly that God has placed a barrier in the way of one species developing into another.

Science has been defined as "verified knowl-edge." Is evolution a scientifically proven fact? The best worked out theory of evolution is that by Darwin; but the names of many distinguished scientists could be given who declare that Darwin's theory has been discarded, because it has not been verified. Writes Dr. Coppens:

Though scientists have now been at work for many years in exploring lands and seas, in examining the fossil remains of countless species of plants and animals, and in applying all the inventive genius of man to obtain and perpetuate new varieties and races, they have never yet been able to exhibit a single decisive proof that a trans-formation of species has ever taken place. Animals are now as they are represented on the pyramids or found mummified in the tombs of Egypt, as they were before they left their fossil forms in the rocks. Many species have become extinct, others are found of which no very ancient specimens have been discovered; but it cannot be proved that any species was ever evolved from another.

There is an impassable chasm between brute and man—between the highest form of animal and the lowest form of human life. No animal exists which uses tools, makes fire, employs articulate speech, or has the capacity for knowing spiritual things. But all these are present in the lower form of human life. The most intelligent ape is only an animal; the most degraded specimen of mankind is certainly a human.

Evolutionists have imagined a type of creature through which the ape passed into the human stage. This is the "missing link," which has been named Pithecanthropus Erectus. Evidence? Some years ago a few bones—two teeth, one thigh bone and a part of a skull cap—were discovered on the island of Java. With the addition of plaster of Paris they reconstructed the link which connects man with the lower creation! Other "links" have been constructed in similar fashion. But Dr. Etheridge, examiner of the British Museum, said, "In all this great museum there is not a particle of evidence of the transmutation of species. This museum is full of proofs of the utter falsity of these views."

Recently Nathan G. Moore has written what may be described as a lawyer's examination of the theory of evolution. His book is based on a survey of the facts set forth in some of the latest scientific works in favor of the theory. Since he belongs to a profession whose members are trained in the laws of evidence, his testimony is of practical value. This writer's purpose was "to collate the governing facts and submit to the judgment of the thoughtful reader, first, whether they fairly prove the hypothesis (an assumed explanation) that man is developed and not created; and second, whether there is any law or complex of laws which can explain the facts on natural grounds. After a detailed examination of the facts this lawyer comes to the following conclusion:

The evolutionary theory does not explain, nor help to explain, the origin of man, or help to prove that he developed from any lower form, even physically. It does not even suggest a method by which he acquired, or might have acquired, those higher qualities which distinguish him from other forms of life.

Another lawyer, Philip Mauro, thus sums up the kind of evidence presented by the proponents of the theory of evolution:

Imagine a litigant in court upon whom rests the burden of proof. He insists that the averments of his declaration are true, and demands a verdict in his favor; but he has no proof to sustain his allegations. In fact, all the evidence presented in court is against him. He demands, nevertheless, that judgment be rendered in his favor upon the supposition: (1) that volumes of proofs, which once existed ("missing links," etc.) have been destroyed, leaving no trace; and (2) that if those proofs could now be produced they would be found to be in his favor! Such is the absurd plight in which the theory of evolution now finds itself, as matters stand at present.

Evolutionists seek to link man with the brute creation; but Jesus Christ came into the world to link man with God. He took upon Himself our nature in order to glorify it for a heavenly destiny. To as many as receive Him, to them gives He power to become the sons of God (John 1:12); and those who share His Divine life become members of a new and higher race—even children of God. This new race, however ("new man," Eph. 2:15), came, not by human nature evolving into the Divine, but by the Divine entering into human nature. To those who have become "partakers of the divine nature" (2 Peter 1:4), John the apostle says, "Beloved, now are we the sons of God." 1 John 3:2.

II. THE NATURE OF MAN.
1. The Human Tri-unity.

According to Gen. 2:7 man is composed of two substances—the material substance, called his body, and the immaterial substance, or his soul. The soul gives life to the body, and when the soul is withdrawn the body dies.

But according to 1 Thess. 5:23 and Heb. 4:12 man is composed of three substances—spirit, soul. and body, and some Biblical scholars have con-tended for this three-part view as against the two-part doctrine of man's constitution held by other scholars.

Both views are correct when properly under-stood. Spirit and soul represent two sides of man's non-physical substance; or, to state it in other words, spirit and soul represent two modes in which the spiritual nature operates. Though sep-arate, spirit and soul are not **separable.** They per-meate and interpenetrate each other. Because they are so closely connected the words "spirit" and "soul" are often used interchangeably (Eccl. 12:7; Rev. 6:9); so that in one place man's spirit-ual substance is described as soul (Matt. 10:28), and in another place as spirit. James 2:26.

Though often used interchangeably, the terms spirit and soul have distinct meanings. For ex-ample: "Soul" is man viewed in relation to this present life. Deceased persons are described as "souls" when the writer is referring back to their previous life. Rev. 6:9, 10; 20:4. "Spirit" is the common description for those who have passed into the other life. Acts 23:9; 7:59; Heb. 12:23; Luke 23:46; 1 Peter 3:19. When persons are "caught up" temporarily out of the body (2 Cor.

12:2) they are described as being "in the spirit." Rev. 4:2; 17:3.

Because man is "spirit," he is capable of God-consciousness, and of communion with God; because he is "soul," he has self-consciousness; because he is "body," he has, through his senses, world-consciousness.—Scofield.

2. The Human Spirit.

Indwelling all flesh is a God-given spirit in an individual form. Num. 16:22; 27:16. This was fashioned by the Creator in the inward part of man's nature and is capable of renewal and development. Psalm 51:10. This spirit is the center and source of human life; the soul possesses and uses this life and expresses it through the body. In the beginning God breathed the spirit of life into an inanimate body and man "became a living soul." Thus soul is embodied spirit, or a human spirit operating through a body, the combination of both constituting man a "soul." The soul survives death because it is energized by the spirit, yet both soul and spirit are inseparable because spirit is woven into the very texture of soul. They are fused and welded into one substance.

The spirit is that which makes man differ from all known created things. It contains human life (and intelligence. Prov. 20:27; Job 32:8) as distinct from animal life. Animals have a soul (Gen. 1:20, in original) but not a spirit. In Eccl. 3:21 the reference seems to be to the principle of life in both man and beast. Solomon is recording a question he raised when he had departed from God. Unlike man, therefore, animals cannot know the things of God (1 Cor. 2:11; 14:2; Eph. 1:17; 4:23) and cannot enter into personal, responsible relations with Him. John 4:24. Man's spirit, when indwelt by God's Spirit (Rom. 8:16), becomes a center of worship (John 4:23, 24); of prayer, song, blessing (1 Cor. 14:15), and service. Rom. 1:9; Phil. 1:27.

The spirit, as representing man's higher nature, is connected with the quality of his character. What gains the mastery of his spirit becomes an attribute of his character. For example, if he allows pride to master him he has a "haughty spirit." Prov. 16:18. According to the respective influences that control him, a man may have a perverse spirit (Isa. 19:14), a provoked spirit (Psalm 106:33), a hasty spirit (Prov. 14:29), a troubled spirit (Gen. 41:8), a contrite and humble spirit. Isa. 57:15; Matt. 5:3. He may be under the spirit of bondage (Rom. 8:15), or impelled by the spirit of jealousy. Num. 5:14. He must therefore take heed to his spirit (Mal. 2:15), rule his spirit (Prov. 16:32), by repentance make himself a new spirit (Ezek. 18:31), and trust God to change his spirit. Ezek. 11:19.

When evil passions are in control and a person manifests a perverse spirit, it means that the soul-life (or the self-life or natural life) has dethroned the spirit. The spirit has fought and lost. The man is a prey to his natural senses and appetites, and is "carnal." The spirit is no longer in control, and its powerlessness is described as a state of death. Hence there is need for a new spirit (Ezek. 18:31; Psalm 51:10); and only He who originally breathed into man's **body** the breath of life can breathe into man's **soul** a new spiritual life—in other words, regenerate him. John 3:8; John 20:22; Col. 3:10. When this occurs man's spirit takes the place of ascendancy, and he becomes "spiritual." Yet, the spirit cannot live of itself but must seek constant renewal by God's Spirit.

3. The Human Soul.

(a) **The Nature of the Soul.** The soul is the life-giving and intelligent principle animating the human body, using the bodily senses as its agents in the exploration of material things, and the bodily organs for its self-expression and communication with the outside world. It originally came into being as a result of the supernatural inbreathing of God's Spirit. We may describe it as spiritual and living, because it came from God; we describe it as natural, because it operates through the body. Yet we must not think that the soul is **part** of God, for the soul sins. It is more correct to say that it is the gift and work of God. Zech. 12:1.

Four distinctions should be noted:

1. The soul distinguishes the life of man and beast from **inanimate** things and also from the **unconscious** life like that of plants.

Both man and beast have souls (in Gen. 1:20, the word "life" is "soul" in the original). We could say that plants have a soul (in the sense of a principle of life), but it is not a **conscious** soul.

2. Man's soul distinguishes him from animals. Animals have a soul, but it is an earthly soul which lives only as long as the body lasts. Eccles. 3:21. Man's soul is of a different quality because it is quickened by a human spirit. As "all flesh is not the same flesh," so it is with the soul; there is a human soul and an animal soul.

Obviously men do what lower animals cannot do, however intelligent they may be; their intelligence is one of instinct, not of reason. Both man and beast build houses. But man has gone on to build cathedrals, schools, and skyscrapers, while animals build today in precisely the same manner as they did when God created them. Animals may chatter (like the monkey), sing (like the bird), and talk (like the parrot); but only man produces art, literature, music, and scientific inventions. The instinct of animals may manifest the wisdom of their Maker, but only man can know and worship his Maker.

To further illustrate man's high place in the scale of life, let us distinguish four degrees of life, which rise in dignity one above the other as they become more independent of matter. First, vegetative life, which needs material organs to assimilate food; second, sensitive life, which uses the organs to perceive and contact material things; third, intellectual life, which perceives the meaning of things by logical thinking, and not merely by the senses; fourth, moral life, which concerns law and conduct. Animals have vegetative and sensitive life; man has vegetative, sensitive, intellectual, and moral life.

3. The soul distinguishes one man from another and thus forms the basis of individuality. The word "soul" is therefore frequently used in the sense of "person." In Ex. 1:5, "seventy souls" means "seventy persons." In Rom. 13:1, "every soul" means "every person." We today have adopted this usage, as for example, when we say, "Not a soul was present."

4. The soul distinguishes man not only from the lower orders but also from the higher orders of life. We find no reference to a soul in angels, because they do not have bodies similar to those of human beings. Man became a "living soul," that is, a soul permeating an earthly body subject to earthly conditions. Angels are described as spirits (Heb. 1:14), because they are not subject to material conditions or limitations. For a similar reason God is called "a Spirit." But angels are created and finite spirits, while God is the eternal and infinite Spirit.

(b) The Origin of the Soul. We know that the first soul came into existence as a result of God's breathing into man the breath of life. But how have souls come into being since that time? Bible students are divided between two views: (1) One group affirms that each individual soul is not received from parents but by immediate Divine creation. They cite the following scriptures: Isa. 57:16; Eccl. 12:7; Heb. 12:9; Zech. 12:1. (2)

Others think that the soul is transmitted from the parent. They point out that the transmission of sinful nature from Adam to posterity militates against the Divine creation of each soul; also the fact that parental characteristics are passed on to the offspring. They cite the following scriptures: John 1:13; John 3:6; Rom. 5:12; 1 Cor. 15:22; Eph. 2:3; Heb. 7:10.

The origin of each soul may be explained by the **co-operation** of both Creator and parents. In the beginning of a new life, a Divine creation and a creative use of means work together. Man begets man in co-operation with "the Father of spirits." God's power controls and permeates the world (Acts 17:28; Heb. 1:3) so that all creatures come into being according to the laws He has ordained. Therefore the normal processes of human reproduction set in motion those Divine laws of life which cause a human soul to be born into the world.

The origin of all forms of life is veiled in mystery (Eccles. 11:5; Psalm 139:13-16; Job 10:8-12), and this fact should warn us against speculating beyond the limits of Scriptural statements.

(c) Soul and Body. The relationship of soul to body may be described and illustrated as follows:

1. The soul is the holder of life; it figures in all that pertains to the sustaining, risking, and loss of life. That is why in many cases the word "soul" has been translated "life." Compare Gen. 9:5; 1 Kings 19:3; 1 Kings 2:23; Prov. 7:23; Ex. 21:23; Ex. 21:30; 30:12; Acts 15:26. Life is the permeation of body with soul. When the soul is gone, the body no longer exists; all that is left is a group of material particles in a state of rapid decay.

2. The soul permeates and inhabits every part of the body and affects more or less directly all its parts. This explains why the Scriptures attribute feelings to the heart, kidneys, or "reins"

(Psalm 73:21; Job 16:13; Lam. 3:13; Prov. 23:16; Psalm 16:7; Jer. 12:2; Job 38:36), intestines (Philemon 12; Jer. 4:19; Lam. 1:20; 2:11; S. of S. 5:4; Isa. 16:11), belly (Hab. 3:16; Job 20:23; 15:35; John 7:38). This same truth that the soul permeates the body explains why in many places the soul is described as performing bodily acts. Prov. 13:4; Isa. 32:6; Num. 21:4; Jer. 16:16; Gen. 44:30; Ezek. 23:17, 22, 28.

"Inward parts" is the general term describing the internal organs as permeated by the soul. Isa. 16:11; Psalm 51:6; Zech. 12:1; Isa. 26:9; 1 Kings 3:28. These scriptures describe the inward parts as the center of feeling, spiritual experience, and wisdom. But notice that it is not the material tissue that thinks and feels, but the soul operating through the tissue. Strictly speaking, it is not the fleshly heart, but the soul through the heart, that feels.

3. Through the body, the soul receives its impressions from the outer world. Impressions are gathered by the senses (sight, hearing, taste, smell, touch) and are conveyed to the brain via the nervous system. By means of the brain, the soul elaborates these impressions, through the processes of intellect, reason, memory, and imagination. The soul then acts on these impressions by sending orders to various parts of the body via brain and nervous system.

4. The soul contacts the world through the body, which is the instrument of the soul. Feeling, thinking, willing, and other acts are all activities of the one soul, or self. It is "I" who see and not merely the eyes; it is "I" who think and not merely the intellect; it is "I" who throw the ball and not merely the arm; it is "I" who sin and not merely the tongue or members. When an organ is injured the soul cannot function properly through it; in the case of brain injury insanity

may result. The soul then becomes like a skilled musician with a broken or damaged instrument.

(d) The Soul and Sin. The soul lives its natural life through what, for want of a better term, we may describe as the instincts. These instincts are the driving forces of the personality, with which the Creator has endowed man in order to fit him for an earthly existence (just as He endowed him with spiritual faculties to fit him for a heavenly existence). We call them instincts because they are inborn impulses implanted within the creature to enable it to do **instinctively** what is necessary for the origination and preservation of natural life. Writes Dr. Leander Keyser: "If the human infant did not have certain instincts to begin with, it could not survive even with the best of parental and medical care."

Let us notice the five most important instincts.

The first is the instinct of self-preservation, which warns us of danger and enables us to care for ourselves. Second, the acquisitive (getting) instinct, which leads us to acquire the necessities for self-support. Third, the food-seeking instinct, an impulse that leads to the satisfying of natural hunger. Fourth, the reproductive instinct which brings about the perpetuation of the race. Fifth, the instinct of dominance, which leads to the exercise of that self-assertion necessitated by one's calling and responsibilities.

The record of man's endowment with these instincts by the Creator is found in the first two chapters of Genesis. The instinct of self-preservation is implied in the prohibition and warning, "But of the tree of the knowledge of good and evil, thou shalt not eat of it: for in the day that thou eatest thereof thou shalt surely die." The instinct of acquisition is apparent in Adam's receiving from the hand of God the beautiful garden of Eden. The food-seeking instinct is assumed in

the words, "Behold, I have given you every herb
bearing seed, which is upon the face of all the
earth, and every tree, in which is the fruit of a
tree yielding seed: to you it shall be for meat."
The instinct of reproduction is referred to in the
statements, "Male and female created he them.
... And God blessed them, and God said unto them,
Be fruitful, and multiply." The fifth instinct,
dominance, is implied in the command, "Replenish
the earth, and subdue it: and have dominion."

God ordained that the lower creatures be
governed primarily by instinct. But man was
dignified with the gift of free will and reason,
wherewith to discipline himself and become arbiter of his own destiny.

As a guide for the regulation of man's faculties, God imposed a **law.** Man's understanding of
this law produced a **conscience,** which means
literally "knowledge with." When man heard the
law, he had an instructed conscience; when he disobeyed God, he suffered from an accusing conscience. In the account of the temptation (Gen.
3) we read how man yielded to the lust of the
eyes, the lust of the flesh, and the pride of life
(1 John 2: 16), and used his powers contrary to
the will of God. The soul knowingly and willing-
ly used the body to sin against God. This combination of a sinning soul with a human body
constituted what is known as "the body of sin"
(Rom. 6:6) or the "flesh." Gal. 5:24. The inclination and desire of the soul to so use the body is
described as the "carnal mind." Rom. 8:7. Because man sinned with the body, he will be judged
according to "the things done in his body." 2 Cor.
5:10. This involves a resurrection. John 5:28, 29.

When the "flesh" is condemned the reference
is not to the material body (material tissue cannot sin), but to the body as used by the sinning
soul. It is the soul that sins. Cut out the slanderer's tongue, and a slanderer he will still be; ampu-

tate a thief's hands, and he will still be a thief at heart. The sinful **impulses** of the soul must be cut off; and that is the work of the Spirit. Compare Col. 3:5; Rom. 8:13.

"Flesh" may be defined as the sum total of man's instincts, not as they first came from the hands of the Creator, but as they have been warped and rendered abnormal by sin. It is human nature in its fallen condition, weakened and disorganized by the racial inheritance derived from Adam, and enfeebled and perverted by known acts of sin. It represents unregenerate human nature whose weaknesses are frequently excused with the words, "It's just human nature after all."

It is the perversion of God-given instincts and faculties that is the basis of sin. For example, selfishness, sensitiveness, jealousy, and anger are perversions of the instinct of self-preservation. Stealing and covetousness are perversions of the instinct of acquisition. "Thou shalt not steal," and "thou shalt not covet" mean, "Thou shalt not pervert the instinct of acquisition." Gluttony is a perversion of the food-seeking instinct, and is therefore a sin. Impurity is a perversion of the instinct of reproduction. Tyranny, injustice, and quarrelsomeness represent abuses of the instinct of dominance. Thus we see that sin is fundamentally the abuse or perversion of the forces with which God has endowed us.

And notice the consequences of this perversion: First, a guilty conscience, telling man that he has dishonored his Maker, and warning him of a fearful penalty. Secondly, the perversion of the instincts reacts against the soul, weakening the will, initiating and strengthening bad habits, and creating evils of disposition. Paul catalogues the symptoms of this soul-crookedness (one Hebrew word for sin means literally "crookedness") in Gal. 5:19-21, "Now the works of the flesh are manifest, which are these: adultery, fornication, uncleanness, lasciviousness, idolatry, witchcraft, hatred, variance, emulations, wrath, strife, seditions, heresies, envyings, murders, drunkenness, revellings, and such like." Paul considers these so serious that he adds the words, "They which do such things shall not inherit the kingdom of God."

Under the guilt and power of sin, the soul becomes "dead in trespasses and sins." Eph. 2:1. Situated between the body and the spirit, between the higher and the lower, between the earthly and the spiritual, it has made the wrong choice. And the choice has brought not profit, but eternal loss. Matt. 16:26. Esau's bad bargain has been made—the bartering of a spiritual blessing for something earthly and perishable. Heb. 12:16. At death such a soul must pass out into the next world, "spotted by the flesh." Jude 23.

But there is a remedy—the "double cure"—for both the guilt and power of sin. (1) Because sin is an offense against God, an atonement is required to remove the guilt and cleanse the conscience. The gospel provision is the blood of Jesus Christ. (2) Since sin brings disease to the soul and disorder into man's being, a healing and corrective power is required. That power is provided in the inward operation of the Holy Spirit who straightens the warp and crookedness of our natures, and sets our life forces moving in the right direction. The results (fruit) are "love, joy, peace, longsuffering, gentleness, goodness, faith, meekness, temperance." Gal. 5:22, 23. In other words, the Holy Spirit makes us **righteous,** which word in the Hebrew means, literally, "straight." Sin is soul-crookedness, righteousness is soul-straightness.

(e) The Soul and the Heart. Both in Scripture and in common usage "heart" denotes the very center of anything. Deut. 4:11; Matt. 12:40; Ex. 15:8; Psalm 46:2; Ezek. 27:4, 25, 26, 27. The "heart" of man is therefore the very center of his personality. It is the center of physical life. In words of Dr. Beck: "The heart is the first thing to live. The first motion is a sure sign of life, its stillness, the sure sign of death." It is also the source and meeting place of all the currents of life, spiritual and soulish. We may describe it as the deepest part of our being, the "engine room," so to speak, of the personality, whence proceed those impulses which determine man's character and conduct.

1. The heart is the center of the life of desire, will, and judgment. Love, hatred, determination, willingness, and gladness (Psalm 105:3) are connected with the heart. The heart knows, understands (1 Kings 3:9), deliberates, estimates; it is set, directed, gives heed, is inclined toward things. Whatever impresses the soul is said to be settled, bound, or written on the heart. The heart is the storehouse of all that is heard or experienced (Luke 2:51). The heart is the "factory," so to speak, for the forming of thoughts and purposes, whether good or bad. See for example Psalm 14:1; Matt. 9:4; 1 Cor. 7:37; 1 Kings 8:17.

2. The heart is the center of the emotional life. To the heart are attributed all degrees of joy from pleasure (Isa. 65:14) to transport and exultation (Acts 2:46); all degrees of pain from discontent (Prov. 25:20) and sorrow (John 14:1) to piercing and crushing woe (Psalm 109:22; Acts 21:13); all degrees of ill-will from provocation and anger (Prov. 23:17) to raging madness (Acts 7:54) and glowing desire of revenge (Deut. 19:6); all degrees of fear from reverential trembling (Jer. 32:40) to blank terror (Deut. 28:28). The heart melts and writhes for anguish (Josh. 5:1), becomes weak through despondency (Lev. 26:36), withers under the weight of sorrow (Psalm 102:4), is broken and crushed by ad-

versity (Psalm 147:3), is consumed by a sacred burning. Jer. 20:9.

3. The heart is the center of the moral life. Concentrated in the heart may be love for God (Psalm 73:26) or blasphemous pride (Ezek. 28:2, 5). The heart is the "workshop" of all that is good or evil in thoughts, words and deeds. Matt. 15:19. It is the meeting place of either good impulses or evil lusts, the seat of a good or evil treasure. Out of its overflow it speaks and acts. Matt. 12:34, 35. It is the place where God's law was originally written (Rom. 2:15), and where the same law is renewed by the operation of the Holy Spirit. Heb. 8:10. It is the seat of conscience (Heb. 10:22) and all the testimonies of the conscience are ascribed to it. 1 John 3:19-21. With the heart man believes (Rom. 10:10) or disbelieves. Heb. 3:12. It is the field where the Divine Word is sown. Matt. 13:19. According as it makes its decisions, it stands under the inspirations of God (2 Cor. 8:16) or of Satan. John 13:2. It is the dwelling place of Christ (Eph. 3:17) and of the Spirit (2 Cor. 1:22), of the peace of God. Col. 3:15. It is the receptacle of the love of God (Rom. 5:5), the place of the rising of the heavenly light (2 Cor. 4:6), the closet of secret communion with God. Eph. 5:19. It is a great mysterious depth which only God can fathom. Jer. 17:9.

It was in view of the tremendous possibilities involved in man's heart-life that Solomon uttered the warning, "Keep thy heart with all diligence; for out of it are the issues of life." Prov. 4:23.

(f) Soul and Blood. "For the life (literally, "soul") of the flesh is in the blood." Lev. 17:11. The Scriptures teach that in both man and beast the blood is the source and holder of physical life. Lev. 17:11; 3:17; Deut. 12:23; Lam. 2:12; Gen. 4:10; Heb. 12:24; Job 24:12; Rev. 6:9, 10; Jer. 2:34; Prov. 28:17. In the words of Harvey, the English physician, who first discovered the circulation of the blood: "It is the first to live, and the last to die; and the primary seat of the soul. It lives and is nourished of itself, and by no other part of the body." In Acts 17:26 and John 1:13 blood is set forth as the original material from which the human organism proceeds. Using the heart as the pump, and the blood as the carrier of life, the soul sends vitality and nourishment to all parts of the body.

The place of the creature in the scale of life determines the value of the blood. First comes the blood of animals; of higher value is the blood of man, because he bears the image of God (Gen. 9:6); of special esteem in the sight of God is the blood of the innocent and of martyrs (Gen. 4:10; Matt. 23:35); and most precious of all is the blood of Christ (1 Peter 1:19; Heb. 9:12), of infinite value because united with Deity.

By God's gracious arrangement, the blood becomes a means of atonement, when sprinkled upon God's altar. "And I have given it to you upon the altar to make an atonement for your souls: for it is the blood that maketh an atonement for the soul." Lev. 17:11.

4. The Human Body.

The following names are applied to the body:

(a) House, or Tabernacle. 2 Cor. 5:1. It is the earthly tent in which man's pilgrim soul dwells in its journey from time to eternity. At death the tent is taken down and the soul departs. Compare Isa. 38:12; 2 Peter 1:13.

(b) Sheath. Dan. 7:15, margin. The body is the sheath of the spirit. Death is the drawing of the sword from its sheath.

(c) Temple. A temple is a place consecrated by the presence of God—a place where the omnipresent God is localized. 1 Kings 8:27, 28. Christ's body was a "temple" (John 2:21) because God was in Him. 2 Cor. 5:19. When God enters into spiritual relationship with a person, that person's body becomes a temple of the Holy Ghost. 1 Cor. 6:19.

Pagan philosophers spoke slightingly of the body; they considered it a hindrance to the soul, and looked forward to the day when the soul should be released from its entangling folds. But the Scriptures everywhere treat the body as God's handiwork, to be presented to God (Rom. 12:1), used for God's glory. 1 Cor. 6:20. Why, for example, does the book of Leviticus contain so many laws governing the physical life of the Israelites? In order to teach them that the body, as the instrument of the soul, must be kept strong and clean.

It is true that this body is earthly (1 Cor. 15:47), and as such a body of humiliation (Phil. 3:21), subject to infirmity and death (1 Cor. 15:53), so that we groan for a heavenly body (2 Cor. 5:2). But at the coming of Christ, the same Power that quickened the soul will transform the body, thus completing man's redemption. And the pledge of this change is the indwelling Spirit. 2 Cor. 5:5; Rom. 8:11.

III. GOD'S IMAGE IN MAN.

"Let us make man in our image, after our likeness." Compare Gen. 5:1; 9:6; Eccles. 7:29; Acts 17:26, 28, 29; 1 Cor. 11:7; 2 Cor. 3:18; 2 Cor. 4:4; Eph. 4:24; Col. 1·15; Col. 3:10; James 3:9; Isa. 43:7; Eph. 2:10. Man was created God-like; he was made like God in character and personality. And throughout the Scriptures the standard and goal set before man is to be like God. Lev. 19:2; Matt. 5:45-48; Eph. 5:1. And to be like God means to be like Christ, who is the image of the invisible God.

Let us consider some of the elements that constitute the Divine image in man.

I. Kinship with God.

The living creatures' relationship to God consisted in blindly obeying the instincts implanted in them by the Creator; but the life that inspired man was a veritable outcome from the personality of God. Man indeed has a body that was made from the dust of the earth; but God breathed into his nostrils the breath of life (Gen. 2:7); thus endowing him with a nature capable of knowing, loving and serving God. Because of this Divine image all men are, by creation, children of God; but since that image has been marred by sin, men must be re-created or born again (Eph. 4:24) in order to be actually sons of God.

A Greek scholar has pointed out that one Greek word for man (anthropos) is a combination of words meaning literally, "the one looking up." Man is a praying creature, and there come times in the lives of the most vicious, when they cry out to some higher Power for help. Man may not understand the greatness of his dignity, and so he may become **like** the beasts that perish (Psalm 49:20), but he is not one. Even in his degradation, he is a witness to his nobler origin, for a beast cannot degrade itself. For example, no one would think of pleading with a tiger by saying, "Now be a tiger!" It always was and always will be, a tiger. But the appeal, "Be a man!" carries a real meaning to one who has degraded himself. However low he may have sunk, he "knows better."

2. Moral Character.

Recognition of right and wrong belongs to man alone. An animal may be taught that it is not to do certain things, but it is because these things are contrary to its master's wish and not because it knows that some things are always right and others always wrong. In other words, animals have no religious or moral nature; they are not capable of being taught truths concerning God and morality. Writes a **great naturalist**:

I fully subscribe to the judgment of those writers who maintain that, of all the differences between man and the lower animals, the moral sense or the conscience is by far the most important. This sense is summed up in that short but imperious "ought," so full of significance. It is the most noble of all the attributes of man.

3. Reason.

The animal is a mere creature of nature; man is above nature. He is capable of self-reflection and reasoning concerning the causes of things. Think of the marvelous inventions that have sprung up from the mind of man—the timepiece, the microscope, steamship, telegraph, radio, adding-machine, and others too numerous to mention. Look at the whole fabric of civilization which is built up by the several arts. Consider the books that have been written, the poetry and music that have been composed. And then adore the Creator for the wonderful gift of reason! The tragedy of history is that man has used this Divine endowment for destructive purposes, even to denying the Creator, who made him a thinking creature.

4. Capacity for Immortality.

The Tree of Life in the garden of Eden indicates that man would never have died had he not disobeyed God. Christ came into the world to bring the Food of Life within our reach so that we need not perish, but live forever!

5. Dominion over the Earth.

Man was designed to be God's image in respect to lordship; and as no man can play the monarch without subjects and kingdom, God gave him both empire and people. "And God blessed them, and God said unto them, Be fruitful, and multiply, and replenish (literally, "fill") the earth, and subdue it: and have dominion over the fish of the sea, and over the fowl of the air, and over every living thing that moveth upon the earth."

Compare Psalm 8:5-8. By virtue of the powers implied in his being formed in God's image, all living beings upon the earth are given into the hand of man. He was to be God's visible representative in relation to the surrounding creatures.

Man has filled the earth with his productions. It is his special privilege to subdue the power of nature unto himself. He has forced the lightning to be his messenger, has put a girdle round the globe, has climbed up to the clouds and penetrated to the depths of the sea. He has turned the forces of Nature against herself; commanding the winds to help him in braving the sea. And marvelous as is man's rule over the external, dead nature, more marvelous still is his rule over animate nature. To see the trained falcon strike down the quarry at the feet of his master and come back, when God's free heaven is before him; to see the hound use his speed in the service of his master, to take a prey not to be given to himself; to see the camel of the desert carrying man through his own home: all these show the creative ability of man and his resemblance to God the Creator.

The Fall of man resulted in the loss of, the marring of, the Divine image. This does not mean that man's mental and psychical (soul) powers were lost; but that the original innocence and moral integrity in which he was created was forfeited by his disobedience. Hence man is utterly unable to save himself and is without hope apart from an act of grace which will restore the Divine image. This subject will be more fully treated in the next chapter.

5

SIN

We read that God, after His work of creation, pronounced every thing "very good." But a little observation will convince us that many things exist which are not good—evil, wickedness, oppression, strife, wars, death, suffering. And naturally the question arises, How did evil enter the world?—a question that has perplexed many thinkers. The Bible has God's answer; more, it tells us what sin really is; better still, we are told of the remedy for sin.

OUTLINE

I. THE FACT OF SIN.

Denied, misconceived or minimized by—

1. Atheism.
2. Determinism.
3. Hedonism.
4. Christian Science.
5. Evolution.

II. THE ORIGIN OF SIN.

1. Temptation: Its Possibility, Source, Subtilty.
2. Guilt.
3. Judgment.
   a. On the serpent.
   b. On the woman.
   c. On the man.
4. Redemption.
   a. Promised.
   b. Pictured.

III. THE NATURE OF SIN

1. Old Testament teaching. Sin viewed—
   a. In the sphere of morals.
   b. In the sphere of brotherly conduct.
   c. In the sphere of holiness.
   d. In the sphere of truth.
   e. In the sphere of wisdom.
2. New Testament teaching. Sin described as—
   a. Missing the mark.
   b. Debt.
   c. Lawlessness.
   d. Disobedience.
   e. Transgression.
   f. Fall.
   g. Defeat.
   h. Ungodliness.
   i. Error.

IV. THE CONSEQUENCES OF SIN.

1. Spiritual weakness.
   a. Marring of the Divine image.
   b. Inborn sin.
   c. Inner discord.
2. Positive punishment.

I. THE FACT OF SIN.

There is no need to argue the question of the reality of sin; history and man's own consciousness bear abundant testimony to the fact. But theories have been advanced which either deny, misconceive, or minimize the nature of sin.

1. Atheism, in denying God denies also sin, for, strictly speaking, we can **sin** only against God, and if there be no God, there can be no sin. Man may be guilty of wrongdoing in relation to others; he may practice vice in relation to himself; but only in relation to God do these constitute sin. In the final analysis, all wrongdoing is directed against God, for wrong is a violation of right, and right is the law of God. "I have sinned against heaven, and in thy sight," cried the Prodigal. Man therefore needs pardon based on a Divine provision of atonement.

2. Determinism is the theory which affirms that free will is a delusion and not a reality. We imagine that we are free to make our choice, but actually our choices are dictated by inner impulses and circumstances beyond our control. The smoke going up the chimney may think that it is free, but it ascends by inexorable laws. This being so, a person cannot help acting the way he does, and, strictly speaking, should not be praised for goodness or blamed for badness. Man is simply a slave of circumstances. So runs this theory.

But the Scriptures consistently affirm that man is free to choose between good and evil—a freedom implied in every exhortation and command. Far from being a victim of fate and chance, man is declared to be the arbiter of his own destiny.

During a discussion of the question of free will, Dr. Johnson, noted English scholar and author, declared: "Sir, we **know** that our wills are free, and that's the end of it!" That ounce of **common sense outweighs a ton of philosophy.**

One practical consequence of Determinism is to treat sin as an infirmity for which the sinner should be pitied rather than as an offense for which he should be punished. But the peremptory "I ought" in the human conscience refutes this theory. Recently a seventeen-year-old murderer refused to enter a plea of insanity; his crime was inexcusable, he declared, because he knew he had committed it in the face of light given him by parents and Sunday School. He therefore insisted on paying the full penalty. Young as he was, and in the face of death, he refused to deceive himself.

3. Hedonism (from the Greek word meaning "pleasure") is a theory of life which maintains that the highest good in life is the securing of pleasure and the avoiding of pain, so that the first question to be asked is not, "Is it right?" but, "Will it bring pleasure?" Not every hedonist lives a vicious life, but the general tendency of hedonism is to wink at sin and sugar-coat it with such designations as: "a harmless weakness"; "side-steppings"; "vagaries of pleasure"; "ebullition of youth." They excuse sin with such sayings as the following: "To err is human"; "what is natural is beautiful, and what is beautiful is right."

This theory is behind the modern teaching of "self-expression." In technical language, man must "release the inhibitions"; in plain language, "yield to temptation because repression is unhealthful." Of course, this often represents an attempt to justify immorality. But these theorists would not be in favor of a person releasing inhibitions of anger, murderous hate, envy, drunkenness or any other evil tendency.

Underlying this theory is the desire to minimize the gravity of sin, and blur the line between good and bad, right and wrong. It represents a modern variation of the old lie, "Ye shall not surely die." And many a descendant of Adam has swallowed the bitter pill of sin, sugar-coated with the soothing assurance, "This won't hurt you." God has made good white and sin black, but some would blend them into a neutral gray. "Woe unto them that call evil good, and good evil," is the Divine warning to those who attempt to confuse the moral distinctions.

4. Christian Science denies the reality of sin; sin, it says, is not a positive thing, but simply the absence of good. That sin has real existence is an "error of the mortal mind." Man **thinks** that sin is real, therefore his thinking needs correction. But after looking over the sin and ruin that are very real in the world, it seems that this "error of the mortal mind" is about as bad as what old-fashioned people call "sin"! The Scriptures denounce sin as a positive violation of God's law, as a real offense meriting real punishment in a real hell.

5. Evolution regards sin as the heritage of man's primitive animalism. Therefore instead of exhorting people to put off the "old man," or the "old Adam," its proponents should admonish them to put off "the old ape" or "the old tiger"! As we have seen, this evolutionary theory is anti-Scriptural. Moreover, animals do not sin; they live according to their nature, and experience no consciousness of guilt for so acting. Comments Dr. Leander Keyser: "If the selfish and bloody struggle for existence in the animal kingdom was the method of progress, bringing man into existence, why should it be wrong for men to continue along that bloody route?" It is true that man has a physical nature, but that lower part of him was the creation of God, and it is intended to be held in subjection to a God-enlightened intelligence.

II. THE ORIGIN OF SIN.

The third chapter of Genesis sounds the keynotes that characterize man's spiritual history. They are: Temptation, Sin, Guilt, Judgment, Redemption.

1. Temptation.

(a) The Possibility of Temptation. The second chapter of Genesis supplies the background for the account of man's fall. It tells of man's first home, his intelligence, his service in the garden of Eden, the two trees, and the first wedding. Particular mention is made of the two trees of Destiny—the tree of the knowledge of good and evil and the tree of life. These two trees represented a sermon in picture form, constantly saying to our first parents: "If ye shall follow the GOOD and reject the EVIL ye shall have LIFE." And is not this the essence of the Way of Life as it is found throughout the Scriptures? Compare Deut. 30:15.

Notice the forbidden tree. Why was it placed there? In order to provide a test whereby man could lovingly and freely choose to serve God and so develop in character. Without free will man would have been a mere machine.

(b) The Source of the Temptation. "Now the serpent was more subtil than any beast of the field which the Lord God had made." It is reasonable to infer that the serpent, which at that time must have been a beautiful creature, was the agent employed by Satan, who had already been cast out of heaven before the creation of man. Ezek. 28:13-17; Isa. 14:12-15. For this reason Satan is described as "that old serpent, called the Devil." Rev. 12:9. Satan generally works through agents. When Peter (without evil intention) attempted to dissuade his Master from the path of duty, Jesus looked beyond Peter, and said, "Get

thee behind me, Satan." Matt. 16:22, 23. In this
case Satan worked through one of Jesus' friends;
in Eden he employed a creature whom Eve did
not mistrust.

(c) The Subtilty of the Temptation. Subtilty is mentioned as an outstanding characteristic
of the serpent. Compare Matt. 10:16. He puts
forth with great artfulness suggestions which,
when embraced, give rise to sinful desires and
sinful acts. He begins by addressing the woman,
the weaker vessel, who, moreover, had not heard
directly the prohibition. Gen. 2:16, 17. And he
waits till Eve is alone. Notice the craftiness of
the approach. He twists God's words (compare
Gen. 3:1 and 2:16, 17) and then pretends to be
surprised at them when so twisted; thus he art-
fully sows doubts and suspicions in the heart of
the unsuspecting woman, and at the same time
insinuates that he himself is well qualified to be a
judge as to the justice of such a prohibition. By
the question in verse 1 he injects a threefold doubt
of God: (1) A doubt of God's goodness. He as
much as says, "God is withholding some blessing
from you." (2) A doubt of God's righteousness.
"Ye shall not surely die." That is, "God does not
mean what He says." (3) a doubt of His holiness.
In verse 5 the serpent says in effect, "God has
forbidden you to eat of the tree because He is
jealous of you. He does not want you to become
as wise as He is, so He keeps you in ignorance.
It is not on **your** account, to save you from death,
but on **His** account, to prevent your becoming
like Him."

2. Guilt.

Notice the evidences of a guilty conscience. (1)
"And the eyes of them both were opened, and they
knew that they were naked." The expression used of
any miraculous or sudden enlightenment. Gen. 21:19;
2 Kings 6:17. The serpent's words (verse 5) were

fulfilled; but the knowledge gained was different from what they had expected. Instead of making them Godlike they experienced a miserable feeling of guilt that made them afraid of God. Notice that the physical nakedness is a picture of a naked or guilty conscience. Emotional disturbances are often reflected in our appearance. Some commentators hold that before their fall Adam and Eve were clothed with a halo or garment of light, which was a sign of their communion with God and the dominance of the spirit over the body. When they sinned communion was broken, the body overcame the spirit, and there began that conflict between spirit and flesh (Rom. 7:14-24) that has been the cause of so much misery. (2) "And they sewed fig leaves together, and made themselves aprons." As the physical nakedness is the picture and sign of a guilty conscience, so the attempt to cover up their nakedness is a picture of man's attempt to cover his guilt by the garment of forgetfulness or the garment of excuses. But only a God-made garment can cover sin. Verse 21. (3) "And they heard the voice of the Lord God walking in the garden in the cool of the day: and Adam and his wife hid themselves from the presence of the Lord God amongst the trees of the garden." It is the instinct of guilty man to flee from God. And as Adam and Eve tried to hide among the trees, so people today try to hide in pleasures and other activities.

3. Judgment.

(a) **Judgment upon the Serpent.** "Because thou hast done this, thou art cursed above all cattle, and above every beast of the field; upon thy belly shalt thou go, and dust shalt thou eat all the days of thy life." All these words imply that at one time the serpent was a beautiful, upright creature. Now, because it has become the instrument for man's fall it is cursed and degraded in the scale of the animal creation. But since the serpent was simply Satan's tool, why should it be punished? Because God has willed to make the curse upon the serpent a type and prophecy of the curse upon the Devil and all the powers of evil. Man must recognize by its punishment how the curse of God rests upon all sin and wickedness; by its crawling in the dust it was to remind man of the day when God should bring down to the dust the power of the Devil. This is an encouragement to man: he, the tempted one, stands erect, while the serpent is under the curse. By God's grace he can crush its head—he can overcome evil. Compare Luke 10:18; Rom. 16:20; Rev. 12:9; 20:1-3, 10.

(b) Judgment upon the Woman. "Unto the woman he said, I will greatly multiply thy sorrow and thy conception; in sorrow thou shalt bring forth children; and thy desire shall be to thy husband, and he shall rule over thee." Says one writer:

The presence of sin has been the cause of much suffering in the ways precisely indicated here. In regard to child-bearing, it is no doubt the case that at this critical and anxious moment of a woman's life, the sense of past wrongdoing weighs particularly upon her, and also men's cruelty and folly have contributed to make the process more painful and perilous for women than it is for animals."

Sin has marred all the relationships of life, and this is true of the marriage relationship. In many countries woman is practically the slave of the man; the position and condition of child-widows and child-mothers in India is a grim commentary on the fulfillment of the curse.

(c) Judgment upon the Man. Work had already been appointed for man (2:15): the penalty is to consist of its laboriousness, and in the disappointments and vexations which often accompany it. Agriculture is specified in particular because it has always been one of the most necessary of human employments. In some mysterious fashion the earth and creation in general have shared the curse and fall of their lord (man), but they are destined to share in his redemption. That is the thought of Rom. 8:19-23. In Isa. 11:1-9 and 65:17-25 we have examples of scriptures that predict the removal of the curse from the earth during the millennium. Besides the physical curse that has overtaken the earth it is also true that human wilfulness and human sin have in many ways embittered toil and made hard and difficult man's working conditions.

Notice the death penalty. "For dust thou art, and unto dust shalt thou return." Man was created capable of not dying physically; he could have lived indefinitely had he preserved his innocence and continued to eat of the tree of life. Even though he return to communion with God (and so overcome **spiritual** death) through repentance and prayer, yet he must return to his Maker by the way of the grave. Because death is part of the penalty of sin, full salvation must include the resurrection of the body. 1 Cor. 15:54-57. However, certain ones will, like Enoch, be privileged to escape physical death. Gen. 5:24; 1 Cor. 15:51.

4. Redemption.

The first three chapters of Genesis contain the three revelations of God, which throughout the Bible figure in all God's relations to man. The Creator, who brought all into existence (chap. 1); the Covenant-God who enters into personal relations with man (chap. 2); the Redeemer who makes provision for man's restoration (chap. 3).

(a) Redemption Promised. Read Gen. 3:15. (1) The serpent attempted to draw Eve into an

alliance with him against God, but God will break
it up. "I will put enmity between thee and the
woman, and between thy seed (descendants) and
her seed." In other words, there will be a struggle between mankind and the evil power that
caused his fall. (2) What will be the result of that
conflict? First, victory for mankind, through
man's representative, the Seed of the woman. "It
(the woman's seed) shall bruise thy head." Christ,
the Seed of the woman, came into the world to
crush the power of the Devil. Matt. 1:23, 25.
Luke 1:31-35, 76; Isa. 7:14; Gal. 4:4; Rom. 16:20;
Col. 2:15; Heb. 2:14, 15; 1 John 3:8; 5:5; Rev.
12:7, 8, 17; 20:1-3, 10. (3) But the victory will
not be without suffering. "And thou (the serpent)
shalt bruise his heel." At Calvary the Serpent
bruised the heel of the Seed of the woman; but
that bruising has brought healing to mankind.
See Isa. 53:3, 4, 12; Dan. 9:26; Matt. 4:1-10; Luke
22:39-44, 53; John 12:31-33; 14:30, 31; Heb. 2:18:
5:7; Rev. 2:10.

(b) Redemption Pictured. Verse 21. God killed
an innocent creature in order to clothe those who
felt naked in His sight because of sin. In like
manner, the Father gave up His Son, the innocent
One, unto death in order to provide an atoning
covering for the souls of men.

III. THE NATURE OF SIN.

What is sin? The Bible has a variety of
terms for moral evil which tells us something of its
nature. A study of these terms in the original
Hebrew and Greek will yield the Scriptural definition of sin.

1. Old Testament Teaching.

The various Hebrew words picture sin as
operating in the following spheres:

(a) The Sphere of Morals. The following are

the words used to express sin in this sphere (for further study consult Young's Concordance):

1. The most commonly used word for sin means "to miss the mark." It conveys the following ideas: (1) To miss the mark, like an erratic archer who shoots but misses. In like manner, the sinner misses the true aim of existence. (2) To miss the way, like a traveler off the right track. (3) To be found wanting when weighed in God's balances.

In Gen. 4:7, where the word is first mentioned, sin is personified as a wild beast ready to spring at any one who gives it inlet.

2. Another word means literally "crookedness" and is often translated by "perverseness." It is thus the opposite of righteousness, which means literally, that which is straight or conformed to a right standard.

3. Another common word, translated "evil," conveys the thought of violence or breaking, and describes the man who "breaks" or does violence to God's law.

(b) The Sphere of Brotherly Conduct. For sins in this sphere the word used means violence or injurious conduct. Gen. 6:11; Ezek. 7:23; Prov. 16:29. Casting off the restraint of the law, man mistreats and oppresses his fellows.

(c) The Sphere of Holiness. Words used to describe sin in this sphere imply that the offender has been in relationship with God. The entire Israelitish nation was constituted "a kingdom of priests," each member being regarded as in touch with God and His holy Tabernacle. Every Israelite, was therefore holy, that is, set apart for God, and every activity and sphere of his life was regulated by the Law of Holiness. The things outside that law were "profane" (the opposite of holy), and the one who partook of them became "unclean" or "defiled." Lev. 11:24, 27, 31, 33, 39.

If he persisted, he was considered a profane or ir-religious person. Lev. 21:14; Heb. 12:16. If he rebelled and deliberately repudiated the jurisdiction of the Law of Holiness, he was considered a "transgressor." Psalm 37:38; 51:13; Isa. 53:12. The Israelite who pursued the last-named course would be considered as belonging to the "criminal" class, and such were the publicans, in the estimate of our Lord's generation.

(d) The Sphere of Truth. Words describing sin in this sphere stress the deceitful and vain element of sin. Sinners deal and speak falsely (Psalm 58:3; Isa. 28:15), misrepresent and bear false witness. Ex. 20:16; Psalm 119:128; Prov. 19:5, 9. Such activity is "vanity" (Psalm 12:2; 24:4; 41:6), that is, empty and worthless.

The first sinner was a liar (John 8:44); the first sin began with a lie (Gen. 3:4); and every sin contains the element of deceitfulness. Heb. 3:13.

(e) The Sphere of Wisdom. Men act wickedly either because they do not or will not reason rightly; either through carelessness or deliberate ignorance they do not guide their lives according to God's will.

1. Many exhortations are directed toward the "simple." Prov. 1:4, 22; 8:5. This word describes the natural man, undeveloped either in the direction of good or evil, without fixed principles, but with a natural inclination to evil which may be worked upon so as to seduce him. He lacks fixity of purpose and moral foundation; he hears but forgets and so is easily led into sin. Compare Matt. 7:26.

2. We often read of those "destitute of understanding" (Prov. 7:7; 9:4), that is, those who from want of understanding rather than from sinful propensity, become victims of sin. Defective in wisdom, they are led to pass rash and hasty

judgments upon God's Providence and things above them. So they run into ungodliness. Both this class and the "simple" are inexcusable, for the Scriptures picture the Lord as freely offering —yea, begging them to accept (Prov. 8:1-10)— that which will make them wise unto salvation.

3. The word often translated "fool" (Prov. 15:20) describes a person who, though capable of good, is bound to fleshly things and is easily led into sin by his fleshly inclinations. He will not discipline himself and guide his propensities according to the Divine law.

4. The "scorner" (Psalm 1:1; Prov. 14:6) is the wicked man who justifies his wickedness with reasoned-out arguments against the existence or reality of God, and against spiritual things in general. Thus, "scorner" is the Old Testament equivalent to our modern "infidel," and the expression "seat of the scornful" probably refers to the local infidel society.

2. New Testament Teaching.

The New Testament describes sin as—

(a) **Missing the mark,** which conveys the same idea as the common Old Testament word.

(b) **Debt.** Matt. 6:12. Man owes (the word "ought" comes from "owe") to God the keeping of His commandments; every sin committed is the contracting of a debt. Unable to pay it, his only hope is for pardon, or remission of the debt.

(c) **Lawlessness.** "Sin is the transgression of the law" (literally, "lawlessness." 1 John 3:4). The sinner is a rebel and an idolater, for he who deliberately breaks a commandment is choosing his own will rather than God's; worse, he is becoming a law unto himself and therefore making a god of Self. Sin began in the heart of that exalted angel who said, "I will," in opposition to God's will. Isa. 14:13, 14. Antichrist is pre-eminently "the lawless one" (literal translation of "wicked one"), because he exalts himself above everything that is worshiped or is called God. 2 Thess. 2:4. Sin is essentially self-will, and self-will is essentially sin.

Sin would cast God from His throne; sin would murder God. Over the cross of the Son of God could well have been written the words, "Sin has done this!"

(d) Disobedience, literally, "hearing amiss"; listening with lack of attention. Heb. 2:2. "Take heed therefore how ye hear." Luke 8:18.

(e) Transgression, literally, "going beyond the limit." Rom. 4:15. God's commandments are fences, so to speak, which would keep men from trespassing on dangerous territory and so suffering injury to their souls.

(f) Fall, or fault, or falling aside. 2 Peter 1:10 in the Greek. Hence the common expression, "to **fall** into sin" To sin is to fall from a standard of conduct.

(g) Defeat is the literal meaning of the word "fall" in Rom. 11:12. In rejecting Christ the Jewish nation suffered a defeat and missed God's purpose.

(h) Ungodliness, from a word meaning "without worship, or reverence." Rom. 1:18; 2 Tim. 2:16. The ungodly man is one who gives little or no thought to God and sacred things. Sacred things bring no feeling of awe and reverence. He is without God because he does not want God.

(i) Error (Heb. 9:7) describes those sins committed through thoughtlessness or ignorance, and so differentiated from those sins committed presumptuously in the face of light. The man who defiantly decides to do wrong incurs a greater degree of guilt than the one who through weakness is overtaken in a fault.

IV. THE CONSEQUENCES OF SIN.

Sin is both an act and a state. As a revolt against God's law it is an **act** of man's will; as separation from God, it becomes a sinful state. A two fold consequence ensues: The sinner brings **evil** upon himself through his own wrongdoing and incurs **guilt** in the sight of God. Two things, therefore, should be distinguished: the evil consequences that follow the acts of sin, and the penalty that will be visited in the judgment. These may be illustrated as follows. A father forbids his little son to smoke cigarets, and warns of a twofold consequence: first, smoking will make him feel sick, and in addition he will be punished for his disobedience. The youngster disobeys and takes his first smoke. The ensuing nausea would represent the evil consequences of his sin, and the subsequent thrashing would represent the positive penalty for guilt.

In like manner, the Scriptures describe two effects of sin upon the guilty: it is followed by disastrous consequences to their souls and will bring upon them God's positive decree of condemnation.

1. Spiritual Weakness.

(a) The Marring of the Divine Image. Man did not lose the Divine image completely, for even in his fallen condition he is regarded as a creature made in the image of God (Gen. 9:6; James 3:9)—a truth expressed in the popular saying, "There is some good in the worst of men." Maudesley, the great English alienist, maintained that the inherent majesty of the human mind was evident even in the ruin wrought by madness.

But though not lost entirely, the Divine image in man is badly marred. Jesus Christ came into the world to make it possible for man to regain the full Divine likeness by being recreated in the image of God. Col. 3:10.

(b) Inborn sin, or "original sin." The effect of the Fall was so deep-seated in human nature that Adam, as the father of the race, passed on to his descendants a tendency or bias to sin. Psalm 51:5. This spiritual and moral handicap under which all men are born is known as original sin. The acts of sin that follow during the age of accountability are known as "actual sin." Christ, the second Adam, came into the world to deliver us from all the effects of the Fall. Rom. 5:12-21.

This moral condition of the soul is described in many ways: all have sinned (Rom. 3:9); all are under the curse (Gal. 3:10); the natural man is stranger to the things of God (1 Cor. 2:14); the natural heart is deceitful and wicked (Jer. 17:9); the mental and moral nature is corrupt (Gen. 6:5, 12; 8:21; Rom. 1:19-31); the carnal mind is at enmity with God (Rom. 8:7, 8); the sinner is a slave of sin (Rom. 6:17; 7:5); is controlled by the prince of the power of the air (Eph. 2:2); is dead in trespasses and sin (Eph. 2:1); and is a child of wrath. Eph. 2:3.

(c) Inner Discord. In the beginning God made man's body from the dust, thus endowing him with a physical or lower nature; He then breathed into his nostrils the breath of life, thus imparting to him a higher nature connecting him with God. It was intended that there should be harmony in man's being, the body being subordinated to the soul. But sin disturbed the relationship, so that man has found himself divided with himself, self opposed to self in a civil war between the higher and lower natures. His lower nature, frail in itself, has rebelled against the higher and opened the gates of his being to the enemy. In the intensity of the conflict man cries out, "O wretched man that I am! who shall deliver me from the body of this death?" Rom. 7:24.

The "God of peace" (1 Thess. 5:23) subdues

the warring elements of his nature, and sanctifies spirit, soul and body. The result is inner
blessedness—"righteousness, and peace, and joy
in the Holy Ghost." Rom. 14:17.

2. Positive Punishment.

"In the day that thou eatest thereof thou shalt
surely die." Gen. 2:17. "The wages of sin is death."
Rom. 6:23.

Man was created with a capacity for immortality; that is, he did not have to die if he
obeyed God's law. In order that he might "lay
hold" on immortality and eternal life, he was
placed under a covenant of works, pictured by the
two trees—the tree of the knowledge of good
and evil and the tree of life. Life was thus conditioned upon obedience; as long as Adam observed the **law of life** he had a right to the **tree
of life.** But he disobeyed, broke the covenant of
life, and became separated from God the Source
of life. Death began from that moment and was
consummated at the disruption of the personality
in the form of separation of soul and body. But
notice the penalty included more than physical
death; the physical dissolution was an indication of God's disfavor, of the fact that man was
out of touch with the Fountain of life. Even
though Adam may have later become reconciled
to his Maker, physical death continued, in accord-
ance with the Divine decree, "In the day that thou
eatest thereof thou shalt surely die." Only through
an act of redemption and a re-creation would man
again have the right to the tree of life which is
in the midst of the paradise of God. Through Christ
righteousness is restored to the soul, which, at
the resurrection, is re-united to a glorified body.

We see, then, that physical death came into
the world as a penalty, and throughout the Scripture, whenever death is threatened as the punishment for sin, it means primarily loss of God's

favor. Thus the sinning person is already "dead in trespasses and in sins," and at physical death he enters the invisible world in the same condition. Then at the Judgment the Judge pronounces the sentence of the second death, which involves "indignation and wrath, tribulation and anguish." Rom. 2:7-12. So then "death" as a penalty is not extinction of the personality but the means of separation from God. There are three phases to this death: spiritual death while man lives (Eph. 2:1; 1 Tim. 5:6), physical death (Heb. 9:27), and the second or eternal death. Rev. 21:8; John 5:28, 29; 2 Thess. 1:9; Matt. 25:41.

On the other hand, when the Scriptures speak of life as a reward of righteousness, more than **existence** is meant, for the wicked exist in hell. Life means living in fellowship and favor with God—a fellowship which death cannot interrupt or destroy. John 11:25, 26. It is a life lived in conscious union with God, the Fountain of life. "And this is life eternal, that they might know (in experience and fellowship) thee the only true God, and Jesus Christ whom thou hast sent." John 17:3. Eternal life is **right** existence; eternal death is **wrong** existence, wretched and debased existence.

Note the word "destruction" used in connection with the fate of the wicked (Matt. 7:13; John 17:12; 2 Thess. 2:3) does not mean extinction. To perish or to be destroyed (according to the Greek) is not to be extinct, but to be **ruined.** For example, that the wineskins "perish" (Matt. 9:17) means that they are no good as wineskins, not that they are annihilated. In like manner, the sinner who perishes or is destroyed is not reduced to nothingness, but is ruined as far as enjoyment of God and eternal life are concerned. The same usage is followed today; when we say, "his life is ruined," we do not mean that the man is dead, but that he has missed the true aim of life.

6

THE LORD JESUS CHRIST

"His birthday is kept across the world. His death-day sets a gallows against every sky-line. Who is He?" With these words a prominent preacher stated a question which is of supreme importance and never-failing interest.

The question was put by the Master Himself when, during a crisis in His ministry, He asked, "Whom do men say that I the Son of man am?" He listened to the statement of current opinion without comment, but His blessing was pronounced upon the answer which Peter had learned from God: "Thou art the Christ, the Son of the living God."

The question still remains and men still attempt answers. But the true answer must come from the New Testament, written by men who knew Him best, and who for that knowledge counted all things but loss.

OUTLINE

I. THE NATURE OF CHRIST.

1. Son of God (Deity).
2. The Word (eternal pre-existence and activity).
3. Lord (exaltation and sovereignty).
4. Son of Man (humanity).
5. Christ (official title and mission).
6. Son of David (royal lineage).
7. Jesus (saving work).

II. THE OFFICES OF CHRIST.

1. Prophet.
2. Priest.
3. King.

III. THE WORK OF CHRIST.

1. His Death.
   a. Its importance.
   b. Its meaning.
2. His Resurrection.
   a. The fact.
   b. The evidence.
   c. The meaning.
3. His Ascension Constituted Him—
   a. The heavenly Christ.
   b. The exalted Christ.
   c. The sovereign Christ.
   d. The way-preparing Christ.
   e. The interceding Christ.
   f. The omnipresent Christ.
   g. Conclusion: values of the ascension.

I. THE NATURE OF CHRIST.

The question, Who is Christ? is best answered by stating and explaining the names and titles by which He is known.

1. The Son of God (Deity).

As "son of man" means one born of man, so "Son of God" means one born of God. Hence this title proclaims the Deity of Christ. Jesus is never called **a** Son of God, in the general sense in which men and angels (Job 2:1) are children of God. He is **the** Son of God in the **unique** sense. Jesus is described as sustaining toward God a relationship not shared by any other person in the universe.

In explanation and confirmation of this truth let us consider:

(a) The Consciousness of Christ. What was the content of Jesus' self-consciousness; that is, what did Jesus know about Himself? Luke, the only writer recording an incident of Jesus' boyhood, tells us that at the age of twelve (at least) Jesus was conscious of two things: a special relationship to God whom He describes as His Father; second, a special mission on earth—His "Father's business."

Just exactly when and how this self-consciousness came must remain a mystery to us. When we think of God coming to us in the form of a man we must reverently exclaim, "Great is the mystery of godliness!" However, the following illustration may prove helpful. Hold an infant before a mirror; he will see himself without recognizing himself. But the time will come when he will know that the reflected image represents himself. In other words, the child has become self-conscious of its identity. May it not have been so with the Lord Jesus? He was always the Son of God; but there came a time when, after studying the Scriptures relating to God's Messiah, the consciousness flashed naturally into

His mind that He, the Son of Mary, was none other than the Christ of God. In view of the fact that the Eternal Son of God lived a perfectly natural human life, it is reasonable to think that the self-consciousness of Deity came about in this fashion.

At the river Jordan Jesus heard the Father's voice corroborating and confirming His inner consciousness (Matt. 3:17), and in the wilderness He successfully resisted Satan's attempt to question His Sonship ("If thou be the Son of God." Matt. 4:3). Later in His ministry He commended Peter for the heaven-inspired testimony to His Deity and Messiahship. Matt. 16:15-17. When before the Jewish council, He might have escaped death by denying the unique sonship and simply affirming that He was a son of God in the same sense that all men are; but put on oath by the high priest, He declared His consciousness of Deity, even though He knew that it meant the death sentence. Matt. 26:63-65.

(b) The Claims of Jesus. He put Himself side by side with the Divine activity. "My Father worketh hitherto, and I work." "I came forth from the Father." John 16:28. "My Father hath sent me." John 20:21. He claimed a Divine knowledge and fellowship. Matt. 11:27; John 17:25. He claimed to unveil the Father's being in Himself. John 14:9-11. He assumed Divine prerogatives: omnipresence (Matt. 18:20); power to forgive sins (Mark 2:5-10); power to raise the dead. John 6:39, 40, 54; 11:25; 10:17, 18. He proclaimed Himself Judge and Arbiter of man's destiny. John 5:22; Matt. 25:31-46.

He demanded a surrender and an allegiance that only God could rightly claim; He insisted on absolute self-surrender on the part of His followers. They must be ready to sever the dearest and closest of ties, for any one who loved even father or mother more than Him was not worthy of Him. Matt. 10:37; Luke 14:25-33.

These tremendous claims were made by One who lived as the humblest of men, and were stated just as simply and naturally as, for example, Paul would say, "I am a man which am a Jew." In order to arrive at the conclusion that Christ was Divine one need make only two concessions: first, that Jesus was not a bad man; and second, that He was not demented. If He said He was Divine when He knew that He was not, then He could not be good; if He falsely imagined that He was God, then He could not be wise. But no sane or wise person would dream of denying either His perfect character or His superior wisdom; consequently one cannot but conclude that He was what He claimed to be—the Son of God in a unique sense.

(c) The Authority of Christ.   In Christ's teaching one notes a complete absence of such expression as: "It is my opinion"; "It may be"; "I think that . . . "; "We may as well suppose," etc.   A rationalistic Jewish scholar admitted that He spoke with the authority of God Almighty Himself.   Dr. Henry van Dyke points out that, in the Sermon on the Mount, for example, we have

the absolutely overwhelming sight of a believing Hebrew placing Himself above the rule of His own faith, a humble Teacher asserting supreme authority over all human conduct, a moral reformer discarding all other foundations and saying, "Whosoever heareth these sayings of mine, and doeth them, I will liken him unto a wise man, which built his house upon a rock (Matt. 7:24)." Nine and forty times, in this brief record of the discourse of Jesus, recurs this solemn phrase with which He authenticates the truth: "Verily I say unto thee."

(d) The Sinlessness of Christ.   No teacher who calls men to repentance and righteousness can avoid some reference to his own sinfulness or imperfection; indeed, the holier he is, the more will he lament and acknowledge his own limitations. But in the words and deeds of Jesus there is a complete absence of consciousness or confession of sin. He had the deepest knowledge of the evil of sin, yet no shadow or stain of it fell upon His own soul. On the contrary, He, the humblest of men, issues the challenge, "Which of you convinceth me of sin?" John 8:46.

(e) The Testimony of the Disciples. No Jew ever made the mistake of thinking that Moses was Divine; even his most enthusiastic disciple would never have dreamed of ascribing to him a statement like, "Baptizing in the name of the Father, and of **Moses,** and of the Holy Ghost." Compare Matt. 28:19. And the reason is that Moses neither spoke nor acted as one coming from God and sharing His nature. On the other hand, the New Testament sets forth this miracle: here are a group of men who walked with Jesus and saw Him in all the characteristic aspects of His humanity—and yet who later worshiped Him as Divine, preached Him as the power unto salvation, and invoked His name in prayer. John, who leaned on Jesus' bosom, has no hesitation in speaking of Him as the eternal Son of God who created the universe (John 1:1, 3), and relates without any hesitancy or apology Thomas' act of worship and cry of adoration, "My Lord and my God." John 20:28. Peter, who had seen his Master eat, drink, and sleep, who had known Him to be hungry and thirsty, who had heard Him pray and watched Him weep—in short, who had witnessed all sides of His humanity, later tells the Jews that Jesus is at the right hand of God; that He possesses the Divine prerogative of imparting the Holy Spirit (Acts 2:33, 36); that He is the only way of salvation (Acts 4:12), the Pardoner of sins (Acts 5:31), and the Judge of the dead. Acts 10:42. In his second epistle (3:18) he worships Him by ascribing unto Him "glory both now and for ever."

There is no record that Paul the apostle saw Jesus in the flesh (although he saw Him in glorified form), but he was in direct contact with those who had. And this Paul, who never lost that reverence for God ingrained into him from youth, nevertheless with perfect calmness describes Jesus as "the great God and our Saviour" (Titus 2:13), represents Him as embodying the fullness of Deity (Col. 2:9), as being the Creator and Upholder of all things. Col. 1:17. As such His name is to be invoked in prayer (1 Cor. 1:2; compare Acts 7:59) and His name coupled with that of the Father and the Holy Spirit in the benediction. 2 Cor. 13:14.

From the very beginning the primitive church regarded and worshiped Christ as Divine. Early in the second century a Roman official reported that the Christians were accustomed to assemble before daybreak and "sing a hymn of praise responsively to Christ, as it were to God." Wrote a pagan author: "The Christians are still worshiping that great man who was crucified in Palestine."

Even the ridicule of the pagans is a testimony to Christ's Deity. An inscription was found in an ancient Roman palace (not later than the third century) representing a human figure with an ass' head hanging on the cross, while a man stands before it in the attitude of worship. Underneath is the inscription: "Alexamenos worships his God." Comments Henry van Dyke:

Thus the songs and prayers of believers, the accusations of persecutors, the sneers of skeptics, and the coarse jests of mockers, all join in proving that beyond a doubt the primitive Christians paid Divine honor to the Lord Jesus. . . . There is no more room for doubt that the early Christians saw in Christ a personal unveiling of God, than that the friends and followers of Abraham Lincoln regarded him as a good and loyal American citizen of the white race.

We must not, however, infer that the primitive church did not worship God the Father, for the contrary is true. Their general practice was to pray to the Father in the name of Jesus, and to thank the Father for the gift of the Son. But so real to them was the Deity of Christ and the oneness between the two Persons, that it came quite natural to them to invoke the name of Jesus. It was their firm adherence to the Old Testament teaching of the unity of God, combined with the firm belief in the Deity of Christ, which led them to formulate the doctrine of the Trinity.

The following words of the Nicene creed (fourth century) have been, and are still, recited by many in a formal manner, but they nevertheless express faithfully the heart-felt conviction of the early church:

We believe in one Lord Jesus Christ, the Son of God, only-begotten of the Father, that is, of the substance of the Father, God of God, Light of Light, very God of very God, begotten not made, being of one substance with the Father; by whom all things were made which are in heaven and earth: who, for us men and for our salvation came down, and was incarnate and was made man, and suffered, and rose the third day, and ascended into the heavens, and shall come again to judge the quick and the dead.

2. The Word (eternal pre-existence and activity).

The word of man is that by which he expresses himself, by which he puts himself in communication with others. By his word he makes his thoughts and feelings known, and by his word he issues commands and gives effect to his will. The word that he speaks carries the impress of his thought and character. By a man's word one could perfectly know him even though one were blind. Sight and information could reveal but little regarding his character if one had not listened to his word. A man's word is his character in expression.

Likewise, the "Word of God" is that by which He communicates with other beings, deals with them; it is the means by which He expresses His power, intelligence, and will. Christ is that Word, because through Him God has revealed His activity, will, and purpose, and because by Him God contacts the world. We express ourselves through words; the eternal God expresses Himself through His Son, who is "the express image of his person." Heb. 1:3. Christ is the Word of God because He reveals God by demonstrating Him in person. He not only **brings** God's message—He **is** God's message.

Consider the need of such a Revealer. Try to comprehend the size of the universe, with its untold millions of heavenly bodies, covering distances that stagger the mind; picture the mighty reaches of space beyond the universe of matter; then try to conceive of the mightiness of the One who is the source of it all. Consider, on the other hand, the insignificance of man. It has been calculated that if everybody in this world were six feet tall and a foot and a half wide and a foot thick, the whole two billion of the human race could be packed into a box measuring a half mile in each direction. God—how mighty and vast! Man—how infinitesimal! Moreover, this God is a Spirit, and therefore not to be apprehended by the eye of flesh and by natural senses. The great question arises, How can man have communion with such a God? how can he even conceive of His nature and character?

It is true that God revealed Himself through the prophetic word, through dreams and visions, and through temporary manifestations. But man yearned for a yet plainer answer to the question, What is God like? To answer this question there occurred the most stupendous event in history—"And the Word was made flesh." John 1:14. The eternal Word of God took upon Himself human nature and became man, in order to reveal the eternal God through a human personality. "God, who at sundry times and in divers manners spake in time past unto the fathers by the prophets, hath in these last days **spoken** unto us by his **Son.**" Heb. 1:1, 2. Therefore to the question, What is God like? the Christian answers, God is like Christ, because Christ is the Word—the idea that God has of Himself. That is, He is the "express image of his person" (Heb. 1:3), "the image of the invisible God." Col. 1:15.

3. Lord (sovereignty).

A glance through a concordance will reveal the fact that "Lord" is one of the commonest titles given to Jesus. This title indicates His Deity, exaltation, and sovereignty.

(a) Deity. The title "Lord" when used before a name, conveyed the thought of Deity to both Jews and Gentiles. The word "Lord" in the Greek ("Kurios") was the equivalent for Jehovah in the Greek translation of the Old Testament; therefore to the Jews "the Lord Jesus" was clearly an ascription of Deity. When the emperor of the Romans referred to himself as the "Lord Cæsar," and required his subjects to say "Cæsar is Lord," the Gentiles understood that the emperor was claiming divinity. The Christians so understood the term, and chose rather to suffer persecution than to ascribe to a man a title which belonged only to One truly Divine. Only to Him whom God had exalted would they ascribe Lordship and render worship.

(b) Exaltation. In **eternity** Christ possesses

the title "Son of God" by virtue of His relationship to God (Phil. 2:9); in **history** He **earned** the title "Lord" by dying and rising for the salvation of men. Acts 2:36; 10:36; Rom. 14:9. He was always Divine by nature; He became Lord by achievement. To illustrate: a young man born into the family of a multi-millionaire is not content with inheriting what others have labored for, but desires to possess only what he has earned by his own achievement. He therefore voluntarily relinquishes his privileges, takes his place as a common worker, and by laborious effort wins for himself a place of honor and wealth. In like manner the Son of God, though He was by nature equal to God, voluntarily subjected Himself to sinless human limitations, by taking man's nature, became a servant to man, and finally died on the cross for his redemption. As a reward He was exalted to Lordship above all creatures—an appropriate recompense, for what better claim could anyone have to rulership over men than the fact that He loved them, and gave Himself for them! Rev. 1:5. The claim has been acknowledged by millions and the Cross has become a stepping-stone by which Jesus has ascended to sovereignty over men's hearts.

(c) Sovereignty. In Egypt Jehovah revealed Himself to Israel as Redeemer and Saviour; at Sinai, as Lord and King. The two go together, for He who became their Saviour has a right to be their Ruler. That is why the Ten Commandments begin with the declaration, "I am the Lord thy God, which have brought thee out of the land of Egypt, out of the house of bondage." Ex. 20:2. In other words, "I the Lord, who redeemed you, have a right to rule you."

And so it was with Christ and His people. The early Christians recognized instinctively—as all true disciples do—that the One who redeemed them from sin and destruction has a right to be Lord of their lives. Bought with a price they are not their own (1 Cor. 6:20), but belong to Him who died and rose for them. 2 Cor. 5:15. Therefore the title "Lord" applied to Jesus by His followers means: "the One who by His death has earned the place of sovereign in my heart, and whom I feel constrained to worship and serve with all my powers."

When the impotent man was reproved for carrying his bed on the sabbath day, he replied, "He that made me whole, the same said unto me, Take up thy bed, and walk." John 5:11. He knew instinctively, with the logic of the heart, that He who had given him life had a right to tell him how to use that life. If Jesus is our Saviour He must be our Lord.

4. The Son of Man (humanity).

(a) **Who?** According to Hebrew usage, "son of" denotes relationship and participation. For example: "the children of the kingdom" (Matt. 8:12) are those who are to share in its truths and blessings. "The children of the resurrection" (Luke 20:36) are those who partake of the resurrection life; a "son of peace" (Luke 10:6) is one possessing a peaceful disposition; a "son of perdition" (John 17:12) is one destined to taste of doom and ruin. Therefore "son of man" means primarily one who shares human nature and human qualities. In this way "son of man" becomes an emphatic designation for man in his characteristic attributes of weakness and helplessness. Num. 23:19; Job 16:21; 25:6. In this sense the title is applied about eighty times to Ezekiel as a reminder of his weakness and mortality, and as an incentive to humility in the fulfillment of his prophetic calling.

Applied to Christ, "Son of man" designates Him as sharing human nature and qualities, and subject to human infirmities. Yet, at the same time, this very title implies His Deity, for, if a person were to declare emphatically, "I am a son of man," people would say, "Why, everybody knows that." But on the lips of Jesus the expression meant a heavenly One who had definitely identified Himself with humanity as representative and Saviour. Notice also that it is **the**—and not **a**—Son of man.

The title is connected with His earthly life (Mark 2:10; 2:28; Matt. 8:20; Luke 19:10), with His sufferings on behalf of humanity (Mark 8:31), and with His exaltation and rule over humanity. Matt. 25:31; 26:24; compare Dan. 7:14.

By referring to Himself as "Son of man," Jesus wished to convey the following message: "I, the Son of God, am Man, in weakness, in suffering, even unto death. Yet I am still in touch with heaven whence I came and hold such relation to the Divine that I can forgive sins (Matt. 9:6), and am superior to religious regulations which have but a temporary and national significance. Matt. 12:8. This manhood shall not cease when I have passed through those last stages of suffering and death, which I must endure for man's salvation and to finish My work. For I shall arise and take it with Me to heaven, whence I shall return to rule over those whose nature I have assumed."

The humanity of the Son of God was real and not make-believe; He is portrayed as actually suffering hunger, thirst, weariness, grief, and as being subject in general to the sinless infirmities of human nature.

(b) How? By what act, or means, did the Son of God become Son of man? What miracle could bring into the world "the second man," who is "the Lord from heaven." 1 Cor. 15:47. The answer is that the Son of God entered the world as the Son of man by being conceived in the womb of Mary by the Holy Spirit, and apart from a human father.

And the quality of the entire life of Jesus is in keeping with the manner of His birth. He who came by the **virgin birth,** lived the **virgin life** (perfect sinlessness)—the latter as great a miracle as the former. He who was born miraculously, lived miraculously, rose from the dead miraculously, and left the world miraculously.

Upon the **fact** of the virgin birth is based the **doctrine** of the Incarnation. John 1:14. The following statement of this doctrine is from the pen of Martin J. Scott, an able scholar:

As all Christians know, the **Incarnation** means that God (that is, the Son of God) became man. This does not mean that God was turned into man, nor that God ceased to be God and began to be man; but that, remaining God, He assumed or took a new nature, namely, human, uniting this to the Divine nature in the one being or person—Jesus Christ, true God and true man.

At the marriage feast of Cana, the water became wine at the will of Jesus Christ, the Lord of Creation (John 2:1-11). Not so did God become man, for at Cana the water ceased to be water when it became wine.

An example which may help us to understand in what sense God became man, but yet one that does not perfectly illustrate the matter, is that of a king who should of his own will become a beggar. If a mighty king should leave his throne and the luxury of the court, and assume the rags of a beggar, live with beggars, share their hardship, etc., in order to improve their condition, we should say that the king became a beggar, yet was still truly a king. It would be correct to say that what the beggar suffered was the suffering of a king; that when the beggar atoned for something, it was the king that atoned, etc.

Since Jesus Christ is God and man, it is evident that God, in some way, is man also. Now in what way is God man? It is clear He was not always man, since man is not eternal and God is. At a certain definite time, therefore, God became man by assuming human nature. What do we mean by **assuming human nature**? We mean that the Son of God, remaining God, took another nature, namely, that of man, and so united it with His own that it constituted one Person, Jesus Christ.

The Incarnation, therefore, means that the Son of God, true God from all eternity, in the course of time became true man also, in the one Person, Jesus Christ, consisting of the two natures, the human and the Divine. This, of course, is a mystery. We cannot understand it any more than we can understand the Trinity.

There are mysteries all about us. We do not understand how the grass and water which cattle live on are converted into their flesh and blood. A chemical analysis of milk shows no ingredient of blood in it, yet the milk which a babe receives from its mother's breast is changed into the flesh and blood of the child. The mother herself does not know how the milk is produced in her which she gives to the child she suckles.

All the wise men in the world cannot explain the connection between thought and speech. We should not be surprised, therefore, if we cannot understand the Incarnation. We believe it because He who has revealed it is God Himself, who can neither deceive nor be deceived.

(c) **Why** did the Son of God become the Son of man, or, what were the purposes of the incarnation?

1. As we have already seen, the Son of God came into the world to be a Revealer of God. He claimed that His deeds and words were God-guided (John 5:19, 20; 10:38); even His evangelistic work was a revelation of the heart of the heavenly Father, and those who criticized His work among sinners thereby showed their lack of harmony with the spirit of heaven. Luke 15:1-7.

2. He took our human nature in order to glorify it and so fit it for a heavenly destiny. He thus fashioned a heavenly pattern, so to speak, by which human nature could be made over into the Divine likeness. He, the Son of God, became the Son of man in order that the children of men might become the sons of God (John 1:12), and one day they shall be like Him (1 John 3:2);

even their bodies shall be "fashioned like unto his glorious body." Phil. 3:21. "The first man (Adam) is of the earth, earthy: the second man is the Lord from heaven" (1 Cor. 15:47); therefore, "as we have borne the image of the earthy (compare Gen. 5:3), we shall also bear the image of the heavenly" (verse 49), because "the last Adam was made a quickening spirit." Verse 45.

3. But the hindrance in the way of the perfection of humanity was sin—which in the beginning deprived Adam of the glory of original righteousness. In order to deliver us from its guilt and power, the Son of God died as an atoning sacrifice.

5. The Christ (official title and mission).

(a) The Prophecy. "Christ" is the Greek form of the Hebrew word "Messiah," which means literally, "the anointed one." The word is suggested by the practice of anointing with oil as a symbol of Divine consecration to service. While priests, and sometimes prophets, were anointed with oil at installation into office, the title "Anointed" was applied particularly to the kings of Israel who ruled as Jehovah's representatives. 2 Sam. 1:14. In some cases the symbol of the anointing was followed by the spiritual reality, so that the person became in a living sense the anointed of the Lord. 1 Sam. 10:1,6; 16:13.

Saul was a failure; but David, who succeeded him, was "a man after God's own heart," a king who placed God's will supreme in his life and who regarded himself as God's representative. But most of the kings departed grievously from the Divine standard, leading the people into idolatry; and even some of the godly kings were not without blemish. Against this dark background the prophets displayed the promise of the coming of a king from the house of David, a king even greater than David. Upon him should rest the Spirit

of the Lord in a power never before known. Isa.
11:1-3; 61:1. Though the Son of David, He would
yet be the Son of Jehovah, bearing Divine names.
Isa. 9:6, 7; Jer. 23:6. Unlike that of David His
reign would be everlasting, and under His sway
should come all nations. This was **the** Anointed,
or the Messiah, or the Christ, and upon Him were
centered the hopes of Israel.

(b) The Fulfilment. It is the consistent testimony of the New Testament that Jesus claimed
to be the Messiah, or Christ, promised in the Old
Testament.

Just as the president of this land is first elected and then publicly inaugurated, so Jesus Christ
was eternally elected to be the Messiah or Christ,
and then publicly inaugurated into His Messianic
office at the Jordan. Just as Samuel first anointed
Saul and then explained to him the meaning of the
anointing (1 Sam. 10:1), so God the Father
anointed His Son with the Spirit of power and
whispered into His ear the meaning of His anointing—"Thou art my beloved Son, in whom I am
well pleased." Mark 1:11. In other words, "Thou
art the Son of Jehovah, whose coming was predicted by the prophets, and I hereby endow Thee
with authority and power for Thy mission, and
send Thee forth with My blessing."

The people among whom Jesus was to minister looked forward to Messiah's coming, but unfortunately their hopes were colored by political
stress. They were expecting a "strong man," who
should be a combination of soldier and statesman.
Would Jesus be that kind of Messiah? The Spirit
led Him into the wilderness to fight the issue out
with Satan, who craftily suggested that He adopt
the popular platform and so take a short and
easy way to power. "Meet their material crav-
ings," suggested the Tempter (compare Matt.
4:3, 4 and John 6:14, 15, 26), dazzle them by leap-

ing from the Temple (and incidentally, "stand in" well with the priesthood), set yourself up as champion of the people and lead them to war. Compare Matt. 4:8, 9 and Rev. 13:2, 4.

Jesus knew that Satan was advocating the popular policy which was inspired by his own selfish and violent spirit. That such a course would lead to bloodshed and ruin was certain. No! He would take God's way and rely solely upon spiritual weapons to conquer the hearts of men, even though that path must lead to misunderstanding, suffering, and death. In the wilderness Jesus chose the cross, and chose it because it was part of God's program for His life.

From this choice the Master never swerved, although often outwardly tempted to forsake the way of the cross. See, for example, Matt. 16:22.

Jesus scrupulously kept Himself from entanglement in the contemporary political situation. At times He forbade those healed by Him to broadcast His fame lest His ministry be misunderstood as a stirring of the people against Rome. Matt. 12:15, 16; compare Luke 23:5, where His success was turned into a charge against Him. He deliberately refused to head a popular movement. John 6:15. He forbade the public proclamation of His Messiahship and the testimony to His transfiguration lest false hopes be raised among the people. Matt. 16:20; 17:9. With consummate wisdom He escaped a skillful trap to either discredit Him before the people as "unpatriotic," or on the other hand, to involve Him in difficulties with the Roman government. Matt. 22:15-21. In all this the Lord Jesus fulfilled the prophecy of Isaiah that God's Anointed should be a proclaimer of Divine truth, and not a violent agitator and self-seeking rabble-rouser (Matt. 12:16-21)—as were some of the false messiahs who preceded and followed Him. John 10:8;

Acts 5:36; 21:38. He faithfully avoided the carnal and followed the spiritual methods, so that Pilate, Rome's representative, could testify, "I find no fault in this man."

We have seen that Jesus began His ministry among a people who had the right hope of a Messiah but a wrong conception of His Person and work. To use a homely illustration: the label was correct but the contents of the bottle did not conform to the label. Knowing this, Jesus did not at first publicly proclaim Himself as Messiah (Matt. 16:20), for He knew this would be a signal for rebellion against Rome. He spoke rather about the Kingdom, describing its standards and its spiritual nature, hoping to inspire the people with a hunger for a spiritual kingdom which would in turn lead them to desire a spiritual Messiah. And His efforts in this direction were not entirely fruitless, for John the apostle tells us (chapter 1) that from the very first there was a spiritual group who recognized Him as the Christ; also, from time to time, He revealed Himself to individuals who were spiritually ready. John 4:25, 26; 9:35-37.

But the nation as a whole did not connect His spiritual ministry with the thought of the Messiah. That He was an able teacher, a mighty preacher, and even a prophet, they freely admitted (Matt. 16:13, 14); but certainly not the one to head their economic, military, and political program—as they thought the Messiah should.

But why blame the people for such an expectation? God had indeed promised to set up an earthly kingdom. Zech. 14:9-21; Amos 9:11-15; Jer. 23:6-8. True, but preceding that event was to take place a moral cleansing and spiritual regeneration of the nation. Ezek. 36:25-27; compare John 3:1-3. And both John the Baptist and Jesus made it plain that the nation, in its present condition, was not fit to enter the kingdom. Hence the exhortation, "Repent ye: for the kingdom of heaven is at hand." But while the words, "kingdom of heaven," profoundly moved the people, the word "repent" made but slight impression. Both the leaders (Matt. 21:31, 32) and the people (Luke 13:1-3; 19:41-44) refused to meet the conditions of the kingdom and consequently lost the privileges of the kingdom. Matt. 21:43.

But God the All-wise had foreseen Israel's failure (Isa. 6:9, 10; 53:1; John 12:37-40), and God the All-powerful had overruled it for the furtherance of a plan hitherto kept secret. The plan was as follows: Israel's rejection would make opportunity for God's taking a Chosen People from among the Gentiles (Rom. 11:11; Acts 15: 13, 14; Rom. 9:25, 26), who, with Jewish believers should constitute a company known as the Church. Eph. 3:4-6. Jesus Himself gave His disciples a glimpse of this period (the Church Age) which was to intervene between His first and second advents, calling these revelations "mysteries" because they were not revealed to Old Testament seers. Matt. 13:11-17. On one occasion the unwavering faith of a Gentile centurion contrasted with the lack of faith in many Israelites and recalled to His inspired vision the spectacle of Gentiles from all lands entering the Kingdom which Israel had rejected. Matt. 8:10-12.

The crisis foreseen in the wilderness had come, and Jesus prepared to break some saddening news to His disciples. He began tactfully by strengthening their faith with a heaven-inspired testimony of His Messiahship, a testimony given by Peter their leader. He then made a remarkable prediction (Matt. 16:18, 19), which may be paraphrased as follows: "The congregation of Israel (or "church," Acts 7:38) have rejected Me as their Messiah, and their leaders will actually excom-

municate Me—the very cornerstone of the nation
Matt. 21:42. But God's plan will not fail thereby, for I will establish another congregation
("church"), composed of men like you, Peter (1
Pet. 2:4-9), who will believe in My Deity and
Messiahship. You shall be a leader and minister
in this congregation, and yours will be the privilege of opening its door with the key of gospel
truth, and you and your brethren shall administer
its affairs."

Then Christ made an announcement which the
disciples did not fully understand until after His
resurrection (Luke 24:25-48); namely, that the
cross was part of God's program for the Messiah.
"From that time forth began Jesus to shew unto
his disciples, how that he must go unto Jerusalem,
and suffer many things of the elders and chief
priests and scribes, and be killed, and be raised
again the third day." Matt. 16:21.

In due time the grim prophecy was fulfilled.
When Jesus might have escaped death by denying
His Deity, when He might have been acquitted by
denying that He was a king, He persisted in His
testimony and died upon a cross bearing the inscription, THIS IS THE KING OF THE JEWS.

But the suffering Messiah (Isa. 53:7-9) rose
from the dead (Isa. 53:10, 11), and as Daniel had
foreseen ascended to the right hand of God (Dan.
7:14; Matt. 28:18), whence He shall come to
judge the quick and the dead.

After this survey of Old and New Testament
teaching, we are in a position to state our full
definition of the title "Messiah"; namely, the One
whom God has authorized to save Israel and the
nations from sin and death, and to rule over them
as the Lord and Master of their lives. That such
a claim implies Deity is understood by thinking
Jews, but is a stumblingblock to them. Said
Claude Montefiore, noted Jewish scholar:

If I could believe that Jesus was God (that is, Divine), then he would obviously be my Master. For my Master—the Master of the modern Jew, is, and can only be, God.

6. Son of David (royal lineage).

This title is equivalent to "Messiah," for an important qualification of the Messiah was His Davidic descent.

(a) The Prophecy. As a reward for his faithfulness David was promised an everlasting dynasty (2 Sam. 7:16), and eternal sovereignty over Israel was given to his house. This was the Davidic or throne covenant. From that time on dates the expectation that, come what might to the nation, there would surely appear, in God's time, a king belonging to the stock and lineage of David. In times of distress the prophets reminded the people of this promise, telling them that the redemption of Israel and the nations was connected with the coming of a great King from the house of David. Jer. 30:9; 23:5; Ezek. 34:23; Isa. 55:3, 4; Psalm 89:34-37.

Notice particularly Isa. 11:1, which may be translated as follows: "A shoot shall come forth from the stump of the tree of Jesse (father of David), and a green branch shall grow out of his roots." In Isa. 10:33, 34, Assyria, Israel's cruel oppressor, is compared to a cedar tree, whose stump never puts out any shoots but rots slowly. Once cut down, the tree has no future. And such describes the fate of Assyria, which has long passed off the scene of history. The house of David, on the other hand, is compared to a tree which will put forth new growth from the stump left in the ground. Isaiah's prophecy is as follows: the Jewish nation will be almost destroyed, and the house of David will cease as a royal house—will be hewn down to a stump. Yet from that stump will come a shoot, from the roots of that stump will come a Branch—the King-Messiah.

(b) The Fulfillment. Judah was taken into captivity, and from this captivity they returned, without a king, without independence, to be subjected successively to Persia, Greece, Egypt, Syria, and after a brief period of independence, to Rome. During these centuries of subjection to Gentiles, there were times of discouragement when the people looked back to the former glories of David's kingdom and cried with the Psalmist, "Lord, where are thy former lovingkindnesses, which thou swarest unto David in thy truth?" Psalm 89:49. But they never lost hope. Gathered around the fire of Messianic prophecy they warmed their hearts and waited patiently for the Son of David.

They were not disappointed. Hundreds of years after the royal house of David had ceased, an angel appeared to a Jewish girl and said, "And, behold, thou shalt conceive in thy womb, and bring forth a son, and shalt call his name JESUS. He shall be great, and shall be called the Son of the Highest: and the Lord God shall give unto him the throne of his father David: and he shall reign over the house of Jacob for ever; and of his kingdom there shall be no end." Luke 1:31-33; compare Isa. 9:6, 7.

A Deliverer had arisen from the house of David. At a time when the house of David seemed reduced to its lowest estate, when the living heirs were a humble carpenter and a simple maiden, then by God's miraculous agency, the Branch sprouted up from the hewn-down stump and grew into a mighty tree that has provided shelter for many people.

The following is the substance of the Davidic covenant as interpreted by the inspired prophets: Jehovah would come down for the salvation of His people, at which time there would be on earth a living descendant of the Davidic family, through whom Jehovah would deliver and then rule His people. That Jesus was this Son of David is shown by the announcement made at His birth, by His genealogies (Matt. 1 and Luke 3), by the fact that He accepted the title when ascribed to Him (Matt. 9:27; 20:30, 31; 21:1-11), and by the testimony of New Testament writers. Acts 13:23; Rom. 1:3; 2 Tim. 2:8; Rev. 5:5; 22:16.

But the title, "Son of David," was not a complete description of the Messiah, for it emphasized mainly His human descent. Therefore the people, ignoring the Scriptures which spoke of the Divine nature of the Christ, looked for a human Messiah who should be a second David. On one occasion Jesus attempted to lift the thoughts of the leaders above this incomplete conception. Matt. 22:42-46. "What think ye of Christ (that is, the Messiah)?" He asked, "whose son is he?" The Pharisees naturally answered, "The son of David." Then Jesus, quoting Psalm 110:1, asked, "If David then call him **Lord,** how is he his son?" How can David's Lord be David's son? was the question that baffled the Pharisees. The answer of course is: the Messiah is **both.** By the miracle of the virgin birth Jesus was born of God and also born of Mary; He was thus the Son of God and Son of man. As Son of God He is David's Lord; as son of Mary He is David's son.

The Old Testament records two lines of Messianic truth. Some portions declare that the Lord Himself will come from heaven to deliver His people (Isa. 40:10; 42:13; Psalm 98:9); others state that a deliverer shall arise from the family of David. Both comings were blended in the appearing of a little Babe in Bethlehem, David's city. For then the Son of the Highest was born as the son of David. Luke 1:32.

Notice how in Isa. 9:6, 7, the Divine nature and Davidic descent of the coming King are combined. The title mentioned here—"the everlasting

Father"—has been misunderstood by some who have deduced therefrom that there is no Trinity but that Jesus is the Father and that the Father is Jesus.

A knowledge of Old Testament language might have saved them from this error. In those days a ruler who governed wisely and righteously was described as a "father" to his people. Thus, the Lord speaking through Isaiah, says of an official: "He shall be a **father** to the inhabitants of Jerusalem, and to the house of Judah. And the key of the house of David will I lay upon his shoulder (note the resemblance to Isa. 9:6, 7 and compare Rev. 3:7)," Isa. 22:21, 22. This title was applied to David, as shown by the people's acclamation at the Triumphal Entry, "Blessed be the kingdom of our **father** David." Mark 11:10. They did not mean that David was their ancestor, for they were not all descended from his family; and of course they had no idea of calling him the heavenly Father. David is described a "father" because as the king after God's own heart he was the real founder of the Israelitish kingdom (Saul was a failure), extending it from 6,000 to 60,000 square miles. In like manner Washington is often referred to as the "Father of our country."

"Father" David was human, and died; his kingdom was earthly, and in time disintegrated. But, according to Isa. 9:6, 7, David's descendant, the King-Messiah, will be Divine, and His kingdom will be an everlasting one. David was a temporary "father" to his people; the Messiah will be an **everlasting** (immortal, Divine, unchangeable) Father to all people—so appointed by God the Father. Psalm 2:6-8; Luke 22:29.

7. Jesus (saving work).

The Old Testament teaches that God Himself is the Source of salvation: He is Israel's Saviour and Deliverer. "Salvation is of the Lord." He delivered His people from Egypt's bondage and ever afterwards Israel knew by experience that He was a Saviour. Psalm 106:21; Isa. 43:3, 11; 45:15, 22; Jer. 14:8.

But God acts through agents, therefore we read of His saving Israel through the mysterious "angel of his presence." Isa. 63:9. At times human instruments were used; Moses was sent to deliver Israel from bondage; from time to time judges were raised up to succor Israel.

"But when the fullness of the time was come, God sent forth his Son, made of a woman, made under the law, to redeem them that were under the law, that we might receive the adoption of sons." Gal. 4:4. On entering the world the Redeemer was given the name expressive of His supreme mission: "And thou shalt call his name JESUS: for he shall save his people from their sins." Matt. 1:21.

The first Gospel preachers did not need to explain to the Jews the meaning of "Saviour"; they had already learned the lesson from their own history. Acts 3:26; 13:23. The Jews understood the Gospel message to mean that just as God sent Moses to deliver Israel from the bondage of Egypt, so He had sent Jesus to deliver His people from their sins. They understood, but refused to believe.

Upon the cross Christ fulfilled the mission indicated by His name, for to save people from their sins implies atonement and atonement implies death. But even during His lifetime He lived up to His name: He was always a Saviour. All over the land were people who could testify: "I was bound by sin, but Jesus delivered me"; Mary Magdalene could say, "He delivered me from seven devils"; the one-time paralytic could testify, "He forgave my sins."

II. THE OFFICES OF CHRIST.

In the Old Testament age there were three classes of mediators between God and His people: the prophet, the priest, and the king. As the perfect Mediator (1 Tim. 2:5) Christ embodies in Himself all three offices. Jesus is the Christ-Prophet, to enlighten the nations; the Christ-Priest to offer Himself as a sacrifice for the nations; the Christ-King to rule over the nations.

1. Christ the Prophet.

The Old Testament prophet was God's earthly representative or agent, who revealed His will in relation to the present and future. That the Messiah should be a prophet to enlighten Israel and the nations is the testimony of the prophets (Isa. 42:1; compare Rom. 15:8), and that Jesus was so regarded is the testimony of the Gospels. Mark 6:15; John 4:19; 6:14; 9:17; Mark 6:4; 1:27. As Prophet—

(a) Jesus Preached Salvation. The prophets of Israel exercised their most important ministry in times of crisis, when rulers, statesmen and priests were confused in judgment and impotent to act. It was then that the prophet stepped forth and with Divine authority pointed the way out of their difficulties, saying, "This is the way, walk ye in it."

The Lord Jesus appeared at a time when the Jewish nation was in a state of restlessness caused by a yearning for national deliverance. Through Christ's preaching the nation was confronted with a choice as to a way of deliverance—war with Rome or peace with God. They made the wrong choice and suffered the disastrous consequence of national destruction. Luke 19:41-44; compare Matt. 26:52. As their disobedient and rebellious forefathers once vainly attempted to force their way into Canaan (Num. 14:40-45), so the Jews, in A.D. 68, tried to force their deliverance from

Rome. Their rebellion was quenched in blood, Jerusalem and the Temple were destroyed, and the wandering Jew began his painful trek through the centuries.

The Lord Jesus showed the way of escape from sin's guilt and power, not only to the nation, but also to the individual. Those who came with the question, What shall I do to be saved? received definite instructions, and these always included a command to follow Him. He not only showed, but made the way of salvation by His death upon the cross.

(b) Jesus Announced the Kingdom. All the prophets spoke of a time when mankind should come under the sway of God's law—a condition of affairs described as the "kingdom of God." This was an outstanding theme of our Lord's preaching. "Repent: for the kingdom of heaven (or God) is at hand." Matt. 4:17. And He enlarged upon this theme by describing the nature of the kingdom, its membership, conditions for entrance, its spiritual history following His ascension (Matt. 13) and the manner of its establishment on earth.

(c) Jesus Predicted the Future. Prophecy is based upon the principle that history does not move with aimless feet but is under the control of God, who knows the end from the beginning. He reveals the course of history to His prophets, thus enabling them to predict the future. As a Prophet, Christ foresaw the triumph of His cause and kingdom through the fleeting changes of human history. Matt. 24 and 25.

The ascended Christ continues His prophetic ministry through His body, the Church, to whom He has promised inspiration (John 14:26; 16:13), and imparted the gift of prophecy. 1 Cor. 12:10. This means not that Christians are to add to the Scriptures, which are "a once for all" revelation (Jude 3); but by inspiration of the Spirit they will speak forth messages of edification, exhortation, and comfort (1 Cor. 14:3) based upon the Word.

2. Christ the Priest.

A priest, in the Biblical sense, is a person Divinely consecrated to represent man before God and to offer sacrifices which will secure the Divine favor. "For every high priest is ordained to offer gifts and sacrifices: wherefore it is of necessity that this man should have somewhat also to offer." Heb. 8:3. At Calvary Christ, the Priest, offered Himself, the sacrifice, in order to secure man's pardon and acceptance before God. His life previous to this was a preparation for His priestly work. The Eternal Son partook of our nature (Heb. 2:14-16) and our experiences, for otherwise He could not represent man to God nor offer sacrifices; nor could He succor tempted humanity without knowing by experience what temptation meant. A priest must therefore be human; for example, an angel could not be a priest for men.

Compare Leviticus, chapter 16 and Hebrews, chapters 8 to 10. Israel's high priest was consecrated to represent man before God and to offer sacrifices which would secure Israel's pardon and acceptance. Once a year the high priest made atonement for Israel; in a typical sense he was their saviour who appeared in God's presence to secure their pardon. The sacrifices of that day were killed in the outer court of the temple; in like manner Christ was crucified on earth. Then the blood was carried into the Holy of holies and sprinkled in the very presence of God; in like manner Jesus ascended into heaven "to appear in the presence of God for us." God's acceptance of His blood gives us the confidence of the acceptance of all who trust in His sacrifice.

Although Christ offered a perfect sacrifice once and for all, His priestly work still continues.

He ever lives to apply the merits and power of His atoning work before God on behalf of sinners. He who died for men now lives for them, to save them, and to intercede for them. And when we pray "in the name of Jesus," we are pleading Christ's sacrificial work as the basis of our acceptance, for only thus are we assured that we are "accepted in the beloved." Eph. 1:6.

3. Christ the King.

The Christ-Priest is also the Christ-King. That both offices be held by one person was God's plan for the perfect Ruler. Thus Melchizedek, because he was both king of Salem and priest of the most high God, became a type of God's perfect King, the Messiah. Gen. 14:18, 19; Heb. 7:1-3. There was a period in the history of the Jewish people when this ideal was nearly realized. About a century and a half before the birth of Christ, the land was ruled by a succession of high priests who were also civil rulers; the ruler of the land was both priest and king. Also, during the Middle Ages the Pope claimed and attempted to exercise both spiritual and temporal power over Europe. As Christ's representative he claimed to rule both the Church and the nations. "Both experiments, the Jewish and the Christian, failed," writes Dr. H. B. Swete; "and so far as can be judged from these examples, neither the temporal nor the spiritual interests of men are promoted by entrusting them to the care of the same representative. The double task is too great for mere man to discharge."

But the inspired writers spoke of the coming of One who was worthy to bear the double burden. That One was the coming Messiah, a ruler and a priest after the order of Melchizedek (Psalm 110:1-4) and a "priest upon his throne." Zech. 6:13. Such an One is the ascended Christ. Compare Psalm 110:1 and Heb. 10:13.

According to the Old Testament, the Messiah was to be a great King of the house of David who should rule Israel and the nations, and usher in the golden age of righteousness, peace, and prosperity. Isa. 11:1-9; Psalm 72.

Jesus claimed to be that King. In the presence of Pilate He testified that He was born to be a King, although He explained that His kingdom was not of this world, that is, not a kingdom founded by human force and governed according to human standards. John 18:36. Some time before His death Jesus predicted His coming in power and majesty to judge the nations. Matt. 25:31. Even upon the cross He looked and spoke as a King, so that the dying thief caught the vision and cried, "Lord, remember me when thou comest into thy kingdom." Luke 23:42. He dimly perceived that death would usher Jesus into a heavenly kingdom.

After His resurrection Jesus declared, "All power is given unto me in heaven and in earth." Matt. 28:18. Following His ascension He was crowned and enthroned with the Father. Rev. 3:21; compare Eph. 1:20-22. This means that in the sight of God Jesus is King; He is not only Head of the church, but also Lord of all the world and Master of men. The earth is His and all that is therein. His and His alone are the power and glory of all those shining kingdoms which Satan the Tempter long ago pointed out from the mountain top. He is Christ the King, Lord of the world, Possessor of its riches, and Master of men.

All this is now true from God's viewpoint; but all men have not yet acknowledged Christ's rule. Though Christ has been anointed King of Israel (Acts 2:30), "His own" (John 1:11) have rejected His sovereignty (John 19:15) and the nations go their way without knowledge of His rule.

This situation was foreseen and predicted by Christ in the Parable of the Pounds. Luke 19:12-25. In those days when a national ruler fell heir to a kingdom he must first go to Rome and receive it from the emperor, after which he was free to return and rule. So Christ compares Himself to a certain nobleman who went into a far country to receive for himself a kingdom and return. He came from heaven to earth, earned exaltation and sovereignty by His atoning death for men, and then ascended to His Father's throne to receive the crown and rulership. "But his citizens hated him, and sent a message after him, saying, We will not have this man to reign over us"; Israel likewise rejected Jesus as their King. Knowing that he would be absent for some time the nobleman entrusted his servants with certain tasks; in like manner, Christ, foreseeing that a period of time would elapse between His first and second advents, has allotted to His servants the task of proclaiming His kingdom and winning members into it, baptizing them into the name of Father, and of the Son, and of the Holy Spirit. Finally, the nobleman, having received his kingdom, returned to reward his servants, assert his sovereignty, and punish his enemies. In like manner will Christ return to reward His servants, assert His sovereignty over the world, and punish the wicked. This is the central theme of the book of Revelation. Rev. 11:15; 12:10; 19:16.

He will then sit upon the throne of David, and there will follow the Kingdom of the Son of David, when for a thousand years the earth shall enjoy a golden reign of peace and plenty. Every sphere of human activity will come under Christ's control, evil-doing will be suppressed with the rod of iron, Satan will be bound, and the earth shall be filled with the knowledge and glory of God "as the waters cover the sea."

III. THE WORK OF CHRIST.

Christ performed many works, but **the** work which He accomplished was to die for the sins of the world. Matt. 1:21; John 1:29. Included in this atoning work are His death, resurrection, and ascension. He must not only die for, but also live for us; He must not only rise from the dead for us, but also ascend to intercede for us. Rom. 8:34; 4:25; 5:10.

1. The Death of Christ.

(a) Its Importance. The outstanding event and central doctrine of the New Testament may be summed up in the words, "Christ died (the event) for our sins (the doctrine)." 1 Cor. 15:3. The atoning death of Christ is the unique feature of the Christian religion. Martin Luther declared that Christian doctrine was distinguished from every other kind, and especially from that which seems to be Christian, by the fact that it is the doctrine of the Cross. The whole battle of the Reformation was for the right interpretation of the Cross. That he who understands the Cross rightly, understands the Christ and the Bible, was the teaching of the Reformers.

It is this unique feature of the Gospels which makes Christianity **the** religion; for **the** problem is the sin problem, and the religion which makes perfect provision for the deliverance from **the** guilt and power of sin has a Divine finality. Jesus is the author of "eternal salvation" (Heb. 5:9), that is, of final salvation; all that salvation can mean is secured by Him.

(b) Its Meaning. There is a certain true relationship between man and his Maker. Something has happened to destroy this relationship. Not only is man far from God, and unlike God in character, but there is an obstacle which blocks the way like a great boulder, an obstacle so great that man cannot remove it by his own efforts.

That obstacle is sin, or rather guilt, which means sin reckoned by God against the sinner.

Man cannot remove this obstacle; if it is removed, deliverance must come from God's side; God must take the initiative and save man if he is to be saved. That God has done this is the testimony of the Scriptures. He sent His Son from heaven to earth to remove that obstacle and so make possible man's reconciliation to God. By dying for our sins He removed the barrier; He bore what we should have borne; He accomplished for us what we were powerless to do for ourselves; this He did because it was the will of the Father. This is the essence of the atonement.

Because of its importance the topic will be considered more in detail in a separate chapter.

2. The Resurrection of Christ.

(a) **The Fact of the Resurrection.** The resurrection of Christ is **the** miracle of Christianity. Once we establish the reality of this event, discussion of the other miracles of the Gospels becomes unnecessary. Furthermore, it is the miracle with which the entire Christian faith stands or falls; for Christianity is a historical religion basing its teachings on definite events that occurred in Palestine about nineteen hundred years ago. These events are the birth and ministry of Jesus Christ, culminating in His death, burial, and resurrection. Of these, the resurrection is the capstone, for, if Christ be not risen, then He was not what He claimed to be; His death was not an atoning death; then Christians have been deceived for centuries; preachers have been declaring error; the faithful have been deceived by a false hope of salvation. But, thank God, instead of the interrogation point, we may place the exclamation point after this doctrine: "But now is Christ risen from the dead, and become the firstfruits of them that slept!"

(b) The Evidence for the Resurrection. "You Christians live on the fragrance of an empty tomb," said a French skeptic. It is a fact that those who came to embalm Jesus' body on that memorable Easter morning, found His tomb empty. This fact has not been and cannot be explained apart from the truth of the resurrection of Jesus. How easily the Jews could have refuted the witness of the first preachers by producing the body of our Lord. But they did not—and could not!

How explain the existence of the Christian church, which would surely have remained buried with her Lord—if He had not risen? The living, radiant church of the Day of Pentecost was not born of a dead Leader!

What shall we do with the testimony of those who saw Jesus after His resurrection, many of whom spoke with Him, handled Him, ate with Him; hundreds of whom Paul said were alive in his day; many of whom have given us their inspired testimony in the New Testament?

How shall we receive the testimony of men too honest and sincere to preach a message they knew to be false, and sacrifice all for it?

How shall we explain the conversion of Paul the apostle, from a persecutor of Christianity to one of its greatest missionaries, unless he actually saw Christ on the Damascus road?

There is but one answer to these questions— **Christ arose!**

Attempts have been made to evade the fact. The Jewish leaders contended that His disciples had stolen the body. As if a small band of timid and discouraged disciples could have mustered up sufficient courage to wrest from hardened Roman soldiers the body of their Master whose death had spelled failure to their hopes!

Modern scholars have their explanations. "The disciples simply experienced a vision." As if hundreds would see the same vision and imagine that they were really seeing Christ! "Jesus did not really die; He simply swooned and was still alive when taken from the cross." As if a pale, bloodless, drooping and weakly Jesus could have persuaded doubting disciples, and above all a doubting Thomas, that He was the risen Lord of life!

These explanations are so weak that they carry their own refutation. Again we affirm, **Christ arose!** De Wette, the liberal theologian, affirmed that, "The resurrection of Jesus Christ cannot be called into doubt any more than the historic certainty of the assassination of Cæsar."

(c) The Meaning of the Resurrection. It means that Jesus is all that He claimed to be—Son of God, Saviour, Lord. Rom. 1:4. The answer of the world to His claims was—a cross; God's answer was—the resurrection.

It means that the atoning death of Christ was a reality, and that man may find forgiveness for past sins, and so find peace with God. Rom. 4:25. The resurrection is really the completion of the atoning death of Christ. How do we know that it was no ordinary death—that it really will take away sin? Because **He arose!**

It means that we have a sympathetic High Priest in heaven, who has lived our life, and known our sorrows and infirmities, and who is able to give us power to live the Christ-life day by day. He who died for us, now lives for us. Rom. 8:34; Heb. 7:25.

It means that we may know that there is a life to come. "But no one has ever come back to tell us about the other world," is a common objection. But Somebody has come back—Jesus Christ. To the question, "If a man die shall he live again?" science can only say, "We don't know." Philosophy can say, "There ought to be a future life." But Christianity can say, "Because He lives, we shall live also; because He arose from the dead, so shall all."

The resurrection of Christ gives not only proof of the fact of immortality, but also the assurance of personal immortality. 1 Thess. 4:14; 2 Cor. 4:14; John 14:19.

It means that there is a certainty of future judgment. As the inspired apostle has said, God "hath appointed a day, in the which he will judge the world in righteousness by that man whom he hath ordained; whereof he hath given assurance unto all men, in that he hath raised him from the dead." Acts 17:31.

As surely as Jesus rose from the dead to be judge of men, so surely shall men rise from the dead to be judged of Him.

3. The Ascension of Christ.

The fact of the ascension is witnessed to by the Gospels, Acts, and the Epistles. What is the meaning of this historical fact? What doctrines are based upon it? What are its practical values?

The ascension teaches that our Master is—

(a) The Heavenly Christ. Jesus left the world because the time had come for Him to return to the Father. His departure was a "going up" as His entrance into the world had been a "coming down." He who had descended now ascended where He was before. And as His entrance into the world was supernatural so was His departure.

Consider the manner of His departure. His appearances and disappearances after the resurrection had been instantaneous, the ascension was gradual—"while they beheld." Acts 1:9. It was followed by no fresh appearances in which the Lord appeared in their midst in Person to eat and drink with them; appearances of this kind ended with the ascension. It was a withdrawal once for all from earthly life which men live on this side of the grave. From now on the disciples must not think of Him as "Christ after the flesh," that is, living an earthly life, but as the glorified Christ living a heavenly life in the presence of God and contacting them through the Holy Spirit. Before the ascension the Master appeared, disappeared and re-appeared from time to time, in order to gradually wean them from dependence on visible and earthly contact with Him, and to accustom them to invisible, spiritual communion with Him.

Thus the ascension becomes the dividing line of two periods of Christ's life: From birth to the resurrection He is the Christ of human history, the One who lived a perfect human life under earthly conditions. Since the ascension He is the Christ of spiritual experience, who lives in heaven and touches men through the Holy Spirit.

(b) The Exalted Christ. In one place Christ is described as "going up," and in another as being "taken up." The first represents Christ as entering the Father's presence in His own will and right; the second lays the emphasis on the Father's act by which He is exalted as the reward of His obedience unto death.

His slow ascent in full view of the disciples brought to them the realization that He was leaving His earthly life, and also made them eyewitnesses to His departure. But once out of their sight, the journey was completed by an act of will. Comments Dr. Swete:

That instant all the glory of God shone about Him, and He was in heaven. The sight was not altogether new to Him; in the depth of His Divine consciousness the Son of man had memories of the glories which in His pre-incarnate life He had had with the Father "before the world was." John 17:5. But the human soul of Christ up to the moment of the Ascension had no experience of the full vision of God which burst upon Him when He was taken up. This was the goal of His human life, the joy set before Him (Heb. 12:2); and in the moment of the Ascension it was attained.

It was in view of His ascension and exaltation that Christ declared, "All power (authority) is given unto me in heaven and in earth." Matt. 28:18. Compare Eph. 1:20-23; 1 Pet. 3:22; Phil. 2:9-11; Rev. 5:12. Quoting again from Dr. Swete:

Nothing is done in that great unknown world, which we call heaven, without His initiating, guiding and determining authority. Processes inconceivable to our minds are being carried forward beyond the veil by agencies equally inconceivable. It is enough for the Church to know that all which is being done there is done by the authority of her Lord.

(c) The Sovereign Christ. Christ ascended to a place of headship over all creatures. He is the "head of every man" (1 Cor. 11:3), the "head of all principality and power" (Col. 2:10); all the authorities of the unseen world as well as the world of men are under His control. 1 Pet. 3:22; Rom. 14:9; Phil. 2:10, 11. He possesses this universal sovereignty to be exercised for the good of the Church which is His body; God "put all things under his feet, and gave him to be the head over all things to the church." In a very special sense, therefore, Christ is the Head of the Church. This headship is manifested in two ways:

1. By the authority exercised by Him over the members of the Church. Paul uses the marriage relationship as an illustration of the relationship between Christ and the Church. Eph. 5:22-33. As the Church lives in subjection to Christ, so wives are to be in subjection to their husbands; as Christ loved the Church and gave Himself for it, so husbands are to exercise their authority in the spirit of love and self-sacrifice. The Church's obedience to Christ is a willing sub-

mission; in like manner should the wife be obedient not only for conscience' sake but out of love
and reverence.

For Christians the marriage bond has become
a "mystery" (a truth with a Divine meaning),
for it reveals the spiritual union between Christ
and His Church; "authority on the part of Christ,
subordination on the part of the church, love on
both sides—love answering to love, to be crowned
by the fullness of joy, when the union is consummated at the coming of the Lord" (Swete).

A prominent characteristic of the early
Church was the attitude of loving submission to
Christ. "Jesus is Lord" was not only the state-
ment of a creed but also the rule of life.

2. The ascended Christ is not only the ruling,
directing Power of the Church, but also the source
of its life and energy. As the vine is to the branches, as the head is to the body, so is the living
Christ to His Church. Although the Head of the
Church is in heaven, He is in the closest union with
His Body on earth, the Holy Spirit being the bond
of communication. Eph. 4:15, 16; Col. 2:19.

(d) The Way-preparing Christ. The separation between Christ and the earthly Church begun
at the ascension, is not permanent; He ascended
as a forerunner to prepare the way for them to
follow Him. His promise was: "Where I am,
there shall also my servant be." John 12:26. The
term "forerunner" is first applied to John the
Baptist as the way-preparer of the Christ. Luke
1:76. As John prepared the way for Christ, so
the ascended Christ prepares the way for the
Church. This hope is likened to "an anchor of the
soul, both sure and stedfast, and which entereth
into that within the vail; whither the forerunner is
for us entered, even Jesus." Heb. 6:19, 20. Though
tossed by the waves of testing and adversity, the
soul of the faithful need not fear shipwreck, so

long as their hope keeps a firm grip upon heavenly realities. In a spiritual sense the Church has already followed the glorified Christ; they have been made to "sit together in heavenly places in Christ Jesus." Eph. 2:6. Through the Spirit believers ascend in heart and mind to their risen Lord; but there will be a literal ascension corresponding to the ascension of Christ. 1 Thess. 4:17; 1 Cor. 15:52. This hope of the believers is no delusion, for already they feel the tug of the anchor chain—they are conscious of the drawing power of the glorified Christ. 1 Pet. 1:8. With this hope Jesus comforted the disciples before His departure. John 14:1-3. "Wherefore comfort one another with these words." 1 Thess. 4:18.

(e) The Interceding Christ. By virtue of His assuming our nature and dying for our sins, Jesus is a Mediator between God and man. 1 Tim. 2:5. But the Mediator is also an Intercessor, and intercession goes a step further than mediation. A mediator may bring two parties together and leave them to settle their difficulties; but an intercessor goes on to say a word on behalf of the person in whose interest he appears. Intercession is an important ministry of the ascended Christ. Rom. 8:34. It forms the climax of His saving activities. He died for us; He rose for us; He ascended for us, and makes intercession for us. Rom. 8:34. Our hope is not in a dead Christ, but in One who lives; and not merely in One who lives, but who lives and reigns with God. Christ's priesthood is eternal, therefore His intercession is permanent.

He can therefore carry on to completion ("to the uttermost," Heb. 7:25) every case He undertakes to defend, thus guaranteeing to those who approach God through his mediation entire restoration to the Divine favor and blessing; indeed, to do this is the very purpose of His life in heaven; He ever lives for this end that He may intercede with God on their behalf. There can be no suspension of His intercessory work as long as the world lasts, . . . for the intercession of the ascended Christ is not a prayer but a **life.** The New Testament does not represent Him as a suppliant standing ever before the Father, and with outstretched arms, and with strong crying and tears, pleading our cause before the presence of a reluctant God; but as a throned Priest-King, asking what He will from a Father who always hears and grants His request."—Swete.

What are the main petitions of Christ in His intercessory ministry? The prayer in John 17 will suggest the answer.

Similar to the office of mediator is that of advocate (in the Greek, "paraclete"). 1 John 2:1. An advocate or paraclete is one who is called to the help of a person in distress or necessity, to administer comfort or give advice and protection. Such was the Lord's relation to the disciples during the days of His flesh. But the ascended Christ is concerned also with the problem of sin. As Mediator, He gains access for us into God's presence; as Intercessor, He bears our petitions before God; as Advocate, He meets the charges laid against us by the "accuser of the brethren," on the score of sin. For true Christians a life of habitual sin is out of the question (1 John 3:6); but isolated acts of sin are possible in the best of Christians and such occasions require the advocacy of the Christ. In 1 John 2:1, 2 there are stated three considerations which give force to His advocacy: first, He is "with the Father," in God's presence; second, He is "the righteous," and as such may be an atonement for others; third, He is "the propitiation for our sins," that is, a Sacrifice which secures God's favor by atoning for sin.

(f) The Omnipresent Christ. John 14:12. While on earth Christ was limited to one place at a time and could not be in contact with each of His disciples all the time. But by ascending to the powerhouse of the universe He was enabled to broadcast His power and Divine personality at all times and in all places and to all His disciples. Ascension to the throne of God gave Him not only omnipotence (Matt. 28:18) but also omnipresence, making it possible for Him to fulfill the promise, "Where two or three are gathered together in my name, there am I in the midst of them." Matt. 18:20.

(g) Conclusion. What are the practical values of the doctrine of the Ascension? (1) Consciousness of the ascended Christ, whom we look forward to seeing some day, is an incentive to holiness. Col. 3:1-4. The upward glance will counteract the downward pull. (2) The knowledge of the ascension makes for a right conception of the Church. Belief in a merely human Christ will cause people to regard the Church as merely a human society, useful for philanthropic and moral purposes, but possessing no supernatural power or authority. On the other hand, a knowledge of the ascended Christ will result in the recognition of the Church as an organism, a supernatural organism deriving Divine life from its risen Head. (3) Consciousness of the ascended Christ will produce a right attitude toward the world and worldly things. "For our conversation (literally, "citizenship") is in heaven; from whence also we look for the Saviour, the Lord Jesus Christ." Phil. 3:20. (4) Faith in the ascended Christ will inspire a deep sense of personal responsibility. Belief in the ascended Christ carries with it the knowledge that an account will have to be rendered to Him some day. Rom. 14:7-9; 2 Cor. 5:9, 10. The sense of a responsibility to a Master in heaven acts as a deterrent to sin and an incentive to righteousness. Eph. 6:9. (5) With faith in the ascended Christ is connected the joyous and blessed hope of His returning. "And if I go and prepare a place for you, I will come again." John 14:3.

7

THE ATONEMENT

"Upon a life I did not live;
Upon a death I did not die;
Upon another's death, another's life,
I risk my soul eternally."

OUTLINE

I. ATONEMENT IN THE OLD TESTAMENT.
1. The Origin of Sacrifice.
   a. Ordained in heaven.
   b. Instituted on earth.
2. The Nature of Sacrifice.
3. The Efficacy of Sacrifice.
   a. Old Testament sacrifices were good.
   b. The New Testament Sacrifice is better.

II. ATONEMENT IN THE NEW TESTAMENT.
1. The Fact of the Atonement.
2. The Necessity for the Atonement.
   a. God's holiness reacts against—
   b. Man's sinfulness, and produces—
   c. Wrath, which is averted by—
   d. Atonement.
3. The Nature of the Atonement. Christ's death is:
   a. An atonement.
   b. A propitiation.
   c. A substitution.
   d. A redemption.
   e. A reconciliation.
4. The Efficacy of the Atonement.
   a. Pardon of transgression.
   b. Freedom from sin.
   c. Deliverance from death.
   d. The gift of life eternal.
   e. The victorious life.

I. ATONEMENT IN THE OLD TESTAMENT.

Why take time and space to describe Old Testament sacrifices? For the simple reason that in the word "sacrifice" we have the key to the meaning of the death of Christ. Many modern theories have been offered to explain that death, but any explanation that leaves out the atoning element is un-Scriptural, for nothing is more marked in the New Testament than the use of sacrificial terms to set forth the death of Christ. To describe Him as "the Lamb of God," to say that His blood cleanses from sin and purchases redemption, to teach that He died for our sins— all this is to say that Jesus' death was a real Sacrifice for sin.

Since the death of Jesus is described in language of Old Testament sacrifice, a knowledge of sacrificial terms helps greatly in its interpretation. For sacrifices (in addition to providing a ritual of worship for the Israelites) were prophetic signs ("types") pointing to the perfect Sacrifice; consequently a clear understanding of the sign will lead to a better knowledge of the One sacrificed. Not only were these sacrifices prophetic of the Christ, but they also served to prepare God's people for the higher dispensation to be ushered in at Christ's coming. When the first gospel preachers declared that Jesus was the Lamb of God whose blood had purchased redemption from sins, they did not have to define these terms to their countrymen, to whom these terms were already familiar.

We, however, who live thousands of years after these events, and who have not been brought up under the Mosaic ritual, must needs study the spelling book, so to speak, by which Israel learned to spell out the great message: Redemption through an Atoning Sacrifice. Such is the justification for this section on the origin, history, nature, and efficacy of Old Testament sacrifice.

1. The Origin of Sacrifice.

(a) Ordained in Heaven. The Atonement was no afterthought on the part of God. The Fall of man did not take Him by surprise, necessitating quick steps to remedy it. Before the creation of the world, He who knows the end from the beginning had made provision for man's redemption. Just as a machine is conceived in the inventor's mind before it is built, so the atonement was in the mind and purpose of God before its actual accomplishment. This truth is borne out by the Scriptures. Jesus is described as "the Lamb slain from the foundation of the world." Rev. 13:8. The Passover Lamb was "foreordained" several days before it was killed (Ex. 12:3, 6); so Christ, the Lamb without blemish and without spot, "verily was foreordained before the foundation of the world, but was manifest in these last times for you." 1 Peter 1:19, 20. He purchased for man eternal life, which God "promised before the world began." Titus 1:2. That there should be a body of people sanctified by this sacrifice was decreed "before the foundation of the world." Eph. 1:4. Peter told the Jews that although they had in their ignorance crucified Christ with wicked hands, they had nevertheless fulfilled the eternal plan of God, for He was "delivered by the determinate counsel and foreknowledge of God." Acts 2:23.

Thus it is evident that Christianity is not a new religion that began nineteen hundred years ago, but is the historical manifestation of an eternal purpose.

(b) Instituted on Earth. Since hundreds of years were to elapse before the consummation of the Sacrifice, what was sinful man to do in the meanwhile? From the very beginning God or-

dained an institution which should both fore-
shadow the Sacrifice and also become a means of
grace for the repentant and believing. We refer
to animal sacrifice, one of the most ancient of
human institutions.

The first mention of a slain animal occurs in
the third chapter of Genesis. After our first
parents sinned they became conscious of physical
nakedness—which was an outward indication of
nakedness of conscience. Their efforts to cover
themselves outwardly with leaves and inwardly
with excuses were in vain. Then we read that the
Lord God took the skins of animals and covered
them. While the record does not state in so many
words that this was a sacrifice, yet in pondering
the spiritual meaning of the act, one cannot avoid
the conclusion that we have here a revelation of
Jehovah the Redeemer making provision for man's
redemption. We see an innocent creature dying
in order that the guilty might be covered; that is
the primary purpose of sacrifice—a divinely provided covering for a guilty conscience. The first
book of the Bible pictures an innocent creature dying for the guilty, and the last book of the Bible
speaks of the spotless Lamb slain in order to loose
the guilty from their sins. Rev. 5:6-10.

2. The Nature of Sacrifice.

This original institution of sacrifice very likely explains why sacrificial worship has been practiced in all ages and lands. Though perverted
from the original pattern, heathen sacrifices are
based upon two fundamental ideas, worship and
atonement. (1) Man recognizes that he is under
the power of a Deity who has certain rights over
him. As a recognition of these rights, and as a
sign of his self-surrender, he offers a gift or a
sacrifice. (2) Frequently, however, becoming
conscious that sin has disturbed the relationship,
he recognizes instinctively that the same God who

made him has the right to destroy him, unless something is done to repair the broken relationship. That the killing of a victim and the shedding of its blood would avert the Divine wrath and secure the Divine favor, was one of the deepest and firmest of ancient beliefs. But how did they learn all this? Paul tells us that there was a time "when they knew God." Rom. 1:21. Just as fallen man bears marks of his divine origin, so even heathen sacrifices bear some marks of an original Divine revelation.

After the Confusion of Tongues (Gen. 11:1-9) Noah's descendants scattered everywhere, carrying with them the true knowledge of God, for as yet there was no record of idolatry. What occurred in course of time is briefly described in Rom. 1:19-32. The nations turned from the pure worship of God and soon lost sight of His glorious Godhead. Spiritual blindness resulted. Instead of seeing God through the heavenly bodies, they began to worship these bodies as deities; instead of seeing the Creator through the trees and animals, they began to worship these as gods; instead of recognizing that man was made in the image of God, they began to make a god in the image of man. Thus spiritual blindness led to idolatry. Idolatry was no mere intellectual matter; the worship of Nature, which forms the basis of most heathen religions, led man to deify (make gods of) his own lusts, and moral corruption was the result.

Yet, in spite of this perversion, man's worship bore dim marks which indicated that there had been a time when he knew better. Back of the idolatries of Egypt, India, and China one discovers a belief in one true God, the Eternal Spirit who made all things.

When spiritual darkness covered the nations, as moral corruption had covered the pre-Flood

world, God made a new start with Abraham as
He had previously done with Noah. God's plan
was to make Abraham the ancestor of a nation
which should restore to the world the light of the
knowledge and glory of God. At Mount Sinai, Israel was set apart from the nations, to be a "holy
nation." In order to direct them in the life of
holiness He gave them a code of laws governing
their moral, national, and religious life. Among
these were the laws of sacrifice (Leviticus, chapters 1-7) which taught the nation the right manner in which God should be approached and worshiped. The nations had a perverted worship;
God restored to Israel the pure worship.

The Mosaic sacrifices were means whereby
the Israelites rendered man's first obligation to
his Maker, namely, worship. They were offered
with the object of attaining to communion with
God, and removing all obstacles to that communion. For example, if the Israelite sinned and
so disturbed the relationship between himself and
God he brought a sin offering—the Sacrifice of
Atonement. Or, if he had wronged his neighbor
he brought a trespass offering—the Sacrifice of
Restitution. Lev. 6:1-7. Now that he was right
with God and man and desired to reconsecrate
himself, he offered a burnt offering—the Sacrifice
of Worship. Leviticus 1. He was now ready to
enjoy happy communion with God who had pardoned and accepted him, so he presented a peace
offering—the Sacrifice of Fellowship. Leviticus 3.

The purpose of these bloody sacrifices is
fulfilled in Christ, the perfect Sacrifice. His death
is described as a death for sin, as a bearing of sin.
2 Cor. 5:21. God made His soul a trespass offering for sin (such is the literal rendering of Isaiah
53:10); He paid the debt we could not pay, and
blotted out the past which we could not undo.
He is our burnt offering, for His death is set forth

as an act of perfect self-giving. Heb. 9:14; Eph.
5:2. He is our peace offering, for He Himself
described His death as a means of our sharing
(having communion with) the Divine life. John
6:53-56; compare Lev. 7:15, 20.

3. The Efficacy of Sacrifice.

To what extent were the Old Testament sacrifices efficacious? Did they really secure pardon
and cleansing? What benefits did they secure for
the offerer? These questions are of real importance, for by comparing and contrasting the
Levitical sacrifices with Christ's Sacrifice we shall
be enabled to better perceive the efficacy and finality of the latter.

The subject is dealt with in the letter to the
Hebrews. The writer is addressing a group of
Hebrew Christians, who, discouraged by persecution are tempted to return to Judaism and the
sacrifices of the Temple. The realities they believe in are invisible; while the Temple with its
gorgeous ritual seems so tangible and real. To
turn their thoughts from such a course of action
the writer makes a comparison between the Old
and New Covenants, showing that the New is
better than the Old, for the Old is imperfect and
temporary while the New is perfect and eternal.
To return to the Temple with its priesthood and
sacrifices would be forsaking substance for
shadow, and perfection for imperfection. The
argument is: the Old Covenant was good, as far
as it went, and for the purpose for which it was
designed; but the New Covenant is better.

(a) **The Old Testament Sacrifices Were
Good.** Else would they not have been divinely ordained. They were good in that they fulfilled a
certain purpose in the Divine plan, namely, to be
a means of grace, that those of Jehovah's people
who had sinned against Him might return to a

state of grace, be reconciled to Him, and continue to enjoy union with Him. When the Israelite had faithfully fulfilled the conditions he could rest upon the promise: "And the priest shall make an atonement for him as concerning his sin, and it shall be forgiven him." Lev. 4:26.

As enlightened Israelites brought their offerings they were aware of two things: first, that repentance in itself was insufficient; a visible transaction must be gone through to indicate that his sin was put away. Heb. 9:22. But on the other hand, he learned from the prophets that the ritual without the right inner disposition of heart was a mere valueless formality. The act of sacrifice must be the outward expression of the inner sacrifices of praise, prayer, righteousness and obedience—the sacrifices of a broken and contrite heart. See Psalm 26:6; 50:12-14; 4:5; 51:16; Prov. 21:3; Amos 5:21-24; Mic. 6:6-8; Isa. 1:11-17. "The sacrifice (blood sacrifice) of the wicked is an abomination to the Lord," declared Solomon. Prov. 15:8. The inspired writers made it clear that ritual motions without righteous emotions were unacceptable devotions.

(b) The One Sacrifice of the New Testament Is Better. While recognizing the Divine ordination of animal sacrifices, enlightened Israelites could not but feel that these were not a perfect means of atonement.

1. There was a wide disparity between an irrational, irresponsible creature and a man made in God's image; and that the animal did not perform the sacrifice either intelligently or voluntarily was evident; there was no fellowship between the offerer and the victim. It was plain that an animal sacrifice could not on the one hand weigh in the balance against a human soul, nor on the other, exercise any spiritual power on the inner man. There was nothing in the blood of

an irrational creature which could effect the spiritual redemption of a soul; that could only be by the offering of a perfect human life. The inspired writer truly voiced what must have been the conclusion of many Old Testament believers when he said, "For it is not possible that the blood of bulls and of goats should take away sins." Heb. 10:4. At best the sacrifices were a temporary and imperfect means of covering sin until a more perfect redemption should come. The law brought the people under conviction for sins (Rom. 3:20), and the sacrifices rendered those sins powerless to provoke the Divine wrath.

2. Animal sacrifices are described as "carnal ordinances," that is, rites which removed bodily defilements, and atoned for the outward acts of sin (Heb. 9:10) but contained no spiritual virtue within themselves. "The blood of bulls and of goats . . . sanctifieth to the purifying of the flesh" (Heb. 9:13); that is, they atoned for those outward defilements which cut off an Israelite from communion in the congregation of Israel. For example, if a person defiled himself physically he was considered unclean and cut off from the congregation of Israel until he had purified himself and offered sacrifice (Lev. 5:1-6); or if he had materially wronged his neighbor, he was under condemnation until he had brought a trespass offering. Lev. 6:1-7. In the first instance the sacrifice cleansed from physical defilement but did not cleanse the soul; in the second instance the sacrifice made atonement for the outward deed but did not change the heart. David himself recognized that he was in the grip of a depravity from which animal sacrifices could not free him (Psalm 51:16; compare 1 Sam. 3:14) and he prayed for that spiritual renewal which they were powerless to effect. Psalm 51:6-10.

3. The repetition of the animal sacrifices

points to their imperfection; they could not make the worshiper perfect (Heb. 10:1, 2), that is, give him a perfect standing or relationship with God upon which he might build his character; they could not give him a "once for all" (Heb. 10:10) experience of spiritual transformation which should be the beginning of a new life.

4. Animal sacrifices were offered by imperfect priests, the imperfection of whose ministry was indicated by the fact that they could not enter at any time into the Holy of Holies, and were therefore unable to lead the worshiper directly into the Divine presence. "The Holy Ghost this signifying, that the way into the holiest of all was not yet made manifest." Heb. 9:8. The priest had no sacrifice to offer whereby he might lead people into a spiritual experience with God, and so make the worshiper "perfect, as pertaining to the conscience." Heb. 9:9.

Had a spiritual Israelite been questioned concerning his hopes for redemption, the same discernment which had revealed to him the imperfection of animal sacrifices would have led him to reply that the solution lay in the future, and that perfect redemption was connected in some way with that perfect order to be ushered in at the coming of the Messiah. Indeed, such a revelation was granted to Jeremiah. That prophet had despaired of the people's ever being able to keep the covenant of the law; their sin was written with an iron pen (17:1), their heart was deceitful and desperately wicked (17:9); they could no more change their hearts than the Ethiopian could change his skin (Jer. 13:23); so calloused and depraved were they that they had passed the state where sacrifices could profit (6:20); indeed, they had forgotten the prime purpose of these sacrifices. From the human viewpoint the people were hopeless, but God comforted Jeremiah with a

promise of the coming of an age when under a
new, better covenant the hearts of the people
would be changed and when there should be a
perfect remission of sins. Jer. 31:31-34. "For I
will forgive their iniquity, and I will remember
their sin no more." In Heb. 10:17, 18 we have the
inspired interpretation of these last words, namely,
that a perfect redemption was to be accomplished
by means of a perfect sacrifice and that therefore
the animal sacrifices were to pass away. Compare
Heb. 10:6-10. Through this one sacrifice man has
a "once for all" experience which gives him a perfect standing with God. What the sacrifices of
the law could not do has been accomplished by
the perfect sacrifice of Christ. "And every priest
standeth daily ministering and offering oftentimes
the same sacrifices, which can never take away
sins: but this man, after he had offered **one sacrifice** for sins **for ever, sat down** on the right hand
of God." Heb. 10:11, 12.

5. One more question remains to be considered. It is certain that people were truly justified before the atoning work of Christ. Abraham
was justified by faith (Rom. 4:23) and entered
the kingdom of God (Matt. 8:11; Luke 16:22);
Moses was glorified (Luke 9:30, 31); and Enoch
and Elijah were translated. There were no doubt
large numbers of godly Israelites who attained
to the spiritual stature of these worthies. Granted
that animal sacrifices were inadequate, and that
Christ's sacrifice was the only perfect Sacrifice, on
what basis were these Old Testament saints justified?

They were saved in anticipation of the future
Sacrifice, just as people today are saved in consideration of the accomplished Sacrifice. Proof
of this truth is found in Heb. 9:15 (compare also
Rom. 3:25), which teaches that the death of Christ
was in some sense retroactive and retrospective;

in other words, it had an efficacy in relation to the past.

Hebrews 9:15 suggests the following line of thought: The Old Covenant was powerless to provide a perfect redemption. Christ closed this covenant and opened the New Covenant with a death which accomplished the "redemption of the transgressions that were under the first testament." That is, when God justified Old Testament believers, He did so in anticipation of Christ's work, "on credit," so to speak; Christ paid the full price on the cross and wiped out the debt. God gave Old Testament saints a standing which the Old Covenant could not purchase, and He did so in view of a coming covenant which could effect this.

If it be asked whether the Old Testament believers during their lifetime enjoyed the same benefits as those living under the New Testament, the answer must be in the negative. There was no permanent gift of the Holy Spirit (John 7:39) to follow their repentance and faith; they did not enjoy the full truth on immortality brought to light by Christ (2 Tim. 1:10), and in general they were limited by the imperfection of the dispensation in which they lived. At best they had but a foretaste of good things to come.

II. ATONEMENT IN THE NEW TESTAMENT.

1. The Fact of the Atonement.

The Atonement which had been foreordained in eternity and typically foreshadowed in the Old Testament ritual was historically accomplished at the crucifixion of Jesus, when God's redemptive purpose was consummated. "It is finished!" The writers of the Gospels describe the sufferings and death of Christ with a minuteness which has no parallel in their narratives of other events of His life, and by referring to the fulfillment of Old Testament prophecies indicate their sense of the importance of the event.

Some writers of the liberal school maintain that the death of Christ was an accident and a tragedy. He began with bright hopes of success, they say, but found Himself enmeshed in a web of circumstances which led to the destruction which He had not foreseen and which He could not escape. But what do the Gospels say about the matter? According to their testimony Jesus knew from the beginning that suffering and death were part of His divinely appointed destiny. In His declaration that the Son of man must suffer, that word "must" indicated Divine vocation and not unforeseen inevitable fate.

At His baptism He heard the words, "Thou art my beloved Son, in whom I am well pleased." These words were taken from two prophecies, the first declaring Messiah's Sonship and Deity (Psalm 2:7), the second describing Messiah's ministry as the Servant of the Lord (Isa. 42:1). Now the Servant mentioned in Isa. 42:1 is the Suffering Servant of Isaiah 53. The conclusion is that even at His baptism Jesus was conscious of the fact that suffering and death were part of His calling. His rejection of Satan's offers in the wilderness implied a tragic issue to His work, for He chose the hard way of rejection rather than the easy one of popularity. The very fact of the Holy One standing with the rest of the people (Luke 3:21) and submitting to baptism was an act of identification with sinful humanity in order to bear the burden of their sins. The Servant of the Lord, according to Isaiah 53, was to be "numbered with the transgressors." The baptism of Jesus may be regarded as "a great act of loving communion with our misery," for in that hour He identified Himself with sinners and thus in a sense His work of atonement began.

Many times during the course of His ministry the Lord referred in a hidden and figurative manner to His coming death (Matt. 5:10-12; Matt. 23:37; Mark 9:12, 13; 3:20-30; 3:6; 2:19); but at Cæsarea-Philippi He plainly told the disciples that He must suffer and die. From that time on He endeavored to brand upon their minds the fact that He must suffer, so that being forewarned they would not suffer shipwreck of faith from the shock of the Crucifixion. Mark 8:31; 9:31; 10:32. He also explained to them the meaning of His death. They were not to regard it as an unfortunate and unforeseen tragedy to which He must resign Himself, but as a death with an atoning purpose. The Son of man had come to "give His life a ransom for many."

At the Last Supper He gave instructions for the future commemoration of His death as the supreme act of His ministry. He ordained a rite which was to commemorate His redemption of mankind from sin as the Passover commemorated Israel's redemption from Egypt.

His disciples, whose minds were as yet under the influence of Jewish ideas about the Messiah and kingdom, were unable to grasp the necessity for His death and could with difficulty be reconciled to the fact. But after the Resurrection and the Ascension they understood, and thereafter they affirm that the death of Christ was a divinely appointed means of atonement. "Christ died for our sins," is their consistent testimony.

2. The Necessity for the Atonement.

The necessity for the atonement follows from two facts: God's holiness and man's sinfulness. The reaction of God's holiness against man's sinfulness is known as His wrath, which may be averted by atonement. Thus the keynotes of our discussion will be as follows: Holiness, sinfulness, wrath, atonement.

(a) Holiness. God is holy in nature, which means that He is righteous in character and in conduct. These attributes of His character are manifest in His dealings with His creation. "He loveth righteousness and judgment." Psalm 33:5. "Justice and judgment are the habitation of thy throne." Psalm 89:14.

God has constituted man and the world according to definite laws. His laws form the very foundation of human personality, being written upon man's heart or nature (Rom. 2:14, 15) before being written on tables of stone. These laws bind man to his Maker in a personal relationship, and form the basis of human responsibility. "In him we live, and move, and have our being" (Acts 17:28), was spoken of mankind in general. Sin disturbs the relationship expressed in this verse, and ultimately the impenitent sinner is cast eternally out of God's presence. This is "the second death."

On many occasions this relationship was reaffirmed, enlarged upon and interpreted under an arrangement known as a covenant. For example, at Sinai God reaffirmed the conditions under which He could have fellowship with man (the moral law) and then enacted a series of regulations by which Israel might observe these conditions in the sphere of national and religious life.

To keep the covenant is to be in right relationship with God, or in grace; for He who is righteous can have fellowship only with those who do right. "Can two walk together, except they be agreed?" Amos 3:3. And to be in fellowship with God means life. From beginning to end, the Scriptures declare this truth, that obedience and life go together. Gen. 2:17; Rev. 22:14.

(b) Sinfulness. This relationship is marred by sin which is a disturbance of the personal relationship between God and man. It is violence done to the constitution, so to speak, under which God and man live, just as unfaithfulness does violence to the covenant under which man and wife live. Jer. 3:20. "Your iniquities have separated between you and your God." Isa. 59:2.

To make amends for violated law and to repair the broken relationship between God and man is the function of atonement.

(c) Wrath. Sin is essentially an attack on God's honor and holiness. It is rebellion against God, for in willfully sinning, man chooses his own will rather than God's, and for the time being, becomes a law unto himself. But should God permit His honor to be attacked, He would then cease to be God. His honor calls for the destruction of the one resisting Him; His righteousness demands satisfaction of the violated law; and His holiness reacts against the sin, this reaction being described as wrath.

But this Divine reaction is not automatic; it does not always react instantly as would fire to a hand thrust into it. God's wrath is governed by personal considerations: He is not hasty to destroy the work of His hands. He pleads with man; He waits to be gracious. He delays judgment in the hope that His goodness shall lead man to repentance. Rom. 2:4; 2 Peter 3:9. But man misunderstands the Divine delays, and scoffs at the thought of judgment. "Because sentence against an evil work is not executed speedily, therefore the heart of the sons of men is fully set in them to do evil." Eccl. 8:11.

But though delayed, retribution must ultimately come, for in a world governed by law there r. 'st be a reckoning. "God is not mocked: for whatsoever a man soweth, that shall he also reap."

Gal. 6:7. This truth was demonstrated at Calvary where God declared "his righteousness for the remission of sins that are past, through the forbearance of God." Rom. 3:25. One scholar translates: "This was to demonstrate the justice of God in view of the fact that sins previously committed during the time of God's forbearance had been passed over." Another paraphrases the words as follows: "He suspended judgment on sins of that former period, the period of His forbearance, with a view to the revelation of His justice under this dispensation, when He, while remaining a just judge, can actually acquit the sinner who makes faith in Jesus his plea." In past ages it seemed that God overlooked the sins of the nations; men sinned on, but they did not seem to reap the wages of sin. And the question arose, Does God ignore sin? But the Crucifixion revealed the awfulness of sin, and pictured the dread penalty upon it. The Cross of Christ declares that God never was, is not, and never can be, indifferent to man's sin. Comments one scholar:

God gave proof of His anger against sin by now and then inflicting punishment on Israel and the Gentiles. But He did not inflict the **full** penalty: else the race would have perished. To a large extent He **passed over** the sins of men. Now for a king to overlook crime, to forbear to punish, or even to delay punishment, is unjust. And God's character was lowered in the eyes of some by His forbearance, which they misinterpreted as an indication that they would escape punishment. God gave Christ to die in order to demonstrate His justice in view of the tolerance of past sins which seemed to obscure it.

(d) Atonement. Man has broken God's laws and violated the principles of righteousness; this knowledge is recorded in memory, and the conscience registers it as guilt. What can be done to remedy the past, and assure the future? Is there an atonement for violated law? To this question three answers have been given:

1. Some contend that atonement is not possible. Life is governed by inexorable law, which punishes violations with a machine-like remorselessness. As a man sows so he must reap, and there is no escape. Sin abides. The sinner can never escape from the past. His future is mortgaged to it and cannot be redeemed. This is the view expressed in the familiar poem:

> The Moving Finger writes; and having writ,
> Moves on; nor all your piety nor wit
> Shall lure it back to cancel half a line,
> Nor all your tears wash out a word of it.

This theory makes man a slave to circumstances; he is powerless to do anything to affect his destiny. If its proponents acknowledge God at all, it is as a God who is enslaved to His own laws, and who cannot provide a way of escape for the sinful.

2. At the other extreme are those who teach that atonement is unnecessary. God is too kind to punish the sinner, and too gracious to demand satisfaction for a broken law. Therefore atonement is unnecessary and forgiveness can be taken for granted.

Said a physician to his patient, who had been speaking to him about the gospel, "I don't need an atonement. When I do wrong I tell God I am sorry and that is sufficient." Some time later his patient came to him and said, "Doctor, I am well now. I am sorry that I fell sick, and I promise you that I will try never to fall sick again." At the same time she hinted that there was no need of considering or even discussing the bill! We trust that the doctor learned the lesson, namely, that mere repentance does not pay the bill, nor repair the damage done by sin.

3. The New Testament teaches that atonement is both possible and necessary: possible, be-

cause God is gracious as well as just; necessary, because God is just as well as gracious.

The two errors referred to are exaggerations of two truths concerning God's character. The first overemphasizes His justice to the exclusion of His grace; the second overemphasizes His grace to the exclusion of His justice. The atonement does justice to both aspects of His character, for in the death of Christ God acts both justly and graciously. In dealing with sin He must needs show His grace, for He desires not the death of the sinner; yet in forgiving sin, He must needs reveal His righteousness, for the very stability of the universe depends upon the sovereignty of God.

In the atonement God does justice to His character as a gracious God. His righteousness called for this punishment of the sinner, but His grace provided a plan for the pardon of the sinner. At the same time He does justice to His character as a righteous God. God would not do justice to Himself if He displayed compassion to sinners in a way which made light of sin, and which ignored its tragic reality. People might think that God was indifferent or indulgent toward sin.

At Calvary the sin penalty was paid and the Divine law honored; God was thus enabled to be gracious without being unjust, and just without being ungracious.

3. The Nature of the Atonement.

"Christ died," expresses the historical fact of the Crucifixion; "for our sins" interprets the fact. In what sense did Jesus die for our sins? How is the fact explained in the New Testament? The answer will be found in the following keywords applied to the death of Christ: Atonement, Propitiation, Substitution, Redemption, Reconciliation.

(a) Atonement. The word "atonement" in the Hebrew means literally "to cover," and is variously translated in our Authorized Version by the following words: make atonement, purge, purge away, reconcile, make reconciliation, pacify, pardon, be merciful, put off.

Atonement (in the original) includes the covering of both the sins (Psalm 78:38; 79:9; Lev. 5:18) and the sinner. Lev. 4:20. To atone for sin is to cover sin from God's sight so that it loses its power to provoke His wrath. We quote from Dr. Alfred Cave:

> The idea expressed by the Hebrew original of the word translated "atone" was cover and covering, not in the sense of rendering invisible to Jehovah, but in the sense of engrossing His sight with something else, of neutralizing sin, so to speak, of disarming it, of rendering it inert to arouse the righteous anger of God. To atone for sin . . . was to throw, so to speak, a veil over sin so dazzling, that the veil, and not the sin, was visible, to place side by side with sin something so attractive as to completely engross the eye. The figure which the New Testament uses when it speaks of the "new robe" (of righteousness) the Old Testament uses when it speaks of "atonement." When an atonement was made under the law it was as though the Divine eye, which had been kindled at the sight of sin and foulness, was quieted by the garment thrown around it; or, to use a figure much too modern, yet equally appropriate, it was as if the sinner who had been exposed to the lightning of Divine wrath had been suddenly wrapped round and insulated. Atonement meant so covering the sinner that his sin was invisible or non-existent in the sense that it could no longer come between him and his Maker. To use the words of a German theologian: "When sinful souls approached the altar of God, where dwelt His holiness, their sinful nature came between them and God, and atonement served the purpose of covering their sins, of canceling the charges on which they were arraigned."

When the blood was applied to the altar by the priest, the Israelite was assured that the promise made to his forefathers, would be realized for him. "And when I see the blood, I will pass over you." Exod. 12:13.

What were the effects of the atonement or covering? The sin was blotted out (Jer. 18:23; Isa. 43:25; 44:22), removed (Isa. 6:7), covered (Psalm 32:1), cast into the depths of the sea (Micah 7:19), cast behind God's back (Isa. 38:17), pardoned (Psalm 78:38). All these terms teach that the sin is covered so as to have all effects from it removed, put out of sight, invalidated, undone. Jehovah sees it no longer and it exerts no influence over Him.

Christ's death was an atoning death because it was death for the removing of sin. Heb. 9:26, 28; 2:17; 10:12-14; 9:14. It was a sacrificial death or a death having relation to sin. What was that relation? "Who in his own self bare our sins in his own body on the tree." 1 Pet. 2:24. "For he hath made him to be sin for us, who knew no sin; that we might be made the righteousness of God in him." 2 Cor. 5:21. To atone for sin is to bear sin and to bear it away, so that it is taken from the transgressor, who is then considered as justified from all unrighteousness, cleansed from defilement and sanctified to belong to God's people. One Hebrew word used to describe cleansing means literally to "un-sin." By Christ's atoning death sinners are "un-sinned" and then "in-Christed" (to coin a word). They die to sin in order to live for Christ.

(b) Propitiation. The word "propitiation" is believed to come from a Latin word "prope," meaning "near." Hence the word means bringing together, making favorable, winning of reconciliation. A sacrifice of propitiation brings man near to God, reconciles him to God by atoning for his transgressions and winning Divine favor and grace. God in mercy accepts the propitiatory gift and restores the sinner to His love. This is also the sense of the Greek word as used in the New Testament. To propitiate is to appease the righteous wrath of a holy God by the offering of an atoning sacrifice. Christ is described as such a propitiation. Rom. 3:25; 1 John 2:2; 4:10. Sin keeps man at a distance from God; but Christ has so dealt with sin on man's behalf that its separative power is annulled; therefore, man may now "draw nigh" to God "in his name." Access to God, the most sublime of privileges, has been purchased at a great price, the blood of Christ. Writes Dr. James Denney:

> And just as in the ancient tabernacle, every object used in worship had to be sprinkled with atoning blood, so all the parts of Christian worship, all our approaches to God, should consciously rest upon the atonement. They should be felt to be a privilege beyond price; they should be penetrated with the sense of Christ's passion, and of the love with which He loved us when He suffered for sins once for all, the just for the unjust, that He might bring us to God.

The word "propitiation" in Rom. 3:25 is the same word used to translate the word "mercy seat" in the Greek. In the Hebrew "mercy seat" means literally "covering," and in both Hebrew and Greek the word conveys the thought of an atoning sacrifice. The reference is to the ark of the covenant (Ex. 25:10-22), which was composed of two parts: first, the ark, representing the throne of Israel's righteous Ruler, and containing the tables of the law as the expression of His righteous will; second, the cover or lid, known as the mercy seat, surmounted by angelic figures known as the Cherubim. Two outstanding lessons were conveyed by this piece of furniture: first, the tables of law taught that God was a righteous God who would not pass by sin and who must enforce His decrees and punish the wicked. But how could a sinful nation live in His sight? The mercy seat, which covered the law, was the place where blood was sprinkled once a year to make atonement for the sins of the people. It was the place of the covering of sin, and taught the lesson that God who is righteous can consistently pardon sin because of an atoning sacrifice. By means of atoning blood, that which is a throne of judgment becomes a throne of grace.

The ark and mercy seat illustrate the problem solved by the atonement. The problem and its solution are stated in Rom. 3:25, 26, where we read that Christ was "set forth to be a propitiation (an atoning sacrifice) through faith in his blood (received by faith), to declare his righteousness for the remission of sins that are past, through the forbearance of God (to show that apparent delays in judgment do not mean that God winks at sin); to declare, I say, at this time his righteousness (His way of making sinners righteous): that he might be just (inflict the punishment for sin), and the justifier (remove the punishment due sin) of him which believeth in Jesus." How can God at the same time both really inflict and really cancel the punishment for sin? In the Person of His Son, God Himself took the penalty, and thus cleared the way for the pardon of the guilty. His law was honored and the sinner was saved. The sin was expiated and God was propitiated. Men can understand how God can be just in punishing and merciful in pardoning; but how God can be just in the act of justifying the **guilty** is a puzzle to them. Calvary solves the problem.

The fact should be emphasized that the propitiation was a real transaction, for there are some who teach that the atonement was simply a demonstration of the love of God and of Christ, intended to move the sinner to repentance. That is indeed one of the effects of the atonement (1 John 3:16) but it does not represent all of the atonement. For example, we might jump into the river and drown in the sight of a poor person in order to convince him of our love; but that act would not pay his rent or his grocery bill! The atoning work of Christ was a real transaction which removed a real obstacle between us and God, and which paid the debt we could not pay.

(c) **Substitution.** The sacrifices of the Old Testament were substitutionary in nature; they were reckoned as doing on the altar for the Israelite what he could not do for himself. The altar represented God; the priest represented the sinner; the victim was the Israelite's substitute to be accepted on his behalf.

In like manner Christ did for us on the cross what we could not do for ourselves, and whatever our need we are accepted "for his sake." Whether we offer God our penitence, thanksgiving or consecration, we do so "in His name," for He is the Sacrifice through whom we approach God the Father.

The thought of substitution is prominent in the Old Testament sacrifices, where the blood of the victim is regarded as covering or making atonement for the soul of the offerer; and in that chapter in which Old Testament sacrifices reach their highest meaning (Isaiah 53) we read: "Surely he hath borne our griefs, and carried our sorrows. . . . But he was wounded for our transgressions, he was bruised for our iniquities: the chastisement of our peace was upon him; and with his stripes we are healed." All these expressions picture the Servant of Jehovah as bearing punishment due to others in order that He might "justify many; for he shall bear their iniquities."

Christ, being the Son of God, was able to offer

a sacrifice of infinite and eternal value. Having assumed human nature, He was able to identify Himself with mankind and so suffer their penalty. He died in our stead; He took the penalty that was ours, in order that we might escape it. This explains the cry, "My God, my God, why hast thou forsaken me?" One who was sinless by nature, and who had never committed a sin in His life, became a sinner (or took the sinner's place). In the words of Paul: "He hath made him to be sin for us" (2 Cor. 5:21); in the words of Peter: He "bare our sins in his own body on the tree." 1 Peter 2:24.

(d) Redemption. The word "redeem" in both Old and New Testaments means to buy back by the paying of a price; to loose from bondage by the paying of a price; to buy in a market and to take from a market. The Lord Jesus is a Redeemer and His atoning work is described as a redemption. Matt. 20:28; Rev. 5:9; 14:3, 4; Gal. 3:13; 4:5; Titus 2:14; 1 Peter 1:18.

The most interesting illustration of redemption is found in the Old Testament law of the kinsman-redeemer. Lev. 25:47-49. According to this law, a man who had sold his property and sold himself into servitude because of debt could regain both his land and liberty at any time on condition that he was redeemed by a man possessing the following qualifications: first, he must be kin to the man; second, he must be willing to redeem or buy back; third, he must have the price. The Lord Jesus Christ measured up to all three qualifications: He became kin to us by taking our nature; He was willing to give up all to redeem us (2 Cor. 8:9), and being Divine He was able to pay the price—His own precious blood.

The fact of redemption reminds us that salvation is costly, and therefore not to be lightly esteemed. When some Corinthian believers became careless in their manner of living, Paul warned them, "Ye are not your own. For ye are bought with a price: therefore glorify God in your body, and in your spirit, which are God's." 1 Cor. 6:19, 20.

Jesus once said, "For what is a man profited, if he shall gain the whole world, and lose his own soul? or what shall a man give in exchange for his soul?" He meant that the soul, or real life, of man could be lost or ruined, and that when it was lost there could be no compensation for it, as there was no means of buying it back. Rich men may boast and trust in their wealth, but their power is limited. Says the Psalmist (49:7-9), "None of them can by any means redeem his brother, nor give to God a ransom for him: (for the redemption of their soul is precious, and it ceaseth for ever:) that he should still live for ever, and not see corruption." But since multitudes have already forfeited their souls by living in sin, and they cannot be redeemed by human means, what is to be done? The Son of man came into the world "to give his life a ransom (or redemption) for many." Matt. 20:28. The supreme object for which He came into the world was to lay down His life as a ransom price that those to whom the forfeited (spiritual) lives belonged might obtain them again. The forfeited lives of many are liberated by the surrender of Christ's life.

Peter tells his readers that they were "redeemed . . . from your vain conversation (literally, conduct, manner of life) received by tradition (that is, from the routine of custom)."

The word "vain" means empty and unsatisfying. Life before the death of Christ touches it is futile and vain; it is a groping or fumbling after something it can never find; and with all its strivings it does not come into contact with reality;

it has no abiding fruit. "What's the use of it all?" cries many a person. From this bondage Christ has redeemed us. When the power of Christ's atoning death enters into any life that life is no longer unsatisfying. It is no longer imprisoned within ruts of ancestral traditions or grooves of established custom. The Christian's actions spring from a new life that has been stirred into being by the power of Christ's death. The death of Christ as a death for sin liberates and re-creates the soul.

(e) Reconciliation. "All things are of God, who hath reconciled us to himself by Jesus Christ, and hath given to us the ministry of reconciliation; to wit, that God was in Christ, reconciling the world unto himself, not imputing their trespasses unto them; and hath committed unto us the word of reconciliation." 2 Cor. 5:18, 19. When we were enemies we were reconciled to God by the death of His Son. (Rom. 5:10). Men who were once alienated and enemies in mind through wicked works, yet now hath he reconciled in the body of His flesh through death. Col. 1:21.

The atonement is often misunderstood and misrepresented. Some imagine the atonement to mean that God was angry at the sinner, and sullenly stood aloof until He was placated by His Son offering to pay the penalty; in other words, God had to be reconciled to the sinner. This, however, is a caricature of the true doctrine. Throughout the Scriptures, it is God, the offended party, who takes the initiative in providing an atonement for man. It is God who clothes our first parents; it is the Lord who ordains the atoning sacrifices; it is God the Father who sends and gives His Son a sacrifice for mankind. God Himself is the author of man's redemption. Though His majesty has been offended by man's sin, and His holiness naturally must react against it, yet He is not willing that the sinner perish (Ezek. 33:11) but that he repent and be saved. Paul does not say that God was reconciled to man, but that God did something in order to reconcile man to Himself.

This act of reconciliation is a finished work; it is a work that has been done in the interests of men so that in the sight of God the entire world is already reconciled. It remains for the evangelist to proclaim it and the individual to receive it. Christ's death has made the reconciliation of all mankind to God **possible;** each individual must make it **actual.**

This is the essence of the gospel message: the death of Christ was a finished work of reconciliation, achieved independently of us, at an infinite cost, and to which men are called by a ministry of reconciliation.

4. The Efficacy of the Atonement.

What does the atoning work of Christ effect for man? what does it produce in his experience?

(a) Pardon of Transgressions. Through His atoning work Jesus Christ paid the debt we could not pay and secured remission of past sins. No longer does the sinful past hang like a dead weight upon the Christian, for his sins are blotted out, taken away, cancelled. John 1:29; Eph. 1:7; Heb. 9:22-28; Rev. 1:5. He has begun life anew, confident that the sins of the past will never meet him at the judgment. John 5:24.

(b) Freedom from Sin. Through the atonement the believer is not only freed from the guilt of past sins but also can be free from the power of sin. The subject is considered in Romans 6 to 8. Paul anticipates an objection which some of his Jewish opponents must have raised often, namely, that if people were saved by merely believing in Jesus, they would think lightly of sin, saying, "If we continue in sin, grace will abound." 6:1. Paul repudiates the very thought and points out that he who truly believes on Christ has, by virtue of his faith, made a clean-cut break with sin—a break so decisive as to be described as "death." Living faith in the crucified Saviour results in the crucifixion of the old sinful nature. The man who believes with all the powers of his soul (and that is what real believing is) that Christ died for sins, has such a conviction of the awfulness of sin that he repudiates it with his entire being. The Cross means the doom of sin in his life. But the Tempter is busy and human nature is frail, hence constant vigilance and daily crucifying of the sinful impulses (6:11) are necessary. And the victory is assured. "For sin shall not have dominion over you: for ye are not under the law, but under grace." 6:14. That is, Law means something is to be done by the sinner; unable to pay the debt or do what the law requires, he remains in the grip of sin. On the other hand, Grace means that something has been done for the sinner—the finished work of Calvary. As he believes what has been done for him, so he receives what has been done for him.

His faith has a powerful ally in the person of the Holy Spirit, who indwells him, helps him to crush the sinful impulses, helps him pray and gives him the assurance of his liberty and victory as a child of God. Romans 8. Indeed, Christ died to remove the obstacle of sin, so that the Spirit of God might come into human life. Gal. 3:13, 14. Being saved by God's mercy revealed in the Cross, the believer receives an experience of cleansing and spiritual quickening. Tit. 3:5-7. Having died to the old life of sin, he is born again to a new life—born of the water (experiencing cleansing) and of the Spirit (receiving Divine life). John 3:5.

(c) Deliverance from Death. Death has both a physical and spiritual meaning. In its physical meaning it denotes the cessation of physical life, consequent upon disease, natural decay or some violent cause. But it is more commonly used in the spiritual meaning, namely, as the penalty attached by God to human sin. The word expresses the spiritual condition of separation from and disfavor with God on account of sin. Dying out of favor with God the impenitent remain separated from God in the other world, and the eternal separation which follows is known as the second death. The threat, "In the day that thou eatest thereof thou shalt surely die," would have failed of fulfillment if death meant simply the physical act of death, for Adam and Eve continued to live after that day. But the proclamation is profoundly true when we remember that the word "death" involved all the penal consequences of sin—separation from God, unrest, inclination toward evil, physical weakness, and finally physical death and consequences beyond death.

When the Scriptures say that Christ died for our sins, they mean that Christ submitted not merely to physical death but to death as the penalty for sin. He humbled Himself to the suffering of death "that he by the grace of God should taste death for every man." Heb. 2:9. Because of His Divine nature and the Divine arrangement He was able to effect this. We may not understand the "how" of the matter, for evidently we are confronted with a Divine mystery. But we accept many facts in this universe without understanding the "how" of them. No sensible person ever deprived himself of the blessings of electricity just because he does not fully understand what electricity is and why it should act as it does. Neither need anyone deprive himself of the benefits of the atonement just because he cannot reason it out as he would a problem of mathematics.

Since death is the penalty of sin, and Christ came to give Himself for our sins, He did so by dying. Concentrated into these few hours of death on the cross was all the awful meaning of that death and the blackness of its penalty, and this explains the cry of abandonment, "My God, my God, why hast thou forsaken me?" These are not the words of a martyr, for martyrs are frequently sustained by the consciousness of God's presence; they are the words of One performing an act which involves the Divine separation. That act was sin-bearing. 2 Cor. 5:21.

While it is true that those who believe on Him may have to suffer physical death (Rom. 8:10), yet for them, the stigma or penalty is taken from death, and it becomes the door to a larger life. In this sense is Jesus' saying true, "Whosoever liveth and believeth in me shall never die." John 11:26.

(d) The Gift of Life Eternal. Christ died that we might not "perish" (the word being used in the Scriptural sense of spiritual ruin), "but have everlasting life." John 3:14-16; compare Rom. 6:23. Eternal life means more than mere existence; it signifies life in favor and fellowship with God. Dead in trespasses and in sins, man is out of favor with God; through Christ's sacrifice the sin is atoned for and he is in full fellowship with God. To be in favor and fellowship with God is life eternal, for it is life with Him who is eternal. This life is possessed now because believers are in fellowship with God now; eternal life is also described as future (Titus 1:2; Rom. 6:22), because the future life will bring perfect fellowship with God. "And they shall see his face."

(e) The Victorious Life. The Cross is the dynamo which generates in the human heart that response which constitutes the Christian life. "I'll live for Him who died for me," well states the dynamic of the Cross. The Christian life is the soul's reaction to the love of Christ.

The Cross of Christ inspires true repentance, which is repentance toward God. Sin may be followed by remorse, shame and anger, but only where there is sorrow for having offended God is there real repentance. This consciousness cannot be produced at will, for it is in the very nature of sin to darken the mind and harden the heart. The sinner needs a powerful motive for repentance—something to make him see and feel that his sin has deeply wronged and offended God. The Cross of Christ supplies that motive, for it demonstrates the awfulness of sin, in that it caused the death of the Son of God; it declares the terrible penalty of sin; but it also reveals the love and grace of God. It has been well said that "all true penitents are children of the Cross. Their penitence is not their own: it is the reaction toward God produced in their souls by this demonstration of what sin is to Him, and what His love does to reach and win the sinful."

It is written of certain saints who had come through great tribulation, that they "have washed their robes, and made them white in the blood of the Lamb." Rev. 7:14. The reference is to the sanctifying power of the death of Christ. They had resisted sin, and were now pure. Where did they secure the strength to overcome sin? From the constraining power of the love of Christ revealed at Calvary. The power of the Cross descending into their hearts enabled them to overcome sin. Compare Gal. 2:20. "They overcame him by the blood of the Lamb, and by the word of their testimony; and they loved not their lives unto the death." Rev. 12:11. The love of Christ constrained them; and enabled them to overcome. The pressure upon them was great, but with the blood of the Lamb as the motive behind them they were unconquerable. "They dared not, with the Cross on which He died before their eyes, betray

His cause by cowardice, and love their lives more than He loved His. They must be His, as He had been theirs."

The victorious life includes victory over Satan. The New Testament declares that Christ conquered Satan on our behalf. Luke 10:17-20; John 12:31, 32; 14:30; Col. 2:15; Heb. 2:14, 15; Rev. 12:11. Christians have the **victory** over the devil as long as they have the **Victor** over the devil!

8

SALVATION

The Lord Jesus Christ, by His atoning death, purchased man's salvation. How is this salvation applied by God and received by man, and so realized in experience? The truths relating to the application of salvation may be grouped under three headings: Justification, Regeneration, Sanctification. The truths relating to man's acceptance of salvation may be grouped under the headings: Repentance, Faith, Obedience.

OUTLINE

I. THE NATURE OF SALVATION.
1. Three Aspects of Salvation.
   a. Justification by the Judge.
   b. Regeneration and adoption by the Father.
   c. Sanctification by the Holy One.
2. Salvation—Outward and Inward.
3. The Conditions of Salvation.
4. Conversion.

II. JUSTIFICATION.
1. The Nature of Justification: Divine Acquittal.
2. The Necessity for Justification: Man's Condemnation.
3. The Source of Justification: Grace.
4. The Ground of Justification: Christ's Righteousness.
5. The Means of Justification: Faith.

III. REGENERATION.
1. The Nature of Regeneration.
   a. A birth. b. A cleansing. c. A quickening. d. A creation. e. A resurrection.
2. The Necessity for Regeneration.
3. The Means of Regeneration.
4. The Effects of Regeneration.
   a. Positional. b. Spiritual. c. Practical.

IV. SANCTIFICATION.
1. The Nature of Sanctification.
   a. Separation. b. Dedication. c. Purification. d. Consecration. e. Service.
2. The Time of Sanctification.
   a. Positional and instantaneous.
   b. Practical and progressive.
3. The Divine Means of Sanctification.
   a. The blood of Christ. b. The Holy Spirit. c. The Word of God.
4. Erroneous Views of Sanctification.
   a. Eradication. b. Legalism. c. Asceticism.
5. The True Method of Sanctification.
6. Entire Sanctification:
   a. Its meaning. b. Its possibilities.

V. THE SECURITY OF SALVATION.
1. Calvinism.
2. Arminianism.
3. A comparison.
4. The Scriptural Balance.

I. THE NATURE OF SALVATION.

The subject of this section is: What constitutes salvation, or the "state of grace."

1. Three Aspects of Salvation.

There are three aspects to salvation, or to the state of grace, and each is characterized by a word conveying a definite picture or illustration of the blessing. The three aspects are: Justification, Regeneration, Sanctification.

(a) Justification is a judicial term bringing to our minds a **court-room** scene. Man, guilty and condemned, before God, is acquitted and declared righteous—that is, justified.

(b) Regeneration (the inward experience) and **adoption** (the outward privilege) suggest a **household** scene. The soul, dead in trespasses and in sins, needs a new life, which new life is imparted by a Divine act of regeneration. The person then becomes a child of God and a member of His household.

(c) The word **sanctification** suggests a **temple** scene, for the word is connected primarily with the worship of God. Set right in relation to God's law and born again to a new life, the person is henceforth dedicated to the service of God. Bought with a price, he is no longer his own; he departs not from the temple (figuratively speaking) but serves God day and night. Luke 2:37. He is sanctified by God and self-given to God.

A saved man, then, is one who has been set right with God, adopted into the Divine family, and is now dedicated to God's service. In other words, his experience of salvation, or state of grace, consists of justification, regeneration (and adoption), and sanctification. Being justified, he belongs to the righteous; being regenerated, he is a child of God; being sanctified, he is a "saint" (literally, a holy person).

Do these blessings follow one another or are they simultaneous as to time? There is indeed a logical order: the sinner is first set right in relation to God's law; his life is disordered, therefore he must be changed; he has been living for sin and the world, and must therefore be separated to a new life and service. Yet, the three experiences are simultaneous in the sense that they cannot be separated actually, although we separate them for the purpose of study. All three constitute "full salvation." The outward change called justification is followed by the inward change called regeneration, and this is followed by dedication to God's service. We cannot conceive of a truly justified person being unregenerate; neither can we conceive of a truly regenerate person being unsanctified (although in actual life a saved person may at times violate his consecration). There can be no full salvation without these three experiences any more than there can be a real triangle without three sides. They represent the three-sided foundation on which the subsequent Christian life is built. From these three beginnings the Christian life progresses to its consummation.

This threefold distinction regulates the language of the New Testament down to very minute shades. To illustrate:

(a) In relation to **justification:** God is the Judge, and Christ the Advocate; sin is transgression of the law; atonement is satisfaction; repentance is conviction; acceptance is pardon or remission; the Spirit's witness is of pardon; the Christian life is obedience and its perfection the fulfillment of the law of righteousness.

(b) Salvation is also a **new life** in Christ. In relation to this new life, God is the Father (Begetter), Christ the elder Brother and Life; sin is self-will, choosing our will rather than that

of the Head of the household; atonement is reconciliation; acceptance is adoption; renewal of life
is regeneration, being born of God; the Christian
life is the crucifying or mortifying of the old
nature, which is opposed to the new nature, and
the raising up of the new; the perfection of this
life is the perfect reflection of the image of Christ,
the only begotten Son of God.

(c) The Christian life is a life dedicated to
the worship and service of God, that is, a sanctified life. In relation to the **sanctified life,** God is
the Holy One; Christ is the high priest; sin is
defilement; repentance is consciousness of defilement; the atonement is an expiatory sacrifice;
the Christian life is dedication on the altar (Rom.
12:1); the perfection of this aspect is entire
sanctification from sin and separation to God.

All three blessings of grace were **procured by
the atoning death of Christ,** and the virtues of that
death are imparted to man by the Holy Spirit. As
satisfying the claims of the law, the atonement
secured man's pardon and righteousness; as abol-
ishing the barrier between God and man, it made
possible our regenerate life; as a sacrifice for
purification from sin, its benefit is sanctification
and holiness.

Note also that all three blessings **flow from
our union with Christ.** The believer is one with
Christ in virtue of His atoning death and in virtue
of His life-giving Spirit. We have become the
righteousness of God in Him (2 Cor. 5:21); and
through Him have the forgiveness of sins (Eph.
1:7); in Him we are new creatures, born again to
a new life (2 Cor. 5:17); we are sanctified in
in Him (1 Cor. 1:2), and He is made unto us sanctification. 1 Cor. 1:30. He is "the author of eternal
salvation."

2. Salvation—Outward and Inward.

Salvation is both objective (outward) and subjective (inward).

(a) Righteousness is first of all a change of position, but it is followed by a change of condition. Righteousness must be both imputed and imparted.

(b) Adoption refers to the conferring of the privilege of Divine sonship; regeneration is the inward life that corresponds to our calling and makes us "partakers of the Divine nature."

(c) Sanctification is both external and internal. Outwardly it is separation from sin and dedication to God; inwardly it calls for purification from sin.

The outward aspect of grace is provided by the atoning work of Christ; the inward aspect is the work of the Holy Spirit.

3. The Conditions of Salvation.

What is meant by conditions of salvation? God's requirements in the man whom He accepts for Christ's sake and on whom He freely bestows the blessings of the gospel of grace.

The Scriptures set forth repentance and faith as the conditions for salvation; water baptism is mentioned as the outward symbol of the convert's inner faith. Mark 1:15; Acts 22:16; 16:31; 2:38; 3:19.

Turning from sin and turning to God are the conditions and preparations for salvation. Strictly speaking, there is no merit to repentance or faith; for all that is necessary for salvation has already been done for the penitent. By repentance the penitent removes the obstacle to the receiving of the gift; by faith he accepts the gift. But though repentance and faith are obligatory because commanded, the helping influence of the Holy Spirit is implied. (Note the expression, "granted repentance." Acts 11:18.) Blasphemy against the

Spirit drives away Him who alone can move the heart to contrition, hence there is no pardon.

What is the difference between repentance and faith? Faith is the instrument by which we receive salvation, which is not true of repentance. Also, repentance is concerned with its sin and misery while faith dwells upon God's mercy.

Can there be faith without repentance? No; only the penitent feels the need of a Saviour and desires the salvation of his soul.

Can there be godly repentance without faith? No one can repent in the Scriptural sense without faith in God's Word, without believing His threats of judgment and promises of salvation.

Are faith and repentance simply preparatory to salvation? They also follow the believer into the Christian life; repentance develops into zeal for soul-purification, and faith works in love and continues to receive from God.

(a) Repentance. Repentance has been defined as follows: "The true sorrow for sin, with sincere effort to forsake it"; "godly sorrow for sin"; "the conviction of guilt produced by the Holy Spirit's application of the Divine law to the heart"; "being sorry enough to quit" (a little boy's definition).

Three elements constitute Scriptural repentance: an intellectual, an emotional, and a practical. They may be illustrated as follows: (1) A traveler learns that he is on the wrong train; this knowledge corresponds to the intellectual element by which a person realizes, through the preaching of the Word, that he is not right with God. (2) The traveler is disturbed at his discovery; he is annoyed, perhaps fearful. This illustrates the emotional side of repentance which is a self-accusation and sincere sorrow for having offended God. 2 Cor. 7:10. (3) He leaves the train at the first opportunity and boards the right train. This illustrates the practical side of repentance, which involves complete "about face" and a traveling in God's direction. One Greek word for "repentance" means literally "a change of mind or a change of purpose." The convicted sinner purposes to mend his ways and turn to God; the practical result is that he brings forth fruits meet for repentance. Matt. 3:8.

Repentance honors the law as faith honors the gospel. How does repentance honor the law? In contrition it mourns over its departure from the holy commandment and over personal defilement revealed in its light; in confession it acknowledges the justice of the sentence; in amendment it turns from sin and makes what reparation is possible and necessary under the circumstances.

How does the Holy Spirit help a person to repent? By applying the Word to the conscience, by touching the heart and by strengthening the will and determination to turn from sin.

(b) Faith. Faith in the Scriptural sense means belief and trust. It is the assent of the mind and the consent of the will. In regard to the intellect it is belief in certain revealed truths concerning God and Christ; in regard to the will it is the acceptance of these truths as directing principles of life. Intellectual faith is not sufficient (James 2:19; Acts 8:13, 21) for salvation; a person may give intellectual assent to the gospel without committing his life to it. Belief in the heart is essential. Rom. 10:9. Intellectual faith means the acknowledgement that the gospel facts are true; heart faith means the willing dedication of one's life to the obligations which those facts involve. Faith as trust implies also an emotional element; thus saving faith is an act of the entire personality, involving intellect, emotion and will.

The meaning of faith may be determined by the manner in which it is employed in the original

Greek. Faith sometimes denotes not only the act of believing a certain body of truth but the entire body of truth itself, as in the following expressions: "preacheth the faith which he once destroyed"; "shall depart from the faith"; "the word of faith which we preach"; the "faith once delivered unto the saints." This is sometimes called objective (or outward) faith. The act of believing these truths is known as subjective faith.

Followed by certain Greek prepositions the word "believe" conveys the thought of reposing or resting on a sure foundation, as for example in John 3:16; followed by another preposition it means a trust which makes a person one with its object. Faith is thus the connecting link between the soul and Christ.

Is faith a human or a Divine activity? The fact that man is commanded to believe implies the ability and obligation to do so. All men have the capacity to place their confidence in somebody and something, so that, for example, one may put his trust in riches, in man, in friends, etc. When belief is directed to the Word of God, and the confidence reposed upon God and Christ, we have saving faith. However, the assisting grace of the Holy Spirit, in co-operation with the Word, is implied in the producing of saving faith. Compare John 6:44; Rom. 10:17; Heb. 12:2; Gal. 5:22.

What is saving faith? The following definitions have been given: "Faith in Christ is a saving grace whereby we receive and rest upon Him alone for salvation as He is offered to us in the gospel." It is "the act of the penitent only, as especially aided by the Spirit, and as resting upon Christ." "That act or habit of mind in the penitent by which, under the influence of the Divine grace, he puts his trust in Christ as the only and sufficient Saviour." "A sure trust and confidence that Christ died for **my** sins, that He loved **me,** and gave Himself for **me**." "It is to believe, to rely on the merits of Christ, that for His sake God is certainly willing to show mercy to us." "The flight of a penitent sinner to the mercy of God in Christ."

4. Conversion.

In its simplest meaning conversion is turning from sin unto God. Acts 3:19. The term is used to denote both the critical period of a sinner's return from the ways of sin to the path of righteousness, and also repentance for some particular transgréssion, on the part of those already in the path of righteousness. Matt. 18:3; Luke 22:32; James 5:20.

It is closely related to repentance and faith, and occasionally it stands for either or both, as representing the sum total of the activities by which man turns from sin to God. Acts 3:19; 11:21; 1 Peter 2:25. The Westminster Catechism, in answer to its own question, gives the following well-rounded definition of conversion:

> What is repentance unto life?
> Repentance unto life is a saving grace, whereby the sinner, out of a true sense of his sin, and apprehension of the mercy of God in Christ, doth with grief and hatred of his sin, turn from it unto God, with full purpose of, and endeavor after, new obedience.

Notice that this definition shows how conversion involves the whole personality—intellect, emotion, and will.

How is conversion to be distinguished from salvation? Conversion describes the human or manward side of salvation. To illustrate: it is observed that a notorious sinner no longer drinks, gambles, or frequents haunts of vice; he hates the things he once loved and loves the things he once hated. His acquaintances say, "He's converted, he's changed." They are describing what they see, namely, the manward side of the event. But from the Godward side we would say that God has pardoned his sin and given him a new heart.

But does this mean that conversion is entirely a matter of human effort? Like faith and repentance, which it includes and involves, conversion is a human activity; but it is also a supernatural effect in that it is man's **reaction** to the drawing power of God's grace and God's Word. Thus conversion is produced by the co-operation of Divine and human activities. "Work out your own salvation with fear and trembling. For it is God which worketh in you both to will and to do of his good pleasure." Phil. 2:12, 13. The following scriptures relate to the Divine side of conversion: Jer. 31:18; Acts 3:26. The following refer to the manward side: Acts 3:19; 11:18; Ezek. 33:11.

Which comes first, regeneration or conversion? The operations involved in conversion are deep and mysterious, and therefore not to be analyzed with mathematical precision. Dr. Strong tells of a candiate for ordination who was asked which came first, regeneration or conversion. He replied: "Regeneration and conversion are like the cannon-ball and the hole—they both go through together."

II. JUSTIFICATION

1. The Nature of Justification: Divine Acquittal.

The word "justify" is a judicial term meaning to acquit, to declare righteous, to pronounce sentence of acceptance. The illustration is taken from legal relations. The guilty one stands before God the righteous Judge; but instead of a sentence of condemnation he receives a sentence of acquittal.

The noun "justification," or "righteousness," means a state of acceptance into which one enters by faith. This acceptance is a free gift of God made available through faith in Christ. Rom. 1:17; 3:21, 22. It is a state of acceptance in which the believer stands. Rom. 5:2. Regardless of his sinful past and of present imperfection, he has a complete and secure position in relation to God; "justified" is God's verdict and none can gainsay it. Rom. 8:34. The doctrine has been defined as follows: "Justification is an act of God's free grace wherein He pardoneth all our sins and accepteth us as righteous in His sight, only for the righteousness of Christ imputed to us and received by faith alone."

Justification is primarily a change of position on the part of the sinner; once condemned, he is now acquitted; once under Divine condemnation he is now the subject of Divine commendation.

Justification includes even more than pardon of sins and removal of condemnation; in the act of justification God places the offender in the position of a righteous man. The governor of a state can pardon a criminal but he cannot reinstate the criminal in the position of one who has not broken the law. But God can do both. He blots out the past with its sins and offences, and then treats the person as if he had never committed a sin in his life! A pardoned criminal is not considered or described as a good or righteous man; but when God justifies the sinner He declares him justified, that is, righteous in His sight. No judge could justly justify a criminal, that is, declare him to be a good and righteous man. And if God were subject to the same limitations and justified only **good** people, then there would be no gospel for sinners. Paul assures us that God justifies the ungodly. "The miracle of the Gospel is that God comes to the ungodly, with a mercy which is righteous altogether, and enables them through faith, in spite of what they are, to enter into a new relationship with Himself in which goodness becomes possible to them. The whole secret of New Testament Christianity, and of every revival of religion and reformation in the church, is that joyous and marvelous paradox, 'God that justifieth the ungodly.'"

Thus we see that justification is first subtraction—the cancellation of sins; second, addition—the imputing of righteousness.

2. The Necessity for Justification: Man's Condemnation.

"How should a man be just with God?" asked Job (9:1). "What shall I do to be saved?" asked the Philippian jailor. Both men voiced one of the greatest questions that can be raised: How can a man get right with God and be sure of His approval?

The answer to the question is found in the New Testament, especially in the epistle to the Romans, which presents the plan of salvation in a detailed and systematic manner. The theme of the book is contained in 1:16, 17, and may be stated as follows: the gospel is God's power for men's salvation, because it tells how sinners can be changed in position and condition so as to be right with God.

One of the outstanding phrases of the book is "the righteousness of God." The inspired apostle describes the kind of righteousness that is acceptable to God so that the man possessing it is considered "right" in God's sight. It is the righteousness which results from faith in Christ. Paul shows that all men need the righteousness of God because the entire race has sinned. The Gentiles are under condemnation. The steps in their downfall were plain: they once knew God (1:19, 20), but failing to worship and serve Him, their minds became darkened. 1:21, 22. Spiritual blindness led to idolatry (verse 23) and idolatry led to moral corruption. Verses 24-31. They are without excuse because they have a revelation of God in nature, and a conscience that approves or disapproves of their deeds. Rom. 1:19, 20; 2:14, 15. The Jew also is under condemnation. True, he belongs to the chosen nation, and has known the law of Moses for hundreds of years, but he has violated that law in thought, deed, and word. Chapter 2. Paul clangs the doors of the prison house of condemnation on the human race, with the words: "Now we know that what things soever the law saith, it saith to them who are under the law: that every mouth may be stopped, and all the world may become guilty before God. Therefore by the deeds of the law there shall no flesh be justified in his sight: for by the law is the knowledge of sin."

What is this "righteousness" that man so needs? The word itself means "rightness," the state of being right. Sometimes the word describes God's character, as being free from imperfection and injustice. Applied to man it means the state of being right with God. The word "right" in the original means "straight," that which is conformed to a standard or rule. Therefore a righteous man is one whose life is lined up with God's law. But what if he discovers that instead of being "straight" he is "perverse" (literally, "crooked") and he cannot straighten himself? Then he needs justification—which is the work of God.

Paul has declared that by the deeds of the law no one can be justified. This is no reflection on the law, which is holy and perfect. It simply means that the law was not given for the purpose of **making** people righteous, but for supplying a standard of righteousness. The law may be compared to a measure which will indicate the length of a piece of material, but will not increase its length. Or it may be compared to a weighing machine, which will tell us how much we weigh, but will not add to our weight. "By the law is the knowledge of sin."

"But now the righteousness of God without the law is manifested." Note the word "now." It has been said that "all time has been divided for Paul into 'Now' and 'Then.'" In other words, the coming of Christ made a change in God's dealings with men. It introduced a new dispensation. For ages men had been sinning and learning the impossibility of putting away or conquering their own sin. But **now** God has plainly and openly revealed the way.

Many Israelites felt that there must be a way of being justified apart from the keeping of the law; for two reasons: (1) They perceived a wide chasm between God's standard for Israel and their actual condition. Israel was unrighteous, and salvation could not come through their own merits and efforts. Salvation must come from God, by His interposition on their behalf. (2) Many Israelites learned from personal experience their inability to keep the law perfectly. They were led to the conclusion that there must be a righteousness independent of their own works and efforts. In other words, they longed for redemption and grace. And God assured them that such a righteousness should be revealed. Paul (Rom. 3:21) speaks about the righteousness of God without the law "being witnessed by the law (Gen. 3:15; 12:3; Gal. 3:6-8) and the prophets (Jer. 23:6; 31:31-34)." This righteousness included both pardon of sins and inward righteousness of heart.

In fact, Paul affirms that justification by faith was God's original method of saving men; the law was added in order to discipline the Israelites and make them feel their need of redemption. Gal. 3:19-26. But the law in itself had no saving power any more than a thermometer has power to allay the fever which it registers. Jehovah Himself was the Saviour of His people and His grace their only hope.

Unfortunately the Jews came to exalt the law as a justifying agent and worked out a scheme of salvation based on merit for the keeping of its precepts and the traditions added to it. "For they being ignorant of God's righteousness, and going about to establish their own righteousness, have not submitted themselves unto the righteousness of God." Rom. 10:3. They had misconceived the purpose of the law. They had come to trust in it as a means of spiritual salvation; ignoring the innate sinfulness of their hearts they imagined that they would be saved by the keeping of the letter of the law, so that when Christ came offering them salvation for their sins, they thought they had no need of such a Messiah. See John 8:32-34. They thought that He would prescribe some rigid requirements whereby they might attain to eternal life. "What shall we **do**," they asked, "that we might work the works of God?" And they were not willing to follow the way indicated by Jesus: "This is the work of God, that ye **believe.**" John 6:28, 29. They were so busy trying to establish and work out their own system of righteousness that they missed God's plan for justifying sinful man. In making a journey a train is a means to an end. We have no intention of making our home on the train; we are concerned simply with reaching our destination, and when we reach the end of our journey we leave the train. The law was given to lead Israel to a certain destination, and that end was trust in God's saving grace. But when the Redeemer came, the self-satisfied Jews acted like a man who refuses to leave the train when the destination has been reached, even though the conductor assures him that it is "the end of the line." The

Jews refused to move from their seats in the Old Covenant "train" although the New Testament assured them that Christ is the "end of the law," and that the Old Covenant was fulfilled. Rom. 10:4.

3. The Source of Justification: Grace.

Grace means primarily favor, or the kindly disposition in the mind of God. It has been called "pure unrecompensed kindness and favor"; "unmerited favor." As such, grace cannot incur a debt. What God bestows He bestows as a gift; we cannot recompense or pay Him for it. Salvation is always presented as a gift, an undeserved and unpayable favor, a pure benefit from God. Rom. 6:23. Christian service, therefore, is not the payment for God's grace; service is the Christian's way to express devotion and love to God. "We love him, because he first loved us."

Grace is God's dealing with the sinner absolutely apart from the question of merit or demerit. "Grace is neither treating a person **as** he deserves, nor treating him as **better** than he deserves," writes L. S. Chafer. "It is treating him graciously without the slightest reference to his deserts. Grace is infinite love expressing itself in infinite goodness."

A misunderstanding should be avoided. Grace does not mean that the sinner is forgiven because God is big-hearted enough to remit the penalty or to waive the righteous judgment. As perfect Ruler of the universe God cannot deal leniently with sin, for that would detract from His perfect holiness and justice. God's grace to sinners is seen in the fact that He Himself, through **the atonement of Christ,** paid the full penalty of sin; therefore He can **justly** pardon sin without regard to the sinner's merit or demerit. Sinners are pardoned not because God is gracious to excuse their sins, but because there is redemption through the blood of Christ. Rom. 3:24; Eph. 1:6. Liberal preachers have gone astray at this point: they have thought that God is gracious in pardoning sin, whereas His pardon of sin is based on strict **justice.** In pardoning sin "He is faithful and just." 1 John 1:9. God's grace is revealed in His providing an atonement whereby He could both justify the ungodly and yet vindicate His holy, unchangeable law.

Grace is independent of man's works or activity. When a person is under law he cannot be under grace; when he is under grace, he is not under law. A person is "under law" when he attempts to secure salvation or sanctification as a a matter of reward, by the performance of good works and the observance of ceremonies; he is "under grace" when he secures salvation by trusting in God's work for him and not in his work for God. The two spheres are mutually exclusive. Gal. 5:4. Law says, "Pay all"; grace says, "All is paid." Law is a work to do; grace is a work done. Law restrains actions; grace changes the nature. Law condemns; grace justifies. Under law a person is a servant working for wages; under grace he is a son enjoying an inheritance.

Deep-rooted in the human heart is the idea that man must do something to make himself worthy of salvation. In the early church certain Jewish Christian teachers insisted that converts are saved by faith **and** the observance of the law of Moses. Among the heathen, and in some sections of the Christian church, this error has taken the form of self-punishment, the performance of rites, the making of pilgrimages, the giving of alms. The idea underlying all this effort is as follows: God is not gracious, man is not righteous, therefore man must make himself righteous in order to make God gracious. That was Luther's error, when by painful self-mortifications he en-

SALVATION235

deavored to work out his own salvation. "O when will you become pious enough that you may have a gracious God," he once cried. But he finally discovered the truth that is at the basis of the gospel: God is gracious and therefore wills to make man righteous. The grace of a loving Father revealed in the atoning death of Christ is an element in Christianity which differentiates it from any other religion.

Salvation is the imputed righteousness of God; it is not the imperfect righteousness of man. Salvation is a Divine reconciliation; it is not a human regulation. Salvation is the canceling of all sin; it is not the cessation from some sin. Salvation is being delivered from and being dead to the law; it is not delighting in or doing the law. Salvation is Divine regeneration; it is not human reformation. Salvation is being acceptable to God; it is not becoming exceptionally good. Salvation is completeness in Christ; it is not competency in character. Salvation is always and only of God; it is never of man.—Lewis Sperry Chafer.

Sometimes the word "grace" is used in an inward sense, to denote the operation of Divine influence (Eph. 4:7), and the effect of the Divine influence. Acts 4:33; 11:23; James 4:6; 2 Cor. 12:9. The operations of this aspect of grace have been classified as follows: **Prevenient** (literally, "going before") grace is the Divine influence preceding a person's conversion, exciting his efforts to return to God. It is the effect of God's favor in drawing men (John 6:44) and striving with the disobedient. Acts 7:51. It is sometimes called **effectual** grace in that it is effectual in producing conversion, if not resisted. John 5:40; Acts 7:51; 13:46. **Actual** grace enables men to live rightly, to resist temptation and do their duty. Thus we speak of praying for grace to perform a difficult task. **Habitual** grace is the effect of the indwelling of the Spirit resulting in a life characterized by the fruit of the Spirit. Gal. 5:22, 23.

4. The Ground of Justification: Christ's Righteousness.

How can God treat a sinner as a righteous person? Answer: God provides him with righteousness. But is it just to give the title of "good" and "righteous" to one who has not earned it? Answer: The Lord Jesus Christ has earned it for and on behalf of the sinner, who is declared righteous "through the redemption that is in Christ Jesus." Redemption means complete deliverance by a price paid.

Christ earned this righteousness for us with His atoning death; "whom God hath set forth to be a propitiation through faith in his blood." A propitiation is that which secures God's favor for the undeserving. Christ died in order to save us from God's righteous wrath and to secure His favor for us. The death and resurrection of Christ represent the outward provision for man's salvation; the term justification has reference to the way in which the saving benefits of Christ's death are made available for the individual; faith is the means whereby the sinner lays hold of the benefits.

Consider the need of righteousness. As the body needs clothing, so the soul needs character. As one must appear before the world clothed in proper garments, so must man appear before God and heaven clothed in the garment of a perfectly righteous character. See Rev. 19:8; 3:4; 7:13, 14. But the sinner's garment is defiled and tattered (Zech. 3:1-4), and were he to clothe himself in his own goodness and merits and plead his own good deeds, they would be considered as "filthy rags." Isa. 64:6. Man's only hope is to have a righteousness which God will accept—a "righteousness of God." Since man naturally lacks this righteousness, it must be provided for him; it must be an imputed righteousness.

This righteousness was purchased by Christ's substitutionary death. Isa. 53:5, 11; 2 Cor. 5:21; Rom. 4:6; 5:18, 19. His death was a perfect act of righteousness, because it satisfied the law of God; it was also a perfect act of obedience. And all this was done on our behalf and placed to our credit. "God accepteth us as righteous in His sight only for the righteousness of Christ imputed unto us," reads one doctrinal statement.

The act by which God charges or reckons this righteousness to our account is called imputation. Imputation is reckoning to a person the consequences of another's act; for example, the consequences of Adam's sin are reckoned to his descendants. The consequences of man's sin were reckoned to Christ, and the consequences of Christ's obedience are reckoned to the believer. He wore our garment of sin that we might wear His garment of righteousness. He "is made unto us righteousness" (1 Cor. 1:30); He becomes "the Lord our Righteousness." Jer. 23:6.

Christ expiated our guilt, satisfied the law, both by obedience and suffering, and became our substitute, so that being united with Him by faith, His death becomes our death, His righteousness our righteousness, His obedience our obedience. God then accepts us not for anything in us, not for anything so imperfect as works (Rom. 3:28; Gal. 2:16) or merit, but for the perfect all-sufficient righteousness of Christ set to our account. For Christ's sake, God treats the guilty man, when penitent and believing, as if he were righteous. Christ's merit is reckoned to him.

The following question may arise in the mind of the thoughtful person: the justification that saves is something external, and concerns the sinner's position; but is there no change in condition? It affects his standing, but what of his conduct? Righteousness is imputed but is it also imparted? In justification Christ is for us, but is He also in us? In other words, it seems that imputation would dishonor the law if it were not bound up with security for future righteousness.

The answer is that justifying faith is the **initial** act of Christian life and this initial act, when the faith is living, is followed by an inward, spiritual change known as regeneration. Faith unites the believer to the living Christ and union with the Author of life results in a change of heart. "If any man be in Christ, he is a new creature: old things are passed away; behold, all things are become new." 2 Cor. 5:17. Righteousness is imputed in justification and imparted in regeneration. The Christ who is for us becomes the Christ in us.

The faith by which a person is actually justified must of necessity be a living faith, and a living faith will produce right living; it will be a "faith which **worketh** by love." Gal. 5:6. Moreover, wearing the righteousness of Christ the believer is called to live a life conformable to that character. "For the fine linen is the righteousness (literally, "righteous deeds") of the saints." Rev. 19:8. Real salvation calls for a life of practical holiness. What would we think of a person who always wore white, clean garments but who never washed himself? Inconsistent, to say the least! No less inconsistent would it be for a person to claim the righteousness of Christ and yet live in a manner unworthy of the Christian calling. They who wear His righteousness will be careful to purify themselves, even as He is pure. 1 John 3:3.

5. The Means of Justification: Faith.

Since the law cannot justify, man's only hope is for a "righteousness without the law" (not an unlawful unrighteousness, or a religion that permits us to sin, but a change of position and condition). This is "the righteousness of God," that is, a righteousness which God imparts; and it is a gift because man lacks the power to develop it or work it out. Eph. 2:8-10.

But a gift must be accepted; how then is the gift of righteousness accepted? Or, in theological language: what is the instrument which appropriates the righteousness of Christ? Answer: "By the faith of Jesus Christ." Faith is the hand, so to speak, which takes what God offers. That faith is the instrumental cause of justification will be seen from the following scriptures: Rom. 3:22; 4:11; 9:30; Heb. 11:7, Phil. 3:9.

Christ's merits are communicated and a saving interest secured through a certain means. Such a means must be divinely appointed, since it is to convey what God Himself and He alone dispenses. This means is faith—the one principle which God's grace makes use of for restoring us to His image and favor. Born in sin, and heir to misery, the soul needs an utter change, both within and without, both in God's sight and in its own sight. The change in God's sight is called justification, and the inward spiritual change that follows is regeneration by the Holy Spirit. This faith is awakened in man by the influence of the Holy Spirit, generally in connection with the Word. Faith lays hold of God's promise and appropriates salvation. It leads the soul to rest on Christ as Saviour and the sacrifice for sins, imparts peace to the conscience and the consoling hope of heaven. Being living and spiritual, and filled with gratitude towards Christ, it abounds in good works of every kind.

"For by grace are ye saved through faith; and that not of yourselves: it is a gift of God: not of works, lest any man should boast." Eph. 2:8, 9. Man had not a single thing wherewith to purchase his justification. God could not come down to what man could offer; man could not measure up to what God demanded. So God graciously saved him for nothing—"freely by his grace." This free grace is received by faith. There is no merit in this faith, any more than a beggar is to be commended for holding out his hand for a gift. This method strikes a blow at man's dignity, but as far as God is concerned, fallen man has no dignity; he has not the power to accumulate enough goodness to buy salvation. "By the deeds of the law shall no flesh be justified."

The doctrine of justification by God's grace through man's faith removes two dangers; first, the pride of self-righteousness and self-effort; second, the fear that one is too weak to "make the grade."

If faith is not meritorious in itself, being simply the holding out of the hand for God's free grace, what gives it its power, and what guarantee does it offer that the one who has received the gift will live a righteous life? Faith is important and mighty because it unites the soul to Christ, and in that union is found the motive and power for a life of righteousness. "For as many of you as have been baptized into Christ have put on Christ. . . . And they that are Christ's have crucified the flesh with the affections and lusts." Gal. 3:27; 5:24.

Faith not only passively receives but also actively uses what God bestows. It is an affair of the heart (Rom. 10:9, 10; compare Matt. 15:19; Prov. 4:23), and to believe with the heart is to enlist all the emotions, affections and desires in response to God's offer of salvation. Through faith Christ dwells in the heart. Eph. 3:17. Faith works by love (the "work of faith." 1 Thess. 1:3); that is, it is an energetic principle as well as a receptive attitude. Faith is therefore a powerful motive to obedience and to every other good work. Faith involves the will and is connected with all good choices and actions, for "whatsoever is not of faith is sin." Rom. 14:23. It includes the choice and pursuit of the truth (2 Thess. 2:12) and implies subjection to the righteousness of God. Rom. 10:3.

The following is Scriptural teaching concerning the relation between faith and works. Faith is opposed to works when by works we mean good deeds upon which a person depends for salvation. Gal. 3:11. However, a living faith will produce works (James 2:26), just as a living tree will produce fruit. Faith is justified and approved by works (James 2:18) just as the soundness of the roots of a good fruit-tree is indicated by its fruit. Faith is perfected in works (James 2:22), just as a flower is completed by its blossom. In brief, works are the result of faith, the test of faith, and the consummation of faith.

A contradiction has been imagined between the teaching of Paul and that of James, one apparently teaching that a person is justified by faith and the other that he is justified by works. Compare Rom. 3:20 and James 2:14-26. However, an understanding of the sense in which they use these terms will quickly dispel the supposed difficulty. Paul is commending a living faith which trusts God alone; James is denouncing a dead, formal faith which is merely an intellectual assent. Paul is rejecting the dead works of the law, or works without faith; James is commending the living works which show that faith is vital. The justification spoken of by Paul refers to the beginning of the Christian life; while James uses the word in the sense of that life of obedience and holiness which is the outward evidence that a person is saved. Paul is combating legalism, or dependence upon works for salvation; James is combating antinomianism, or the teaching that it does not matter so much how one lives so long as he believes. Paul and James are not two soldiers opposed to each other; they are standing back to back facing enemies coming from opposite directions.

III. REGENERATION.

1. The Nature of Regeneration.

Regeneration is the Divine act which imparts to the penitent believer the new and higher life in personal union with Christ.

The New Testament describes regeneration as—

(a) A Birth. God the Father is He "that begat," and the believer is "begotten" of God (1 John 5:1), "born of the Spirit" (John 3:8), and "born from above" (literal translation of John 3:7). These terms refer to the act of creative grace which makes the believer a child of God.

(b) A Cleansing. God saved us by the "washing (literally, laver or bath) of regeneration." Titus 3:5. The soul was completely bathed from the defilements of the old life and made to live in newness of life—an experience pictured by water baptism. Acts 22:16.

(c) A Quickening. We were saved not only by the "washing of regeneration" but also by "the renewing of the Holy Ghost." Titus 3:5. Compare also Col. 3:10; Rom. 12:2; Eph. 4:23; Psalm 51:10. The essence of the regeneration is a new life imparted by God the Father, mediately through Christ and by the operation of the Spirit.

(d) A Creation. He who created man in the beginning and breathed into his nostrils the breath of life, recreates him by the operation of His Holy Spirit. 2 Cor. 5:17; Eph. 2:10; Gal. 6:15; Eph. 4:24; compare Gen. 2:7. The practical result is a radical change in the individual's nature, character, desires, and purposes.

(e) A Resurrection. Rom. 6:4, 5; Col. 2:13; 3:1; Eph. 2:5, 6. As God quickened the lifeless clay and made it alive to the physical world, so He quickens a soul dead in sins and makes it alive to the realities of the spiritual world. This act of resurrection from spiritual death is symbolized in water baptism. Regeneration is "that great change which God works in the soul when He brings it into life; when He raises it from the death of sin to the life of righteousness" (Wesley).

It will be noticed that the above terms are simply variants of one great basic thought of regeneration, namely, the Divine impartation of a new life to the soul of man. And three scientific facts true of natural life also apply to spiritual life, namely, that it comes suddenly, appears mysteriously, and develops progressively.

Regeneration is a unique feature in New Testament religion. In heathen religions the permanence of character is universally recognized. Though these religions prescribe penances and rituals whereby man may hope to atone for his sins, there is no promise of life and grace to transform his nature. The religion of Jesus Christ "is the only religion which professes to take man's fallen nature and regenerate it by bringing into it the life of God." And it professes to do this because Christianity's Founder is a living, Divine Person, who lives to save to the uttermost.

There is no analogy between Christian religion and, say, Buddhism or the Mohammedan religion. There is no true sense in which a man can say, "He that hath Buddha hath life." (See 1 John 5:12.) He may have something to do with morality. He may stimulate, impress, teach, and guide, but there is no distinctly new thing added to the souls of those who profess Buddhism. These religions may be developments of the natural and moral man. But Christianity professes to be more. It is the mental or moral man **plus** something else or Some One else.

2. The Necessity for Regeneration.

Our Lord's interview with Nicodemus (John 3) provides a fine background for the study of the above topic. Nicodemus' opening words reveal a number of emotions struggling in his heart; and our Lord's abrupt statement (verse 3), which seems to be a sudden changing of the subject, is explained by the fact He answered the **heart** rather than the words of the lips. Nicodemus' opening words reveal: (1) Spiritual hunger. Had the ruler put into words the desire of his soul, he might have said: "I am tired of the lifeless services of the synagogue; I attend, but leave as hungry as I enter. Alas, the glory has departed from Israel; there is no vision and the people perish. Master, my soul is hungry for reality! I know little concerning you personally, but your words have touched a deep place in my heart. Your miracles convince me that you are a God-sent Teacher. I would like to join your company." (2) Lack of depth of conviction. Nicodemus feels his need, but it is the need of a **teacher** rather than of a **Saviour.** Like the Samaritan woman, he wants the water of life (4:15), but like her, he must realize that he is a sinner needing cleansing and transforming. 4:16-18. (3) One detects in the words a touch of self-complacency, natural in a man of his age and position. He would say to Jesus: "I believe that you are sent to restore the kingdom of Israel, and am come to advise you on your plan of operation and to urge upon you certain lines of action." Very likely he took it for granted that being an Israelite and a son of Abraham would be sufficient qualifications for becoming a member of the kingdom of God.

"Jesus answered and said unto him, Verily, verily, I say unto thee, Except a man be born again, he cannot see the kingdom of God." To paraphrase these words: "Nicodemus, you cannot

join My company as one would join an organization. Whether you belong to My company or not depends on the quality of the life that you live; My cause is none other than that of the kingdom of God, and you cannot enter without a spiritual change. The kingdom of God is quite another thing than you are thinking of, and the way to establish it, enlist citizens in it, is very different from the way upon which you have been meditating."

Jesus pointed out the deepest and universal need of all men—a radical, out-and-out change of the whole nature and character. Man's entire nature has been warped by sin, the heritage of the Fall, and that warp and twist is reflected in his individual conduct and his various relationships. Before he can live a life pleasing to God, in time and eternity, his nature must undergo a change so radical that it is actually a second birth. Man cannot change himself; the transformation must come from above.

Jesus did not attempt to explain the **how** of the new birth, but He did explain the **why** of the matter. "That which is born of the flesh is flesh, and that which is born of the Spirit is spirit." Flesh and spirit belong to different realms, and one cannot produce the other; human nature can generate human nature, but only the Holy Spirit can generate a spiritual nature. Human nature can produce only human nature, and no creature can rise beyond its own nature. Spiritual life does not descend from father to child by way of natural generation; it descends from God to man by way of spiritual generation.

Human nature cannot rise above itself. Writes Marcus Dods:

Every creature has a certain nature according to its kind and determined by its parentage. This nature which the animal receives from its parents determines from the first the capabilities and sphere of the animal's life. The mole cannot soar in the face of the sun like the eagle; neither can the bird that comes from the eagle's egg burrow like the mole. No training can possibly make the tortoise as swift as the antelope, or the antelope as strong as the lion. . . . Beyond its nature no animal can act.

The same principle may be applied to man. Man's highest destiny is to live with God forever; but human nature in its present condition does not possess the capacities for living in a heavenly kingdom; therefore heavenly life must come down from above to transform it for membership in that kingdom.

3. The Means of Regeneration.

(a) **Divine Agency.** The Holy Spirit is the special Agent in regeneration, who so acts upon a person as to produce the change. John 3:6; Titus 3:5. However, each Person of the Trinity is involved. Indeed, the three Persons are involved in every Divine operation, although each Person has certain offices which are His in a special sense. Thus the Father is pre-eminently the Creator, yet both the Son and the Spirit are also mentioned as agents. The Father begets (James 1:18) and throughout the Gospel according to John, the Son is set forth as the Life-giver. See chapters 5 and 6.

Note especially Christ's relation to man's regeneration. He is the Giver of Life. And how does He bring life to men? By dying for them, so that they by eating His flesh and drinking His blood (believing in His atoning death) may have eternal life. How does He actually impart life to men? Part of His reward was the prerogative of imparting the Holy Spirit (compare John 3:3, 13; Gal. 3:13, 14), and He ascended in order to become the Source of spiritual life (John 6:62) and energy. Acts 2:33. The Father has life in Himself (John 5:26); so He gives the Son to have life in Himself; the Father is the source of the Holy

Spirit, but He gives the Son the power to impart the Spirit; thus the Son is a "quickening Spirit" (1 Cor. 15:45), having power not only to raise the physically dead (John 5:25, 26) but also to quicken the dead souls of men. Compare Gen. 2:7, John 20:22, and 1 Cor. 15:45.

(b) The Human Preparation. Strictly speaking, man cannot co-operate in the act of regeneration, which is the sovereign act of God; but he has part in the **preparation** for the new birth. What is that preparation? Repentance and faith.

4. The Effects of Regeneration.

We may group them under three heads: positional (adoption); spiritual (union with God); practical (righteous living).

(a) Positional. When a person has undergone the spiritual change known as regeneration he becomes a child of God and beneficiary of all the privileges of that sonship. Writes Dr. William Evans: "In adoption, the believer, already a child, receives a place as an adult son; thus the child becomes a son, the minor becomes an adult." **Gal. 4:1-7.** The word "adoption" means literally "the giving the position of sons," and refers in ordinary usage to a man's taking into his household children not born to him.

Doctrinally, adoption and regeneration should be distinguished: the first is a legal term indicating the imparting of the privilege of sonship to one that is not a member of a family; the second denotes the inner spiritual change that makes one a child of God, and a partaker of the Divine nature. However, it is difficult to separate the two in regard to experience, for regeneration and adoption represent the twofold experience of sonship.

In the New Testament the common sonship is sometimes defined by the term "sons" ("uioi") which word lies at the root of the word "adoption," and sometimes by the word "children" ("tekna"), which means literally, "begotten ones," and which implies regeneration. The two ideas are distinguished yet combined in the following verses: "But as many as received him, to them gave he power (implying adoption) to become the sons of God . . . which were born . . . of God." John 1:12, 13. "Behold, what manner of love the Father hath bestowed upon us, that we should be called (implying adoption) the sons of God (the word used for those born of God)." 1 John 3:1. In Rom. 8:15, 16, the two ideas are blended: "For ye have not received the spirit of bondage again to fear; but ye have received the Spirit of adoption, whereby we cry, Abba, Father. The Spirit itself beareth witness with our spirit, that we are the children of God."

(b) Spiritual. Because of its very nature regeneration involves spiritual union with God and with Christ through the Holy Spirit; and this spiritual union involves a Divine indwelling. 2 Cor. 6:16-18; Gal. 4:5, 6; 1 John 3:24; 4:13; Gal. 2:20. This union results in a new type of life and character, described in various ways: Newness of life (Rom. 6:4); a new heart (Ezek. 36:26); a new spirit (Ezek. 11:19); the new man (Eph. 4:24); partakers of the divine nature. 2 Pet. 1:4. The believer's duty is to maintain his contact with God through the various means of grace and so preserve and nourish his spiritual life.

(c) Practical. The person born of God will demonstrate that fact by his hatred of sin (1 John 3:9; 5:18), righteous deeds (1 John 2:29), brotherly love (1 John 4:7) and victory over the world. 1 John 5:4.

Two extremes should be avoided: first, making the standard too low so that regeneration becomes a matter of natural reformation; second,

raising the standard too high and failing to make
allowance for the frailties of believers. Young
converts, when learning to walk in Christ may
stumble—like a babe learning to walk; older believers may be overtaken in a fault. John declares
that it is utterly inconsistent that one born of God
and bearing the Divine nature should live habitual-
ly in sin (1 John 3:9), yet he is careful to write,
"If any man sin, we have an advocate with the
Father." 1 John 2:1.

IV. SANCTIFICATION.

1. The Nature of Sanctification.

In a previous study we affirmed that the key
to the meaning of the New Testament doctrine
of atonement was found in Old Testament sacrificial ritual; in like manner we shall reach the
meaning of the New Testament doctrine of sanctification by a study of the Old Testament usage of
the word "holy."

At the outset let it be observed that "sanctification," "holiness," "consecration" are synonymous terms; so are "sanctified" and "holy"; to
sanctify is the same as to make holy or to consecrate. The word "holy" conveys the following
ideas:

(a) **Separation.** "Holy" is a word descriptive of the Divine nature. Its root meaning is
"separation"; therefore holiness represents that
in God which makes Him separate from all that
is earthly and human—namely, His absolute moral
perfection and Divine majesty.

When the Holy One wills to use a person or
object in His service, He separates him or it from
common use, and by virtue of this separation
the person or object becomes "holy."

(b) **Dedication.** Sanctification includes both
a separation **from** and a dedication **to;** it is "the
condition of believers as they are separated from

sin and the world and made partakers of the Divine nature, and consecrated to the fellowship and service of God through the Mediator."

The word "holy" is used mainly in connection with worship. When applied to men or things it expresses the thought that they are used in His service and dedicated to Him, in a special sense His property. Israel is a holy nation because dedicated to the service of Jehovah; the Levites are holy because specially dedicated to the services of the tabernacle; the Sabbath and feast days are holy because they represent the dedication or consecration of time to God.

(c) Purification. While the primary meaning of holy is that of separation to service, the idea of purification is also involved. Jehovah's character reacted upon whatever was devoted to Him. Hence men dedicated to Him must share His nature. Things devoted to Him must be clean. Cleanliness is a **condition** of holiness, but not the holiness itself, which is primarily separation and dedication.

When Jehovah selects and separates a person or object for His service, He does something or causes it to be done, which constitutes the person or object holy. Inanimate objects were consecrated by being anointed with oil. Ex. 40:9-11. The Israelitish nation was sanctified by the blood of a covenant sacrifice. Ex. 24:8, compare Heb. 10:29. The priests were sanctified by Jehovah's representative, Moses, who washed them with water, and anointed them with oil and sprinkled them with the blood of consecration. Read Leviticus, chapter 8.

As Old Testament sacrifices were typical of the one sacrifice, so the various washings and anointings of the Mosaic system were typical of the real sanctification made possible through the work of Christ. Thus, as Israel was sanctified by the blood of the covenant so "Jesus also, that he might sanctify the people with his own blood, suffered without the gate." Heb. 13:12.

Jehovah sanctified the sons of Aaron to the priesthood through the mediation of Moses and by means of water, oil and blood. God the Father (1 Thess. 5:23) sanctifies believers to spiritual priesthood (1 Pet. 2:5) through the mediation of the Son (1 Cor. 1:2; 1:30; Eph. 5:26; Heb. 2:11), and by means of the Word (John 17:17; 15:3), the blood (Heb. 10:29; 13:12) and the Spirit. Rom. 15:16; 1 Cor. 6:11; 1 Peter 1:2.

(d) Consecration, in the sense of living holily and righteously. What is the difference between righteousness and holiness? Righteousness represents the regenerate life as conformed to **the Divine law;** the children of God live right. 1 John 3:6-10. Holiness is the regenerate life as conformed to the **Divine nature** and dedicated to the Divine service; and this calls for the removal of any defilement which would hinder that service. "But as he which hath called you is holy, so be ye holy in all manner of conversation." 1 Pet. 1:15. Thus sanctification includes the removal of the spot or defilement which is contrary to the holiness of the Divine nature.

Following Israel's consecration the question would naturally arise, How should a holy people live? In order to answer this question, God gave them the code of holiness laws which are found in the book of Leviticus. Thus from Israel's consecration followed the obligation to live a holy life. The same is true of the Christian. Those who are declared to be sanctified (Heb. 10:10) are exhorted to follow holiness (Heb. 12:14); those who have been cleansed (1 Cor. 6:11) are exhorted to cleanse themselves. 2 Cor. 7:1.

(e) Service. The covenant is a state of relationship with God and men in which He is their

God and they are His people, which means His worshiping people. The word "holy" expresses this covenant relationship. To serve God in this relationship is to be a priest; hence Israel is described as a holy nation and as a kingdom of priests. Ex. 19:6. Any defilement that marred this relationship must be washed away with water or with the blood of purification.

In like manner New Testament believers are "saints," that is, consecrated holy people. By means of the blood of the covenant they have become "a royal priesthood, an holy nation . . . an holy priesthood, to offer up spiritual sacrifices, acceptable to God by Jesus Christ" (1 Pet. 2:9, 5); they offer the sacrifice of praise (Heb. 13:15) and dedicate themselves as living sacrifices upon God's altar. Rom. 12:1.

Thus we see that service is an essential element of sanctification or holiness, because this is the only sense in which men can belong to God, namely as His worshipers doing Him service. Paul expressed perfectly this aspect of holiness when he spoke of God, "whose I am, and whom I serve." Acts 27:23. Sanctification involves possession by God and service toward God.

2. The Time of Sanctification.

Sanctification is: (1) Positional and instantaneous. (2) Practical and progressive.

(a) Positional and Instantaneous. The following is a statement of the "second definite work" teaching on sanctification, made by one who taught the doctrine for years:

Justification is supposed to be a work of grace by which sinners are made righteous and freed from their sinful habits when they come to Christ. But in the merely justified there remains a corrupt principle, an evil tree, "a root of bitterness," which continually provokes to sin. If the believer obeys this impulse and wilfully sins, he ceases to be justified; therefore the desirability of its removal that the likelihood of backsliding be thereby lessened. The eradication of this sinful root is sanctification. It is therefore the cleansing of the nature from all inbred sin by the blood of Christ (applied through faith when a full consecration is made), and the refining fire of the Holy Spirit who burns out all dross, when all is laid upon the altar of sacrifice. This, and this only, is true sanctification—a distinct second definite work of grace, subsequent to justification, and without which that justification is very likely to be lost.

The above definition teaches that a person may be saved or justified without being sanctified. This theory, however, is contrary to the New Testament. The apostle Paul addresses **all** believers as "saints" (literally, "sanctified ones") and as already sanctified (1 Cor. 1:2; 6:11); yet the same letter was written to correct those Christians because of carnality and even open sin. 1 Cor. 3:1; 5:1, 2, 7, 8. They were "saints" and "sanctified **in Christ,**" but some of them were far from being such in daily conduct. They had been called to be saints but were not walking worthy of the vocation wherewith they had been called.

According to the New Testament, then, there is a sense in which sanctification is simultaneous with justification.

(b) Practical and Progressive. But does sanctification consist **only** of the giving of the position of saints? No, this initial setting apart is the **beginning** of a progressive life of sanctification. All Christians are separated to God in Jesus Christ; and from this springs the responsibility to live for Him. This separation is to be followed daily, the believer seeking to become more and more conformed to the image of Christ. "Sanctification is the work of God's free grace, whereby we are renewed in the whole man after the image of God, and are enabled more and more to die unto sin, and live unto righteousness." This does not mean that we grow **into** sanctification, but that we progress **in** sanctification.

Sanctification is both absolute and progressive —absolute in the sense that it is a work done once for all (Heb. 10:14), progressive in the sense that the Christian must follow after holiness (Heb. 12:14) and perfect his consecration by cleansing himself from all defilement. 2 Cor. 7:1.

Sanctification is positional and practical— positional in that it is primarily a change of position whereby a defiled sinner is changed to a holy worshiper; practical in that it calls for righteous living. Positional sanctification is indicated by the fact that all the Corinthians are addressed as "sanctified in Christ Jesus, called to be saints." 1 Cor. 1:2. Progressive sanctification is implied in the fact that some of them are described as carnal (1 Cor. 3:3), which means that their present condition did not measure up to their God-given position; hence they are exhorted to cleanse themselves from all defilement and so bring their consecration to perfection. The two aspects of sanctification are implied in the fact that those addressed as sanctified and holy (1 Pet. 1:2; 2:5) are exhorted to be holy (1 Pet. 1:15); those who are dead to sin (Col. 3:3) are exhorted to mortify (make dead) their sinful members (Col. 3:5); those who have put off the old man (Col. 3:9) are exhorted to put off the old man. Eph. 4:22; Col. 3:8.

3. The Divine Means for Sanctification.

The Divinely appointed means for sanctification are the blood of Christ, the Holy Spirit and the Word of God. The first provides primarily absolute and positional sanctification; it is a finished work which gives the penitent a perfect position in relation to God. The second is internal, effecting the transforming of the believer's nature.

The third is external and practical, dealing with the believer's practical conduct. Thus God has made provision for both external and internal sanctification.

(a) The Blood of Christ. (Eternal, absolute, and positional.) Heb. 13:12; 10:10; 10:14; 1 John 1:7. In what sense is a person sanctified by the blood of Christ? As a result of the finished work of Christ the penitent is changed from a defiled sinner into a holy worshiper. Sanctification is the result of that "wondrous work accomplished by the Son of God when He offered Himself to put away sin by His sacrifice on Calvary. By virtue of that sacrifice the believer is forever set apart to God, his conscience is purged, and he himself is transformed from an unclean sinner into a holy worshiper, linked up in an abiding fellowship with the Lord Jesus Christ; for 'both he that sanctifieth and they who are sanctified are all of one: for which cause he is not ashamed to call them brethren.'" Heb. 2:11.

That there is also a continuous aspect to sanctification by the blood is implied in 1 John 1:7: "the blood of Jesus Christ his Son cleanseth us from all sin." If there is to be fellowship between a holy God and man, there must necessarily be some provision for removing the sin that is a barrier to that fellowship, for even the best of men are imperfect. When Isaiah received his vision of the holiness of God he was smitten with a sense of his own unholiness, and was in no condition to hear God's message until a coal from the altar had cleansed his lips. Consciousness of sin mars fellowship with God; confession and faith in the eternal sacrifice of Christ removes the barrier. 1 John 1:9.

(b) The Holy Spirit. (Internal sanctification.) 1 Cor. 6:11; 2 Thess. 2:13; 1 Pet. 1:1, 2; Rom. 15:16. In these passages sanctification by the Holy Spirit is treated as the beginning of God's work in the souls of men, leading them to the full knowledge of justification through faith in the blood-sprinkling of Christ. As the Spirit brooded over the primeval chaos (Gen. 1:2), and was followed by the Word of God bringing order, so the Spirit of God broods over the regenerate soul, opening it to receive the light and life of God. 2 Cor. 4:6.

The tenth chapter of Acts gives a concrete instance of sanctification by the Holy Spirit. During the first years of the church, the evangelization of the Gentiles was delayed, for many of the Jewish Christians considered the Gentiles "unclean" and unsanctified because of their non-conformity to the food laws and other Mosaic regulations. It required a vision to convince Peter that what the Lord had cleansed he must not call common or unclean. This meant that God had made provision for the sanctification of the Gentiles to be His people. And when the Spirit of God fell upon the Gentiles assembled in the house of Cornelius, there was no doubt about the matter. Regardless of whether or not they followed the Mosaic ordinances, they were sanctified by the Holy Ghost (Rom. 15:16), and Peter challenged the Jews who were with him to deny the outward symbol of their spiritual cleansing. Acts 10:47; 15:8.

(c) **The Word.** (External and practical sanctification.) John 17:17; Eph. 5:26; John 15:3; Psalm 119:9; James 1:23-25. Christians are described as having been "born of the word of God." 1 Pet. 1:23. The Word of God awakens men to a realization of the folly and wickedness of their lives. When they respond to the Word, repent, and believe in Christ, they are clean through the word which was spoken unto them. This is the beginning of a cleansing which must continue throughout the believer's life. At his consecration the Israelite priest received a complete priestly bath which was never repeated; it was a work done once for all; but he was required to wash his hands and feet daily. In like manner the regenerate have been bathed (Titus 3:5); but there must be a daily putting away of defilements and imperfections as these are revealed by the Word of God, which is the mirror of the soul. James 1:22-25. He must wash his hands, that is, his deeds must be right; he must wash his feet, that is, keep himself from "those earth-stains which are so readily contracted by sandaled pilgrim feet pressing along this world's highways."

4. Erroneous Views of Sanctification.

Many Christians become aware of the fact that the greatest hindrance to holiness is the "flesh," which thwarts them in their progress toward perfection. How may one realize deliverance from the "flesh"? Three erroneous views have been advanced:

(a) **Eradication** of "inbred" sin is one view taught. Writes Lewis Sperry Chafer: "If eradication of the sin-nature were accomplished there would be no physical death; for physical death is the result of that nature. Rom. 5:12-21. Parents who had experienced eradication would of necessity generate unfallen children. But even if eradication were secured there would still be the conflict with the world, the flesh (apart from the sin-nature) and the devil; for eradication of these is obviously un-Scriptural and is not included in the theory itself."

Eradiction is also contrary to experience.

(b) **Legalism,** or the keeping of rules and regulations. Paul teaches that the law cannot sanctify (Rom. 6) any more than it can justify. Rom. 3. The truth is stated and developed in the letter to the Galatians. Paul is in nowise depreciating the law. He is defending it against a mistaken conception of its purpose. If a man is to be saved from sin it must be by a power apart from him. Let us employ the illustration of a thermometer. The glass and the red fluid will represent the individual. The record of degrees will represent the law. Imagine the thermometer saying: "I am not quite up to the mark today; I ought to be up to 80 degrees." Could the thermometer raise itself to the required temperature? No, it would have to depend on a condition **outside** of itself. In like manner, a man who perceives he has come short of the Divine standard cannot raise himself up to the standard; he must be acted upon by a force apart from him; and that force is the power of the Spirit.

(c) Asceticism represents the attempt to subdue the flesh and attain to sanctity by means of self-inflicted deprivations and sufferings—a method followed by Roman Catholic and Hindu ascetics.

This method seems based on the ancient heathen belief that all matter, including the body, is evil. The body is therefore a clog to the spirit, and the more it is beaten and subdued the quicker will the spirit be released. This is contrary to the Scripture, which teaches that God created everything very good. It is the soul and not the body that sins; therefore the sinful impulses, not the material flesh, must be crushed. Asceticism is an attempt at self-deadening; but self cannot overcome self. That is the work of the Spirit.

5. The True Method of Sanctification.

The Scriptural method of dealing with the flesh must obviously be based upon the objective provision for salvation, the blood of Christ, and the subjective provision, the Holy Spirit. Deliverance from the power of the flesh must therefore come through faith in the atonement and a response to the moving of the Spirit. The first is dealt with in the sixth chapter of Romans, and the second in the first section of the eighth chapter.

(a) **Faith in the Atonement.** Let us imagine that there were Jews present (which was often the case) while Paul was expounding the doctrine of purification by faith. We imagine them saying in protest: "This is heresy of the most dangerous kind! Telling people that they need only to believe in Jesus, and that they can do nothing about their salvation- because it is by God's grace, will result in their becoming careless in their living. They will think that what they do matters little, as long as they **believe.** Your doctrine of faith promotes sin. If justification be by grace alone without works, why break off sin? Why not continue in it in order to obtain more grace?" Paul's enemies actually accused him of preaching this doctrine. Rom. 3:8; 6:1. He indignantly repudiates such a perversion. "God forbid. How shall we, that are dead to sin, live any longer therein?" Continuance in sin is impossible to a really justified man because of his union with Christ in death and life. Compare Matt. 6:24. By virtue of his faith in Christ the saved man has had an experience which includes such a clean-cut break with sin as to be described as death to sin, and a transformation so radical as to be described as a resurrection. The experience is pictured in water baptism. The convert's immersion testifies to the fact that because of his union with the crucified Christ he has died to sin; his being raised from the water testifies that his contact with the risen Christ means that "as Christ was raised up from the dead by the glory of the Father, even so we also should walk in newness of life." Christ died **for** sin in order that we might die **to** sin.

"For he that is dead is freed from sin." Death

cancels all obligations and breaks all ties. Through union with Christ the Christian has died to the old life, and the fetters of sin have been broken. As death put an end to the bondage of the literal slave, so the believer's death to the old life has freed him from the bondage to sin. To continue the illustration: The law has no jurisdiction over a dead man; regardless of what crime he may have committed, once dead he is beyond the power of human justice. In like manner, the law of Moses often violated by the convert cannot "arrest" him, for by virtue of his experience with Christ he is "dead." Rom. 7:1-4; 2 Cor. 5:14.

"Knowing that Christ being raised from the dead dieth no more; death hath no more dominion over him. For in that he died, he died unto sin once: but in that he liveth, he liveth unto God. Likewise reckon ye also yourselves to be dead indeed unto sin, but alive unto God through Jesus Christ our Lord." Christ's death ended that earthly state in which He had contact with sin, and His life is now one of unbroken communion with God. Christians, though still in the world, may share His experience, because they are united to Him. How? "Likewise reckon ye also yourselves to be dead indeed unto sin, but alive unto God through Jesus Christ our Lord." What does this mean? God has said that through our faith in Christ we **are** dead to sin and alive to righteousness. There remains one thing to be done, and that is to believe God and reckon or conclude that we are dead to sin. God says that when Christ died we died to sin; when Christ arose we arose to live a new life. We are to keep on reckoning these facts as absolutely true, and then, as we reckon them, they will become powerful in our lives, for we become what we reckon ourselves to be. An important distinction has been pointed out, namely, that between the **promises** and the **facts** of the

Bible. Jesus said, "If ye abide in me, and my words abide in you, ye shall ask what ye will, and it shall be done unto you." That is a promise, because it lies in the future; it is something **to be done.** But when Paul says, "Christ died for our sins according to the scriptures," he is stating a fact, something that **has been done.** Compare Peter's statement, "by whose stripes ye **were** healed." And when Paul declares that "our old man **is** crucified," he is stating a fact—something that has been done. The question that remains is: Are we willing to believe what God declares to be facts about ourselves? For faith is the hand that accepts what God freely offers.

May it not be that the awakening to one's position in Christ constitutes what some persons have described as a "second definite work of grace"?

(b) Response to the Spirit. Romans, chapters 7 and 8, continue the subject of sanctification; they deal with the believer's deliverance from the power of sin and his growth in holiness. In chapter 6 we saw that victory over sin's power was achieved by **faith.** Chapter 8 introduces another ally in the battle against sin—the **Holy Spirit.**

As a background for chapter 8 study the line of thought in chapter 7, which pictures a man turning to the law for sanctification. Paul here shows that the law is powerless to save and sanctify, not because the law is not good, but because of the sinful bias in human nature known as the "flesh." He points out that the law reveals the fact (v. 7), the occasion (v. 8), the power (v. 9), the deceitfulness (v. 11), the effect (vv. 10, 11) and the sinfulness of sin. Verses 12, 13.

Paul, who seems to be describing his own past experience, tells us that the very law, which he earnestly desired to observe, stirred sinful impulses within him. The result was a "civil war" in the soul. He is hindered from doing the good that he wants to do, and is impelled to do the things he hates. "I find then a law, that, when I would do good, evil is present with me. For I delight in the law of God after the inward man: but I see another law in my members, warring against the law of my mind, and bringing me into captivity to the law of sin which is in my members."

The latter part of chapter 7 evidently presents the picture of a man under law who has discovered the heart-searching spirituality of the law, but who in every attempt to keep it finds himself thwarted by the indwelling sin. Why does Paul describe this conflict? To show that the law is just as powerless to sanctify as it is to justify.

"O wretched man that I am! who shall deliver me from the body of this death?" Compare 6:6. And Paul, who has been describing experience under law, joyfully testifies to his experience under grace: "I thank God (that deliverance comes) through Jesus Christ our Lord." With this cry of triumph we enter the wonderful eighth chapter, which has as its dominant theme, deliverance from the sinful nature by the power of the Holy Spirit.

There are three deaths in which the believer must take part: (1) Death **in** sin—our condemnation. Eph. 2:1; Col. 2:13. Sin had brought the soul to that condition the penalty of which is spiritual death or separation from God. (2) Death **for** sin—our justification. Christ endured upon the cross the sentence of a violated law on our behalf and we therefore are counted as having endured it in Him. What He did **for** us is reckoned as having been done **by** us. 2 Cor. 5:14, R. V.; Gal. 2:20. We are held legally or judicially free from the penalty of a violated law if by personal faith we consent to the transaction. (3) Death

to sin—our sanctification. Rom. 6:11. What is true
for us must be made real **in** us; what is judicial
must be made practical; death to the penalty of
sin must be followed by death to the power of
sin. And this is the work of the Holy Spirit. Rom.
8:13. As the ascending sap in a tree crowds off
dead leaves which cling in spite of frost and storm,
so the indwelling Spirit crowds out the imperfections and habits of the old life.

6. Entire Sanctification.

This truth is often discussed under the topic
of "Christian Perfection."

(a) The Meaning of Perfection. There are
two kinds of perfection, absolute and relative.
That is absolutely perfect which cannot be im-
proved upon; this belongs only to God. That is
relatively perfect which fulfills the end for which
it was designed; this perfection is possible to man.

The word "perfection" in the Old Testament
has the meaning of "sincere and upright." Gen.
6:9; Job 1:1. In avoiding the sins of the surrounding nations Israel might be "perfect." Deut.
18:13. The essence of perfection in the Old Testament is the whole-hearted desire and determination to do the will of God. Regardless of the sins
that mar his record David may be truly called a
perfect man or a "man after God's own heart,"
because the supreme aim of his life was to do
God's will.

The word "perfect" and its derivatives have a
variety of applications in the New Testament, and
therefore must be interpreted according to the
sense in which the terms are used. Various Greek
words are used to convey the idea of perfection:
(1) One word means being complete in the sense
of being apt or fit for a certain task or end. 2 Tim.
3:17. (2) Another word denotes a certain end attained through growth in mental and moral
development. Matt. 5:48; 19:21; Col. 1:28; 4:12;

Heb. 11:40. (3) The word used in 2 Cor. 13:9; Eph. 4:12, and Heb. 13:21 means thorough equipment. (4) The word used in 2 Cor. 7:1 means to terminate, or to bring to a termination. (5) The word used in Rev. 3:2 signifies to make replete, to fulfill, to cram (as a net), to level (as a hollow).

The word is descriptive of the following aspects of the Christian life: (1) Positional perfection in Christ (Heb. 10:14)—the result of Christ's work **for** us. (2) Spiritual maturity and understanding, as opposed to spiritual childhood. 1 Cor. 2:6; 14:20; 2 Cor. 13:11; Phil. 3:15; 2 Tim. 3:17. (3) Progressive perfection. Gal. 3:3. (4) Perfection in certain particulars: the will of God, the love for man, and service. Col. 4:12; Matt. 5:48; Heb. 13:21. (5) The ultimate perfection of the individual in heaven. Col. 1:28, 22; Phil. 3:12; 1 Pet. 5:10. (6) The ultimate perfection of the church, or the corporate body of believers. Eph. 4:13; John 17:23.

(b) The Possibilities of Perfection. The New Testament presents two general aspects of perfection: (1) Perfection as a gift of grace, which is the perfect position or standing given the penitent in response to faith in Christ. He is counted perfect because he has a perfect Saviour and a perfect righteousness. (2) Perfection as actually wrought in the believer's character. One may overemphasize the first aspect to the neglect of practical Christianity. Such an one was that individual who, after a lecture on the Victorious Life, said to the speaker, "I have all that in Christ." "But do you have it in Glasgow?" was the quiet question. On the other hand, by overemphasizing the second aspect some have practically denied any perfection apart from that which they find in their own experience.

John Wesley seems to have taken a middle road between the two extremes. He acknowledged that a person was sanctified at conversion, but affirmed the necessity of **entire sanctification** as another work of grace. What made this experience seem necessary was the power of sin which caused the Christian to be defeated. The blessing comes in response to faithful seeking; pure love fills the heart and governs all the work and action, with the result that the power of sin is broken. This perfection in love was not considered sinless perfection, neither does it exempt the believer from constant vigilance and care. Wrote Wesley: "I believe that a person filled with the love of God is still liable to involuntary transgressions. Such transgressions you may call sins if you please; I do not." Concerning the time of entire sanctification, Wesley wrote:

Is this death to sin, and renewal in love, gradual or instantaneous? A man may be dying for some time; yet he does not, properly speaking, die till the instant the soul is separated from the body; and in that instant he lives the life of eternity. In like manner, he may be dying to sin for some time; yet he is not dead to sin, till sin is separated from his soul; and in that instant he lives the full life of love. And as the change undergone, when the body dies, is of a different kind, and infinitely greater than any we had known before, yea, such as till then it was impossible to conceive; so the change wrought when the soul dies to sin, is of a different kind, and infinitely greater than any before, and than any can conceive till he experiences it. Yet he still grows in grace, in the knowledge of Christ, in the love and image of God; and will do so, not only till death, but to all eternity. How are we to wait for this change? Not in careless indifference, or indolent activity; but in vigorous, universal obedience, in a zealous keeping of the commandments, in watchfulness and painfulness, in denying ourselves, and in taking up our cross daily; as well as in earnest prayer and fasting, and a close attendance on the ordinances of God. And if any man dreams of attaining it any other way (yea, of keeping it when it is attained, when he hath received it even in the largest measure) he deceiveth his own soul.

John Calvin, who stressed the believer's perfection because of Christ's finished work, and who was no less zealous for holiness than Wesley, gives the following account of Christian perfection:

> When God reconciles us to Himself through the righteousness of Christ, and reckons us righteous through the free remission of our sins, He also dwells within us by His Spirit, and sanctifies us by His power, mortifying the lusts of our flesh and forming our hearts unto obedience to His Word. It thus becomes our principal desire to obey His will and to promote His glory. But even after this, there still remains in us enough of imperfection to check pride and constrain us to humility. Eccl. 7:20; 1 Kings 8:46.

Both views, perfection as a gift in Christ and perfection as an actual work wrought in us, are taught in the Scriptures; what Christ has done for us must be wrought in us. The New Testament holds up a high standard of practical holiness and affirms the possibility of deliverance from the power of sin. It is therefore the Christian's duty to strive after perfection. Phil. 3:12; Heb. 6:1.

In this connection it must be acknowledged that progress in sanctification often involves a crisis experience almost as definite as that of conversion. By one means or another the believer receives a revelation of the holiness of God and the possibility of a closer walk with Him, and this is followed by a consciousness of defilement. Compare Isaiah 6. He has come to a crossroad in his Christian experience where he must decide either to go back or go forward with God. Confessing past failures, he makes a reconsecration and as a result receives a new accession of peace, joy, and victory, and also the witness that God has accepted his consecration. Some have called this experience a second work of grace.

There will still be temptation from without and within, hence the need of vigilance (Gal. 6:1; 1 Cor. 10:12); the flesh is frail and the

Christian is free to yield, for he is in a state of probation (Gal. 5:17; Rom. 7:18; Phil. 3:3); his knowledge is partial and faulty and he may therefore be subject to sins of ignorance. Nevertheless, he may press on with the following assurance: that he may resist and overcome every recognized temptation (James 4:7; 1 Cor. 10:13; Rom. 6:14; Eph. 6:13, 14); he may be always glorifying to God and filled with the fruits of righteousness (1 Cor. 10:31; Col. 1:10); he may possess the graces and power of the Spirit and walk in unbroken fellowship with God (Gal. 5:22, 23; Eph. 5:18; Col. 1:10, 11; 1 John 1:7); he may ever have the constant cleansing of the Blood and thus be blameless before God. 1 John 1:7; Phil. 2:15; 1 Thess. 5:23.

V. THE SECURITY OF SALVATION.

We have studied the preparations for salvation and considered the nature of salvation. In this section we shall consider the question: Is the final salvation of Christians unconditional, or may it be forfeited because of sin?

Experience proves the possibility of a temporary fall from grace popularly known as backsliding. "Backsliding" is not found in the New Testament; it is an Old Testament word. One Hebrew word used means to "turn back" or to "turn away"; another word means to "turn around" or "be refractory." Israel is compared to a backsliding heifer that refuses to be led and becomes refractory under the yoke; Israel has turned from Jehovah and has stubbornly refused to take upon her the yoke of His commandments.

The New Testament warns against such an attitude, but uses other terms. A backslider is one who once had zeal for God but who has become cold (Matt. 24:12); he once obeyed the Word but worldliness and sin impeded its growth and prevented fruit (Matt. 13:22); he once put his hand to the plough, but looked back (Luke 9:62); like Lot's wife he has been delivered from the City of Destruction but his heart has returned there (Luke 17:32); he was once in vital contact with Christ, but is now out of touch, and is withered and barren and good for nothing spiritually (John 15:6); he once heeded the checks of conscience but now has thrown away that guiding compass, and as a result, his ship of faith has become wrecked on the rocks of sin and worldliness (1 Tim. 1:19); he was once happy to call himself a Christian, but is now ashamed to confess his Lord (2 Tim. 1:8; 2:12); he was once delivered from the world's defilements, but has returned like "the sow that was washed to her wallowing in the mire." 2 Peter 2:22; compare Luke 11:21-26.

Lapses from grace are possible; but may a person who was once saved lapse and be finally lost? Those who follow the Calvinistic system of doctrine answer in the negative; those who follow the Arminian system (named after Arminius, a Dutch theologian who brought the question to an issue) answer in the affirmative.

1. Calvinism.

John Calvin's doctrine was not new with him; it was taught by Augustine, the great saint and theologian of the fourth century. Neither was it new with Augustine, who claimed to be interpreting Paul's doctrine of free grace.

The Calvinistic doctrine is as follows. Salvation is entirely of God; man has absolutely nothing to do about it. If he repents and believes and comes to Christ, it is entirely because of the drawing power of God's Spirit. This is due to the fact that man's will has become so corrupt since the Fall that, without God's help, he cannot even repent and believe, or choose rightly. This was Calvin's starting point—the complete bondage of man's will to evil. Salvation therefore can be nothing but the execution of a Divine decree which fixes its extent and conditions.

The question naturally arises: If salvation is entirely the work of God, and man has nothing to do about it, and is helpless unless God's Spirit deals with him, why does not God save all men, since all are lost and helpless? Calvin's answer was: God has predestined some to be saved and others to be lost. "Predestination is the eternal decree of God, by which He has decided what is to become of each and every individual. For all are not created in like condition; but eternal life is foreordained for some, eternal condemnation for others." In so acting God is not unjust for He is under no obligation to save anybody; man's responsibility remains, for Adam's fall was his own fault and man is always responsible for his own sins.

Since God has predestined certain individuals to salvation, Christ died only for the "elect"; the atonement would fail were any to be lost for whom Christ died.

From the doctrine of predestination follows the teaching of "once in grace always in grace," for if God has predestined a man to salvation, and he can be saved and kept only by God's grace, which is irresistible, then he can never be lost.

Advocates of the "eternal security" doctrine present the following scriptures in support of their position: John 10:28, 29; Rom. 11:29; Phil. 1:6; 1 Pet. 1:5; Rom. 8:35; John 17:6.

2. Arminianism.

The Arminian teaching is as follows. God's will is that all men be saved because Christ died for all. 1 Tim. 2:4-6; Heb. 2:9; 2 Cor. 5:14; Tit. 2:11, 12. To that end He offers His grace to all. While salvation is the work of God, absolutely free, and independent of our good works or merits, yet man has certain conditions to fulfill. He can either choose to accept God's grace or he can resist or reject it. The power of choice ever remains.

The Scriptures do teach a predestination, but not that God predestines some to eternal life and others to eternal suffering. He predestines "whosoever will" to be saved—and that plan is wide enough to include everybody who really wants to be saved. This truth has been explained as follows: Outside the door of salvation we read the words, "Whosoever will may come"; when we enter and are saved, we read the words, "Elect according to the foreknowledge of God." God, because of His knowledge, foresaw those persons who would accept the gospel and stay saved, and predestined such to a heavenly inheritance. He **foreknew** their destiny but did not **fix** it.

The doctrine of predestination is mentioned not for a speculative, but for a practical purpose. When God called Jeremiah to the ministry, He knew that he was going to have a very difficult task, and that he might be tempted to give up. In order to encourage him, the Lord assured the prophet that He had known and called him before he was born. Jer. 1:5. The Lord as much as says, "I already know what is ahead of you; but I also know that I can give you grace to meet every future test and to take you through victoriously." When the New Testament describes Christians as objects of God's foreknowledge, its purpose is to assure us of the fact that God has foreseen every difficulty that will confront us, and that He can and will keep us from falling.

3. A Comparison.

Is salvation conditional or unconditional? Once saved, is a person eternally saved? The answer will depend on the way we can answer the following "key questions": On whom does salvation depend? Is grace irresistible?

(1) On whom does salvation ultimately depend—on God or man? Certainly it must depend on God, for who could be saved if salvation depended on a person's own strength? We may be sure of this—God will take us through no matter how weak or blundering we are—provided we honestly desire to do His will. His grace is ever present to warn, check, encourage and sustain.

However, is there not a certain sense in which salvation does depend on man? The Scriptures consistently teach that man has the power of freely choosing between life and death, and that power God will never violate.

(2) Can God's grace be resisted? One of the fundamental principles of Calvinism is that God's grace is irresistible. When God decrees the salvation of a person, His Spirit draws, and that drawing cannot be resisted. Therefore a true child of God will certainly persevere to the end and be saved; even though he fall into sin God will chastise him and strive with him. Speaking figuratively: the man may fall on the ship but he cannot fall overboard.

But the New Testament does teach that Divine grace may be resisted, and resisted to eternal loss (John 6:40; Heb. 6:4-6; 10:26-30; 2 Pet. 2:21; Heb. 2:3; 2 Pet. 1:10), and that perseverance is conditional upon keeping in contact with God.

Note especially Heb. 6:4-6 and 10:26-29. These words were spoken to Christians; Paul's letters were not addressed to the unregenerate. Those addressed are described as being once enlightened, having tasted of the heavenly gift, being made partakers of the Holy Ghost, having tasted the good word of God and the powers of the world to come. These words certainly describe regenerate persons.

Those addressed were Hebrew Christians, who, discouraged and persecuted, (10:32-39) were tempted to return to Judaism. Before being received again into the synagogue they would be publicly required to make the following statements (10:29): that Jesus was not the Son of God; that His blood was rightly shed as that of a common malefactor; and that His miracles were done by the power of the evil one. All this is implied in 10:29. (That such a repudiation would have been insisted on is illustrated by the case of a Hebrew Christian in Germany, who desired to return to the synagogue, but was refused when he desired to hold on to some of the New Testament truths.) Before their conversion they had belonged to the nation which had crucified Christ; to return to the synagogue would be to crucify to themselves the Son of God afresh and put Him to an open shame; it would be the awful sin of apostasy (Heb. 6:6); it would be like the unpardonable sin for which there is no forgiveness, because the one so hardened as to commit it cannot be "renewed unto repentance"; it would be worthy of a worse punishment than that of death (10:28); it would mean incurring the vengeance of the living God. 10:30, 31.

It is not stated that any have gone that far; indeed, the writer is "persuaded better things" of them. 6:9. However, if the terrible sin of apostasy on the part of saved people were not at least remotely possible, all these warnings would have been meaningless.

Read 1 Cor. 10:1-12. The Corinthians had been boasting of the Christian liberty and the possession of spiritual gifts, yet many of them were living on a low plane. They were evidently trusting in their "standing" and privileges in the Gospel. But Paul warns them that privileges may be lost by sin, and cities the examples of the Israelites. They were supernaturally delivered from the land of Egypt, through the agency of Moses, and as a result accepted him as their leader to the Promised Land. Their passing through the Red Sea was a sign of their dedication to his leadership.

Overshadowing them was the supernatural symbol of God's guiding presence. After saving them from Egypt God sustained them with supernatural food and drink. All this meant that the Israelites were in grace, that is, in favor and fellowship with God.

But "once in grace always in grace" was not true in their case; for the route was dotted with the graves of those who had been smitten for their murmurings, rebellion and idolatries. Sin broke their fellowship with God and as a result they fell from grace. Paul declares that these events were recorded to warn Christians of the possibility of forfeiting the most exalted privileges through wilful sin.

4. A Scriptural Balance.

The respective fundamental positions of both Calvinism and Arminianism are taught in the Scriptures. Calvinism exalts the grace of God as the only source of salvation—and so does the Bible; Arminianism emphasizes man's free will and responsibility—and so does the Bible. The practical solution consists in avoiding the unscriptural extremes of either view, and in refraining from setting one view in antagonism to the other. For when two scriptural doctrines are set squarely in opposition to each other the result is a reaction that leads to error. For example: overemphasis of God's sovereignty and grace in salvation may lead to careless living, for if a person is led to believe that his conduct and attitude have nothing to do with his salvation, he may become negligent. On the other hand, overemphasis of man's free will and responsibility, in reaction against Calvinism, may bring people under the bondage of legalism and rob them of all assurance. Lawlessness and legalism—these are the two extremes to be avoided.

When Finney ministered in a community where grace had been overemphasized he bore down heavily on the doctrine of man's responsibility. When he held a meeting in a community where human responsibility and works had been stressed he emphasized the grace of God. And as we leave the mysteries of predestination and set ourselves to the practical task of getting people saved, we shall not be troubled by the matter. Wesley was an Arminian and Whitefield was a Calvinist. Yet both led thousands to Christ.

Godly Calvinistic preachers of the type of Spurgeon and Finney have preached the perseverance of the saints in such a manner as to discourage carelessness. They were careful to point out that while a true child of God was certain to persevere to the end, the fact that he did not so persevere would put in question the fact as to whether he had really been born again! If a person did not follow after holiness, said Calvin, he would do well to question his election.

We are bound to be confronted with mystery as we set out to relate the mighty truths of God's foreknowledge and man's free-will; but as we keep to the practical exhortations of the Scripture and set ourselves to the definite duties commanded, we shall not go wrong. "The secret things belong unto the Lord our God; but those things which are revealed belong unto us." Deut. 29:29.

In conclusion may we suggest that it is unwise to dwell unduly on the perils of the Christian life. The emphasis should rather be placed upon the means of security—the power of Christ as Saviour, the faithfulness of the indwelling Spirit, the certainty of the Divine promises, and the unfailing efficacy of prayer. The New Testament teaches a true "eternal security," assuring us that regardless of weakness, imperfections, handicaps, or outward troubles, the Christian can be secure and victorious in Christ. With the apostle Paul he can cry, "Who shall separate us from the love of Christ? shall tribulation, or distress, or persecution, or famine, or nakedness, or peril, or sword? . . . Nay, in all these things we are more than conquerors through him that loved us. For I am persuaded that neither death, nor life, nor angels, nor principalities, nor powers, nor things present, nor things to come, nor height, nor depth, nor any other creature, shall be able to separate us from the love of God, which is in Christ Jesus our Lord." Rom. 8:35-39.

We append John Wesley's views regarding the final perseverance of the saints.

Having found for some time a strong desire to unite with Mr. Whitefield as far as possible, to cut off needless dispute, I have written down my sentiments, as plain as I could, in the following terms:

There are three points in debate: 1. Unconditional Election. 2. Irrisistible Grace. 3. Final Perseverance.

With regard to the first, Unconditional Election, I believe—

That God, before the foundation of the world, did unconditionally elect certain persons to do certain works, as Paul to preach the gospel;

That He has unconditionally elected some nations to receive peculiar privileges; the Jewish nation in particular;

That He has unconditionally elected some nations to hear the gospel, as England and Scotland now, and many others in past ages;

That He has unconditionally elected some persons to many peculiar advantages, with regard to both temporal and spiritual things;

And I do not deny (though I cannot prove it is so)

That He has unconditionally elected some persons to eternal glory.

But I cannot believe—

That all those who are not thus elected to glory must perish everlastingly; or

That there is one soul on earth who has not ever had a possibility of escaping eternal damnation.

With regard to the second, Irresistible Grace, I believe—

That the grace which brings faith, and thereby salvation, into the soul, is irresistible at that moment;

That most believers may remember some time when God did irresistibly convince them of sin;

That most believers do at some other times find God irresistibly acting upon their souls;

Yet I believe, that the grace of God, both before and after those moments, may be and hath been resisted; and

That in general it does not act irresistibly, but we may comply therewith or may not.

And I do not deny—

That in some souls the grace of God is so far irresistible, that they cannot but believe and be finally saved.

But I cannot believe—

That all must be damned, in whom it does not thus irresistibly work; or

That there is one soul on earth, who has not, and never had any other grace, than such as does in fact increase his damnation, and was designed of God so to do.

With regard to the third, Final Perseverance, I incline to believe—

That there is a state attainable in this life, from which a man cannot finally fall; and

That he who has attained this can say, "Old things are passed away: all things in me are become new."

9

THE HOLY SPIRIT

The doctrine of the Holy Spirit, judged by the place it occupies in the Scriptures, stands in the foremost rank of redemption truths. With the exception of 2 and 3 John, every book in the New Testament contains a reference to the Spirit's work; every Gospel begins with a promise of His outpouring.

Yet it is admittedly the "neglected doctrine." Formalism and fear of fanaticism have produced a reaction against emphasis on the Spirit's work in personal experience.

Naturally this has resulted in spiritual deadness, for there can be no vital Christianity apart from the Spirit. Only He can make actual what Christ's work has made possible. In the words of Ignatius, a leader of the ancient church:

The grace of the Spirit brings the machinery of redemption into vital connection with the individual soul. Apart from the Spirit the Cross stands inert, a vast machine at rest, and about it lie the stones of the building unmoved. Not till the rope has been attached can the work proceed of lifting the individual life through faith and love to the place prepared for it in the church of God.

OUTLINE

I. THE NATURE OF THE SPIRIT.

1. The Names of the Spirit.
   a. The Spirit of God.
   b. The Spirit of Christ.
   c. The Comforter.
   d. The Holy Spirit.
   e. The Holy Spirit of promise.
   f. The Spirit of truth.
   g. The Spirit of grace.
   h. The Spirit of life.
   i. The Spirit of adoption.

2. Symbols of the Spirit.
   a. Fire.
   b. Wind.
   c. Water.
   d. A seal.
   e. Oil.
   f. The dove.

II. THE SPIRIT IN THE OLD TESTAMENT.

1. The Creative Spirit.
2. The Dynamic Spirit, Producing—
   a. Workers for God.
   b. Speakers for God.
3. The Regenerative Spirit, in the Old Testament Is—
   a. Operative but not emphasized.
   b. His general bestowal is a future blessing,
   c. Connected with Messiah's coming, and
   d. Exhibiting special features.

III. THE SPIRIT IN CHRIST.

1. Birth.
2. Baptism.
3. Ministry.
4. Crucifixion.
5. Resurrection.
6. Ascension.

IV. THE SPIRIT IN HUMAN EXPERIENCE.

1. Conviction.
2. Regeneration.
3. Indwelling.
4. Sanctification.

I. THE NATURE OF THE SPIRIT

Who is the Holy Spirit? The answer to this question will be found in studying the names He bears, and the symbols which illustrate His workings.

1. The Names of the Spirit.

(a) The Spirit of God. The Spirit is the executive of the Godhead—working in every sphere, both physical and moral. Through the Spirit God created and preserves the universe. Through the Spirit—"the finger of God" (Luke 11:20)—God works in the spiritual sphere, converting sinners and sanctifying and sustaining believers.

(1) Is the Holy Spirit divine in the absolute sense? His Deity is proved from the following facts: Divine attributes are ascribed to Him; He is eternal, omnipresent, omnipotent, and omniscient. Heb. 9:14; Psalm 139:7-10; Luke 1:35; 1 Cor. 2:10, 11. Divine works are ascribed to Him such as creation, regeneration and resurrection. Gen. 1:2; Job 33:4; John 3:5-8; Rom. 8:11. He is placed in co-ordinate rank with the Father and the Son. 1 Cor. 12:4-6; 2 Cor. 13:14; Matt. 28:19; Rev. 1:4.

(2) Is the Holy Spirit a person or just an influence? The Spirit is often described in an impersonal way—as the Breath that fills, the Unction that anoints, the Fire that lights and heats the Water that is poured out, the Gift of which all partake. However, these are merely descriptions of His operations. The Spirit is described in such a way as to leave no doubt as to His personality. He exercises the attributes of personality—mind (Rom. 8:27), will (1 Cor. 12:11), feeling (Eph. 4:30). Personal activities are ascribed to Him: He reveals (2 Peter 1:21), teaches (John 14:26), witnesses (Gal. 4:6), intercedes (Rom. 8:26), speaks (Rev. 2:7), commands (Acts 16:6-7),

testifies. John 15:26. He may be grieved (Eph. 4:30), lied to (Acts 5:3), and blasphemed. Matt. 12:31, 32.

His personality is indicated by the fact that He was manifested in the visible form of a dove (Matt. 3:16) and also by the fact that He is distinguished from His gifts. 1 Cor. 12:11.

Perhaps some have denied personality to the Spirit because He is not described as having body or shape. But personality and corporeality (possessing a body) must be distinguished. Personality is that which possesses intelligence, feeling, and will; it does not necessarily require a body. Moreover, lack of definite form is no argument against reality. The wind is real though without form. John 3:8.

It is not difficult to form a conception of God the Father or of the Lord Jesus Christ, but some have confessed to an inability to form a clear conception of the Holy Spirit. The reason is twofold: First, throughout the Scriptures the Spirit's operations are invisible, secret, and internal. Second, the Holy Spirit never speaks of Himself or represents Himself; He always comes in the name of and as representing another. He is hidden behind the Lord Jesus Christ and in the depths of our inner man. He never calls attention to Himself but to the will of God and the saving work of Christ. "He shall not speak of himself." John 16:13.

(3) Is the Holy Spirit a personality separate and distinct from God? Yes; the Spirit proceeds from God, is sent from God, is God's gift to men. Yet the Spirit is not independent of God. He always represents the one God acting in the spheres of thought, will, and activity. How the Spirit can be one with God and yet distinct from God is part of the mystery of the Trinity.

(b) **The Spirit of Christ.** Rom. 8:9. There is

no essential distinction between the Spirit of God, the Spirit of Christ, and the Holy Spirit. For there is only one Holy Spirit, as there can be only one God and one Son. But the one Spirit has many names descriptive of His various ministries.

Why is the Spirit called the Spirit of Christ? (1) Because He is sent in the name of Christ. John 14:26. (2) Because He is the Spirit sent by the Christ. The Spirit is the principle of spiritual life by which men are born into the kingdom of God. This new life of the Spirit is imparted and maintained by Christ (John 1:12, 13; 4:10; 7:38), who is also the Baptizer with the Holy Spirit. Matt. 3:11. (3) The Holy Spirit is called the Spirit of Christ because His special mission in this age is to glorify Christ. John 16:14. His special work is connected with Him who lived, died, rose, and ascended. He makes real **in** believers what Christ has done **for** them. (4) The glorified Christ is present in the church and in believers by the Holy Spirit. It is often said that the Spirit has come to take the place of Christ, but it is more correct to say that He has come to make Christ real. The Holy Spirit makes possible and real the omnipresence of Christ in the world (Matt. 18:20) and His indwelling in believers. The connection between Christ and the Spirit is so close, that both Christ and the Spirit are said to dwell in the believer (Gal. 2:20; Rom. 8:9, 10); and the believer is both "in Christ" and "in the Spirit."

Thanks to the Holy Spirit, the Life of Christ becomes our life in Christ.

(c) The Comforter. This is the title given to the Spirit in John, chapters 14-17. A study of the background of these chapters will reveal the significance of the gift. The disciples had taken their last meal with the Master. Their hearts were sad at the thought of His departure, and they were oppressed with a sense of weakness and helplessness. Who will help us when He is gone? Who will teach and guide us? Who will stand by us as we preach and teach? How shall we be able to face a hostile world? These unspoken fears Jesus quieted with the promise, "I will pray the Father, and he shall give you **another** Comforter, that he may abide with you for ever." John 14:16.

The word Comforter ("paracletos" in the Greek) bears the following literal meaning: one called to the side of another for the purpose of helping him in any way, particularly in legal and criminal proceedings. It was the custom in ancient tribunals for parties to appear in court attended by one or more of their most influential friends, who were called in Greek, "Paracletes," and in Latin, "Advocatus." These gave their friends—not for fee or reward, but from love and interest—the advantage of their personal presence and the aid of their wise counsel. They advised them what to do, what to say, spoke for them, acted on their behalf, made the cause of their friends their own cause, stood by them and for them in the trials, difficulties, and dangers of the situation.

Such was the relationship that the Lord Jesus had sustained to the disciples during His earthly ministry, and naturally they were dismayed at the thought of His departure. But He comforted them with the promise of another Comforter who should be their defender, helper, and teacher during His absence. He is called "another" Comforter because He was to be invisibly to the disciples what Jesus had been to them visibly.

The word "another" distinguishes the Holy Spirit from Jesus, yet puts Him on the same plane. Jesus sends the Spirit, yet Jesus comes spiritually to the disciples through the Spirit; the Spirit is thus both Christ's Successor and also His Presence. The Holy Spirit makes possible and real the continued presence of Christ in the church.

It is He who causes the person of Christ to dwell in them so that they acquire the right to say with Paul, "Christ liveth in me." It is therefore the life of Christ, the nature of Christ, the sentiments of Christ, the virtues of Christ, that the Spirit communicates to believers; it is after the likeness of Christ that He fashions them, and after the model which He had left us. Without Christ the Spirit has nothing to produce in the heart of the believer. Take away Christ, and His Word, and it is like removing from the photographer's studio the person whose features the sun is about to fix on the plate prepared to receive them.

The sending of the Comforter does not mean that Christ has ceased to be the Helper and Advocate of His people. John tells us that He still fulfills that office. 1 John 2:1. Christ, whose sphere of work is in heaven, defends the disciples against the charges of the "accuser of the brethren"; at the same time the Spirit, whose sphere of work is on earth, "silences the earthly adversaries of the Church through the victory of faith which overcomes the world." As Christ is Paraclete in heaven, so the Holy Ghost is Paraclete on earth.

The ascended Christ not only sends the Spirit but also manifests Himself by means of the Spirit. In the flesh He could be in only one place at a time; in His ascended life He is omnipresent by the Spirit. During His earthly life He was external to men; by the Spirit He can dwell in the very depths of their souls. One writer has stated this truth as follows:

If He had remained on earth in His physical life, He would have been only an example to be copied; but if He went to His father and sent His Spirit, then He would be a life to be lived. If He had remained visibly and tangibly with us, He would have been related to us merely as a model is related to an artist who chisels his marble, but never as the idea and inspiration which produces the work of art. If he had remained on earth, He would have been merely the subject of prolonged observation of scientific study, and He would always have been outside of us, external to us; an external voice, an external life, an external example. . . . But thanks to His Spirit, He can now live in us as the very Soul of our souls, the very Spirit of our spirits, the Truth of our minds, the Love of our hearts, and the Desire of our wills.

If the Spirit's work is to communicate the work of the Son, what gain could there be in the departing of the one in order to make possible the coming of the other? Answer: It is not the **earthly** Christ that the Spirit communicates, but the **heavenly** Christ—the Christ reinvested with His eternal power, reclothed with heavenly glory. Employing an illustration suggested by Dr. A. J. Gordon:

It is as if a father, whose kinsman had died, had said to his children: "We are poor and I have become an heir. If you will submit cheerfully to my leaving you and crossing the sea and entering into my inheritance, I will send you back a thousand times more than you could have had by my remaining with you."

Christ's life on earth represented the days of His poverty (2 Cor. 8:9) and humiliation; on the Cross He secured the riches of His grace (Eph. 1:7); on the Throne He secured the riches of His glory. Eph. 3:16. After His ascension to the Father He sent the Spirit to convey the riches of the inheritance. By His ascension Christ would have more to give and the church would have more to receive. John 16:12; 14:12. "The stream of life will have higher power because of the higher source from which it proceeds."
The Comforter teaches only the things of Christ, yet teaches more than Christ taught. Until the Crucifixion, Resurrection, and Ascension the Christian doctrine was not yet complete and therefore could not be fully communicated to the disciples of Christ. In John 16:12, 13 Jesus says in

effect: "I have brought you a little way in the knowledge of my doctrine; He shall bring you all the way." The Ascension was to bring a larger impartation of **truth** as well as a greater impartation of **power.**

(d) The Holy Spirit. The Spirit is called holy because He is the Spirit of the Holy One, and because His chief work is sanctification. We need a Saviour for two reasons: to do something **for** us, and something **in** us. Jesus did the first by dying for us; through the Holy Spirit He lives in us, transmitting to our souls His Divine life. The Holy Spirit has come to reorganize the nature of man and to pit Himself against all its evil tendencies.

(e) The Holy Spirit of Promise. The Holy Spirit is so called because His grace and power is one of the outstanding blessings promised in the Old Testament. Ezek. 36:27; Joel 2:28. It is the highest prerogative of the Christ, or the Messiah, to impart the Spirit, and this Jesus claimed when He said, "Behold, I send the promise of my Father upon you." Luke 24:49; Gal. 3:14.

(f) The Spirit of Truth. The purpose of the Incarnation was to reveal the Father; the mission of the Comforter is to reveal the **Son.** When we gaze upon a picture, we may for ourselves see much that is beautiful and attractive in its modes of exhibiting color and form; but to understand the inner meaning of the picture and appreciate its real purpose, we need some skilled interpreter to open our eyes.

The Holy Spirit is the Interpreter of Jesus Christ. He does not bestow a new or different revelation, but rather opens the minds of men to see the deeper meaning of Christ's life and words. As the Son did not speak of Himself, but spoke

288 KNOWING THE DOCTRINES OF THE BIBLE

what He had received from the Father, so the Spirit will not speak of Himself as from a separate store of knowledge, but will declare what He hears in that inner life of the Godhead.

(g) The Spirit of Grace. Heb. 10:29; Zech. 12:10. The Holy Spirit gives man grace to repent by striving with him; He imparts the power for sanctification, endurance, and service. He who does despite unto the Spirit of grace, drives away Him who alone can touch or move the heart, and thus cuts himself off from God's mercy.

(h) The Spirit of Life. Rom. 8:2; Rev. 11:11. "I believe in the Holy Ghost, the Lord, and Giver of life," reads an ancient creed. The Spirit is that Person of the Godhead whose special function is the creation and preservation of natural and spiritual life.

(i) The Spirit of Adoption. Rom. 8:15. When a person is saved, he is not only given the name of child of God, and adopted into the Divine family, but he also receives within his soul the consciousness that he is a partaker of the Divine nature. Writes Bishop Andrews: "As Christ is our witness in heaven, so is the Spirit here on earth witnessing with our spirits that we are the children of God."

2. Symbols of the Spirit.

It has been well said that "words are often but lame vehicles for the conveyance of truth. At their best, they but half reveal, half conceal the hidden depths of thought." God has chosen to illustrate with symbol what otherwise, because of the poverty of language, we could never know. The following symbols are employed to describe the operations of the Holy Spirit:

(a) Fire. Isa. 4:4; Matt. 3:11; Luke 3:16. Fire illustrates the purging, purification, fiery boldness, and zeal produced by the anointing of the Spirit. The Spirit is compared to fire because fire warms, illuminates, spreads, and purifies. Compare Jer. 20:9.

(b) Wind. Ezek. 37:7-10; John 3:8; Acts 2:2. Wind symbolizes the regenerative work of the Spirit and is indicative of His mysterious, independent, penetrating, life-giving and purifying operation.

(c) Water. Ex. 17:6; Ezek. 36:25-27; 47:1; John 3:5; 4:14; 7:38, 39. The Spirit is the fountain of living water, the purest, the best, because He is a veritable River of life—flooding, gushing over our souls, cleansing away the dust of sin. The power of the Spirit does in the spiritual what water does in the material order. Water purifies, refreshes, quenches thirst and renders sterility fruitful. It purifies what is soiled and restores cleanliness; it is an apt symbol of Divine grace which not only cleanses the soul but adds to it a Divine beauty. Water is an indispensable element of physical life; the Holy Spirit is an indispensable element of spiritual life.

What is the meaning of the expression, "living water"? It is living in contrast with the stagnant water of cisterns or marshes; it is water that bubbles up, flows along always in communication with its source and always bearing evidences of life. If this water is caught in a reservoir, if its flow is interrupted, if it is cut off from its source, it can no longer bear the name of living water. Christians have the "living water" only to the extent that they are in contact with its Divine source in Christ.

(d) A Seal. Eph. 1:13; 2 Tim. 2:19. This illustration conveys the following thoughts: (1) Ownership. The impress of a seal implies a relation to the owner of the seal, and is a sure token of something belonging to him. Believers are God's property and known to be so by the Spirit dwelling in them. The following custom was common in Ephesus in Paul's day. A merchant would go to the harbor, select certain timber and then stamp it with his seal—an acknowledged sign of ownership. Later he would send his servant with his signet who looked for the timber bearing the corresponding impress. See 2 Tim. 2:19. (2) The idea of security is also involved. Eph. 1:13; compare Rev. 7:3. The Spirit inspires the sense of security and assurance in the believer's heart. Rom. 8:16. He is an earnest or first part of our heavenly inheritance, an assurance of the glory to come. Christians have been sealed, but must beware of doing anything to break the seal. Eph. 4:30.

(e) Oil. Oil is perhaps the most familiar and common symbol of the Spirit. Whenever oil was used ritually in the Old Testament it spoke of usefulness, fruitfulness, beauty, life, and transformation. It was commonly used for food, light, lubrication, healing, and soothing of the skin. In like manner, in the spiritual order, the Spirit strengthens, illumines, liberates, heals and soothes the soul.

(f) The Dove. The dove, as a symbol, speaks of gentleness, tenderness, loveliness, innocence, mildness, peace, purity, and patience. Among the Syrians it is an emblem of the life-giving powers of nature. A Jewish tradition translates Gen. 1:2 as follows: "The Spirit of God like a dove brooded over the waters." Christ spoke of the dove as the embodiment of the harmlessness which was characteristic of His own disciples.

II. THE SPIRIT IN THE OLD TESTAMENT

The Holy Spirit is revealed in the Old Testament in three ways: first, as the creative or cosmic Spirit through whose power the universe and all living creatures were created; second, as the dynamic or power-giving Spirit; third, as the regenerative Spirit by which human nature is changed.

1. The Creative Spirit.

The Holy Spirit is the Third Person of the Trinity by whose power the universe was created. He brooded over the face of the waters and shared the glory of creation. Gen. 1:2; Job 26:13; Psa. 33:6; 104:30. Writes Dr. Denio:

> The Holy Spirit as Deity immanent (abiding) in all creation manifests His presence by what we call the laws of nature. He is the principle of order and life, the organizing power in created nature. All the forces of nature are but evidences of the presence and operation of the Spirit of God. Mechanical forces, chemical action, organic life in plant and animal, energy connected with nervous action, intelligence, and moral conduct are but tokens of the immanence of God of which the Holy Spirit is the agent.

The Holy Spirit created and sustains man. Gen. 2:7; Job 33:4. Every individual whether or not he serves God, is sustained by the creative power of God's Spirit. Dan. 5:23; Acts 17:28. Man's existence is like the note of an organ, lasting only as long as the Creator's finger is upon the key. Man owes his being to the "two hands of God," the Word (John 1:1-3) and the Spirit, for it was to these that the words, "Let us make man," were spoken.

2. The Dynamic Spirit.

The Creator-Spirit made man in order that he might form a society governed by God; in other words, the kingdom of God. After sin had entered and human society was organized apart from and in opposition to God, God made a new start by calling Israel, organizing them under His laws, so constituting them the kingdom of Jehovah. 2 Chron. 13:8. As we study the history of Israel we read of the Holy Spirit inspiring certain individuals, to rule and guide the members of that kingdom, and to supervise their progress in the life of consecration.

The dynamic operation of the Spirit created two kinds of ministers: first, workers for God—men of action, organizers, executives; second, speakers for God, prophets, and teachers.

(a) Workers for God. As examples of Spirit-inspired workers we mention Joseph (Gen. 41:38-40), Bezaleel (Ex. 35:30, 31), Moses (Num. 11:16, 17), Joshua (Num. 27:8-21), Othniel (Judges 3:9, 10), Gideon (Judges 6:34), Jephthah (Judges 11:29), Samson (Judges 13:24, 25), Saul. 1 Sam. 10:6.

It was very likely in the light of these examples that the leaders of the early church insisted that even those charged with waiting on tables should be filled with the Holy Ghost. Acts 6:3.

(b) Speakers for God. The prophet of Israel may be described as a speaker for God—one who received messages from God and passed them on to the people. He was conscious of a heavenly power coming upon him from time to time, enabling him to utter messages not conceived in his own mind, a feature which distinguished him from false prophets. Ezek. 13:2. The word "prophet" is indicative of inspiration, coming from a word meaning "to bubble up"—a testimony to the torrential outbursts of eloquence which often flowed from the prophet's lips. Compare John 7:38.

(1) The expressions employed to describe the manner in which the inspiration came to them convey the thought of suddenness and supernaturalness. In referring to the origin of their power, the prophets said that God poured out the Spirit, gave the Spirit, put His Spirit upon them, filled them with His Spirit, and put His Spirit

within. Describing the variety of influence, they declared that the Spirit was on them, rested upon them, laid hold of them. To indicate the influence exerted on them, they said they were filled with the Spirit, moved by the Spirit, taken up by the Spirit, and that the Spirit spoke through them.

(2) When the prophet prophesied, he was sometimes in an exalted condition known as "ecstasy"—a dignified form of the old expression "under the power," that state of being in which one is lifted above ordinary consciousness and into the spiritual realm, the realm of prophecy. Ezekiel said, "The hand of the Lord God (the power of the Lord God) fell there upon me, . . . and the spirit lifted me up between the earth and the heaven, and brought me in the visions of God to Jerusalem." Ezek. 8:1-3. It is very likely that Isaiah was in this condition when he beheld the glory of Jehovah. Isaiah 6. John the apostle states that he was "in the Spirit on the Lord's day." Rev. 1:10; compare Acts 22:17.

The expressions used to describe the inspiration and ecstasy of the prophets are similar to those describing the New Testament experience of being filled or baptized with the Spirit (see the Acts). It seems that in this latter experience the Spirit made so direct an impact on the human spirit that the person was lifted into a condition of ecstasy, in which condition he gave utterance to ecstatic speech.

(3) The prophets did not always prophesy in an ecstatic condition; the expression, "the word of the Lord came," implies that the revelation came by a supernatural illumination of the mind. The divine message may be received and delivered in either way.

(4) The prophet did not exercise the gift at his discretion; the prophecy came not "by the will of man." 2 Peter 1:21. Jeremiah said he knew

not that people had been plotting against him.
Jer. 11:19. The prophets never supposed, nor
did Israelites believe, that the power of prophecy was possessed by any man as a constant or
uninterrupted gift to be used at will. They understood that the Spirit was a personal agent and
that therefore inspiration was by the sovereign
will of God. The prophets could, however, bring
themselves into a condition of receptivity to the
Spirit (2 Kings 3:15), and in times of crisis they
could ask God for guidance.

3. The Regenerative Spirit.

We shall consider the following truths relative to the regenerative Spirit. His presence is
recorded in the Old Testament, but not emphasized; His bestowal is described mainly as a future
blessing; this outpouring is connected with Messiah's coming; and exhibits distinctive features.

(a) Operative but Not Emphasized. The Holy
Spirit in the Old Testament is also described as
being associated with the transformation of
human nature. In Isa. 63:10, 11 reference is made
to the Exodus and the wilderness life. When the
prophet says that Israel grieved God's holy Spirit,
when it is said that He gave His "good Spirit" to
instruct them (Neh. 9:20), the reference is to
the Spirit as inspiring moral goodness. Compare
also Psalm 143:10. David recognized the Spirit
as being everywhere, searching out men's ways
and throwing the light of God on the darkest re-
cesses of their lives. After his great sin he prayed
that God's Holy Spirit, God's sanctifying Presence, the Spirit that influences character, might not
be taken from him. Psa. 51:11.

However, this aspect of the Spirit's work is
not emphasized in the Old Testament. The name
Holy Spirit occurs only three times in the Old
Testament, but eighty-six times in the New, sug-

gesting that in the Old Testament the emphasis is on the dynamic operations of the Spirit, while in the New the emphasis is upon His sanctifying power.

(b) His General Bestowal, a Future Blessing.

The general bestowal of the Spirit as the source of holiness is spoken of as a thing of the future, one of the blessings of the promised kingdom of God. In Israel the Spirit of God was given to certain chosen leaders, and doubtless wherever there was real godliness it was due to the working of His Spirit. But the mass of the people were generally lapsing into paganism and iniquity, and though revived from time to time through the ministry of prophets and godly kings, it became evident that the nation was bad at heart and that a general outpouring of the Spirit was needed to turn them back to God.

Such an outpouring was predicted by the prophets, who told of the Spirit being outpoured upon the people in unprecedented measure. Jehovah would cleanse the hearts of the people, put His Spirit within them, and write His law on their inward parts. Ezek. 36:25-29; Jer. 31:34. In those days the Spirit should be outpoured in power upon all flesh (Joel 2:28), that is, upon all sorts and conditions of men without distinction of age, sex or rank. Moses' prayer that all of God's people should become prophets would then be fulfilled. Num. 11:29. As a result many would be converted, for, "whosoever shall call on the name of the Lord shall be delivered." Joel 2:32.

The distinguishing feature of God's people under the old dispensation was the possession and revelation of the law of God; the distinguishing feature of His people under the new dispensation should be the writing of the law and the abiding of the Spirit in their hearts.

(c) Connected with Messiah's Coming. The great outpouring would find its culminating point and climax in the King-Messiah, on whom the Spirit of Jehovah should rest permanently as the Spirit of wisdom and understanding, counsel and might, knowledge and holy fear; He would be the perfect Prophet who should proclaim Good News of liberation, healing, comfort and joy.

What is the connection between these two great events of prophecy—the coming of the Anointed One and the universal effusion of the Holy Spirit? John the Baptist answers: "I indeed baptize you with water unto repentance: but he that cometh after me is mightier than I, whose shoes I am not worthy to bear: he shall baptize you with the Holy Ghost and with fire." In other words, the Messiah is the Giver of the Holy Spirit. This is what marked Him as the Messiah or the Founder of the kingdom of God; the great blessing of the new age was to be the outpouring of the Spirit and it was Messiah's highest privilege to impart the Spirit. During His earthly ministry Christ spoke of the Spirit as the Father's best gift (Luke 11:13); He invited the spiritually thirsty to come and drink, and offered them an abundant supply of the water of life; in His farewell discourses He promised to send the Comforter to His disciples.

Note especially the connection of the gift with the work of Christ as Redeemer. The giving of the Spirit is connected with Christ's departure (John 16:7) and glorification (John 7:39), which imply His death. John 12:23, 24; 13:31, 33; Luke 24:49. Paul states the connection clearly in Gal. 3:13, 14; Gal. 4:4-6, and Eph. 1:3, 7, 13, 14.

(d) And Exhibiting Special Features. Perhaps this is the place to enquire concerning the meaning of the statement: "For the Holy Ghost was not yet given; because that Jesus was not yet glorified." John 7:39. (The word "given" is in italics, indicating that it has been supplied by the translators.) John certainly did not mean that no one in Old Testament times experienced manifestations of the Spirit; every Jew knew that the mighty deeds of Israel's leaders and the messages of the prophets were due to the operations of God's Spirit. He evidently refers to a certain aspect of the Spirit's work which was not known in previous dispensations. What, then, are the distinct features of the Spirit's work in this dispensation?

(1) The Spirit was not yet given as the Spirit of the crucified and glorified Christ. This mission of the Spirit could not begin until the mission of the Son was ended; Jesus could not be manifest in the Spirit until He ceased to live in the flesh. The gift of the Spirit could be claimed by Him for men only when He had taken His place as their Advocate in the presence of God. When Jesus spoke there was as yet no spiritual force in the world such as was brought into it at Pentecost and afterward swept the whole earth like a great tidal wave. For Jesus had not yet ascended whither He was before the incarnation (John 6:62), He was not yet with His Father (John 16:7; 20:17); and there could not be a universal spiritual presence until the presence in the flesh had been withdrawn, and until the Son of man had been crowned by His exaltation to the right hand of God. The Spirit was kept in the hands of God for this general outpouring until He could be claimed for humanity by a victorious Christ.

(2) In Old Testament times the Spirit was not given universally but limited generally to Israel and imparted according to God's sovereign will to certain individuals, such as prophets, priests, kings and other workers in His kingdom. But in

this age the Spirit is available for all regardless of age, sex or race.

In this connection note that in the Old Testament God's Spirit is rarely referred to by the brief designation, "the Spirit." One reads of the "Spirit of Jehovah" or "the Spirit of God." But in the New Testament the brief title, "the Spirit" is of frequent occurrence, suggesting that His operations are no longer isolated manifestations but familiar occurrences.

(3) It is believed by some scholars that the impartation of the Spirit in Old Testament times did not involve the permanent indwelling and abiding which is characteristic of the New Testament gift. They point out that the word "gift," implies possession and permanence, and that in this sense there was no **gift** of the Spirit in the Old Testament. It is true that John the Baptist was filled with the Holy Ghost from his mother's womb, and this implies a permanent anointing. Perhaps this, and other similar cases, could be regarded as exceptions to the general rule. For example, when Enoch and Elijah were translated, they were exceptions to the general Old Testament rule that entrance into God's presence was through the grave and Sheol (the realm of departed spirits).

III. THE SPIRIT IN CHRIST.

The New Testament ushers in the Dispensation of the Spirit, fulfilling the promise that God would pour out of His Spirit on all flesh, put His Spirit within His people's hearts, and so write His laws there. This was to be done in the days of the Messiah, who was to be anointed with the Holy Spirit. Accordingly we find in the New Testament that the Holy Spirit is represented as working upon, in and through Jesus Christ.

The designations, "Spirit of Christ," "Spirit of Jesus Christ," indicate a relation between Christ and the Holy Spirit which is not shared by His disciples. For example, we would not think of speaking of the "Spirit of Paul."

From the beginning to the end of His earthly life the Lord Jesus was intimately connected with the Holy Spirit. So close is the connection that Paul describes Christ as a "quickening Spirit." The meaning is not that Jesus is the Spirit, but that He gives the Spirit and through the same Spirit exercises omnipresence.

The Spirit is mentioned in connection with the following crises and aspects of Christ's ministry:

1. Birth.

The Holy Spirit is described as the Agent in the miraculous conception of Jesus (Matt. 1:20; Luke 1:35); Jesus was in relation with the Spirit of God from the first moment of His human existence. The Holy Spirit came upon Mary, the Power of the Most High overshadowed her, and that which was born of her was entitled to be called holy, Son of God. For John the Forerunner it sufficed that he be filled with the Holy Ghost from his mother's womb, whereas Jesus is to be conceived by the power of the Spirit in the womb and for that reason to bear names and titles such as could not be given to John. God, working by His Spirit, is the Father of the humanity of Jesus, in the sense that its origination from the substance of the Virgin Mother was a Divine act.

The effect of this Divine intervention is to be seen in Christ's sinlessness, His entire consecration, His uninterrupted sense of the Fatherhood of God. The power of sin was broken at last, and One born of a woman was, even as a man, holy, and a Son of God. The second Man is from heaven. 1 Cor. 15:47. His life was from above (John 8:23), its course was a victory over sin and its issues in the quickening of the race. 1 Cor. 15:45. He who has no sin and saves His people from their sin must needs have been begotten of the Holy Ghost.

2. Baptism.

As years went by a fresh relation with the Spirit began. He who had been conceived of the Spirit and conscious of the Divine indwelling, was anointed with the Spirit. As in the conception the Spirit descended upon Mary, at the baptism the Spirit descended upon her Son anointing Him to be Prophet, Priest and King. The first operation sanctified His humanity; the second consecrated His official life. As His conception was the beginning of His human existence, so His baptism was the beginning of His active ministry.

3. Ministry.

Then He was led by the Spirit into the wilderness (Mark 1:12) to be tempted by Satan. Here He overcame those suggestions of the prince of this world that would have led Him to attempt His work in a selfish, vainglorious and worldly spirit, and to use His power along natural lines.

He carried on His ministry in the consciousness of the indwelling of the Divine power. He knew that the Spirit of the Lord God was upon Him to fulfill the ministry predicted of the Messiah (Luke 4:18); by the finger of God He cast out demons. Luke 11:20; compare Acts 10:38. He testified to the fact that the Father within Him performed the miraculous works.

4. Crucifixion.

The same Spirit who led Him into the wilderness and sustained Him there, also gave Him strength to consummate His ministry upon the cross, where, "through the eternal Spirit He offered Himself without spot unto God." Heb. 9:14. He went to the cross with the anointing still upon Him. The Spirit kept before Him the inflexible claims of God and enflamed Him with love for man and zeal for God, to go forward in spite of hindrance, pain and difficulty, to effect the world's redemption. The Holy Spirit filled His mind with unflagging ardor, zeal and love, which led Him to complete His sacrifice. His human spirit was so penetrated and elevated by the Spirit of God that it lived in the eternal and invisible, and was able to "endure the cross, despising the shame."

5. Resurrection.

The Holy Spirit was the quickening Agent in Christ's resurrection. Rom. 1:4; Rom. 8:11. Some days after this event Christ appeared to His disciples, breathed on them and said, "Receive ye the Holy Ghost." John 20:22; compare Acts 1:2. These words cannot mean the enduement of power for which the Lord, before His ascension, had commanded them to tarry. Some students believe that the breathing was merely symbolic of what was to occur fifty days hence, that is, a reminder of the coming Pentecost. Others believe that something definite was imparted to the disciples.

A comparison with Gen. 2:7 indicates that the Divine inbreathing symbolizes a creative act. Christ is later described as a quickening or life-giving Spirit. 1 Cor. 15:45. May it not be that on this occasion the Lord of life made these disciples to know by experience "the power of His resurrection?" The eleven were to be sent into the world to fulfill a new commission; they were to continue the work of Christ. Of such a mission they were in themselves incapable, just as an inanimate body is incapable of performing the functions of a living man. Hence the act symbolizing the giving of life. As the old humanity was inbreathed by the Lord God so the new humanity is inbreathed by the Lord Christ.

If we grant a real impartation on this occasion, it must be remembered, however, that it is not the Person of the Comforter but the inspiration of His life which was communicated. Bishop Wescott thus states the distinction between "The Gift of Easter" and the "Gift of Pentecost"—"The one answers to the power of the Resurrection, and the other to the power of the Ascension." That is, the one is the grace of quickening, and the other is the grace of endowment.

6. The Ascension.

Note the following three degrees in the impartation of the Spirit to Christ: (1) At His conception the Spirit of God was from that moment the Spirit of Jesus, the vivifying, sanctifying power by which He entered on His life as the Son of man and lived it to the end. (2) As years went by a fresh relation with the Spirit began. The Spirit of God became the Spirit of Christ in the sense of resting upon Him for His Christ-ministry. (3) After the ascension the Spirit became the Spirit of Christ in the sense of being imparted to others.

The Spirit came to abide upon Christ not only for His own needs, but that He might bestow Him upon all believers. (See John 1:33 and note especially the word "remaining.") After the ascension the Lord Jesus exercised the great prerogative given Him as Messiah—the sending of the Spirit upon others. Acts 2:33; compare Rev. 5:6. Hence He gives the blessing that He Himself has received and enjoys, and makes us joint-partakers with Himself. Thus we read not only of the gift but the "communion" of the Holy Spirit, that is, partaking in common of the privilege and blessing of having the Spirit of God given to us. It is not only fellowship of believers with one another but also with Christ; they receive the same anointing as He did; it is like the precious anointing on the head of Aaron, that flowed down his beard and descended even to the skirts of his garments. All the members of Christ's body, as a kingdom of priests, partake of the anointing of the Spirit flowing from its Head, our great High Priest who has passed into the heavens.

IV. THE HOLY SPIRIT IN HUMAN EXPERIENCE.

This section concerns itself with the varied operations of the Spirit in relation to the individual.

1. Conviction.

In John 16:7-11 Jesus describes the work of the Comforter in relation to the world. The Spirit will act as Christ's "Prosecuting Attorney," so to speak, working to secure a Divine conviction against the rejecters of Christ. To convict means to bring home truths otherwise doubted or discarded; or to bring home charges made against conduct and life. Men do not know what sin, righteousness and judgment really are and therefore need to be convinced of spiritual truth. For example, it would be useless to argue with a person who declared he could see no beauty in a rose, for his inability would argue lack of appreciation of beauty. A sense of beauty must be awakened within him; he must be "convinced" of the beauty of the flower. In like manner, the darkened mind and soul sees nothing in spiritual truths until convinced and awakened by the Holy Spirit. He will convince men of the following truths:

(a) The Sin of Unbelief. When Peter preached on the day of Pentecost he had nothing to say of the people's looseness of life, their worldliness, their covetousness; he did not go into details of their depravity in order to bring a blush of shame to their cheeks. **The** sin he charged them with, and commanded them to repent of, was the crucifixion of the Lord of glory; the peril he warned them against was the refusal to believe on Him in the face of evidence.

The sin of unbelief is here described as the only sin because, in the words of one scholar, "where it continues all other sins are retained, and when it departs all other sins are removed." It is the "mother sin," because it produces new sins and because it is the sin against the remedy for sin. Writes Dr. Smeaton, "But however great and perilous this sin may be, such is the ignorance in which man is naturally involved, that its criminality is utterly unknown till it is brought home by the influence of the Holy Ghost, the Comforter. Conscience may convince a man of ordinary sins, but never of the sin of unbelief. Of the enormity of this sin no man was ever convinced but by the Holy Ghost Himself."

(b) The Righteousness of Christ. "Of righteousness, because I go to my Father, and ye see me no more." Jesus Christ was crucified as a malefactor and a deceiver of the people. But after the day of Pentecost, the outpouring of the Spirit and the performing of miracles in His name convinced thousands of Jews that He was not only righteous but also the only heavenly source and way of righteousness. Through Peter the Spirit convinced them that they had crucified the Lord of righteousness (Acts 2:36, 37), but He also assured them that there was pardon and salvation in His name. Acts 2:38.

(c) The Judgment of Satan. "Of judgment, because the prince of this world is judged." How are people today convinced that crime will be judged and punished? By the manifested crime of the criminal and the subsequent punishment; in other words, by a demonstration of justice. The Cross was a demonstration of the truth that the power of Satan over the lives of men was broken, and that his complete destruction was decreed. Heb. 2:14, 15; 1 John 3:8; Col. 2:15; Rom. 16:20. Satan has been judged in the sense that the great cause has gone against him so that he has no more right to hold men in bondage as his subjects. By His death Christ has delivered all men from Satan's dominion, and it remains for them to accept their deliverance. Men are convinced by the Holy Spirit that they are free indeed (John 8:36), no more subjects of the tempter, no more bound to obey him, but loyal subjects of Christ and made willing in the day of His power. Psalm 110:3.

Satan contended that he had a right to possess men who had sinned and that the righteous Judge must leave them in his hands. The Mediator, on the other hand, appealed to the fact that He bore man's penalty and took his place, therefore justice as well as mercy required that Satan's right of conquest should be reversed and that the world should be given to Him who was its second Adam and Lord of all. The verdict was given against the prince of this world—and he was judged. He can no longer keep his goods in peace when the stronger than he comes upon the scene. Luke 11:21, 22.

2. Regeneration.

The creative work of the Spirit upon the soul may be illustrated by the creative work of God's Spirit upon man's body in the beginning. Picture the scene suggested by Gen. 2:7. God takes the dust of the earth and forms a body. There it lies, inanimate and still. Though in the world and surrounded by its beauties, it does not react because it has no life. It neither sees nor hears nor understands. Then "God breathed into his nostrils the breath of life; and man became a living soul." At once he reacted to the world, saw its beauties and heard its sounds.

As with the body, so with the soul. Man is surrounded by the spirit world and by God who is not far from any of us. Acts 17:27. Yet he lives and acts as if that world did not exist because he is spiritually dead and therefore cannot react to it. But when the same Lord who quickened the body quickens the soul, the person awakens to the spiritual world and begins to live the spiritual life. Any one who has witnessed the reactions of a real convert following the radical experience known as the new birth knows that regeneration is not merely a doctrine but a practical reality.

3. Indwelling.

See John 14:17; Rom. 8:9; 1 Cor. 6:19; 2 Tim. 1:14; 1 John 2:27; Col. 1:27; 1 John 3:24; Rev. 3:20.

God is always and necessarily present everywhere; in Him all men live, move and have their being. But indwelling means that He is present in a new way, sustaining a **personal** relation to the individual. This union with God, which is called indwelling, is produced in reality by the presence of the whole Trinity, as will be seen by an examination of the above texts. But since it is the special ministry of the Holy Spirit to indwell the hearts of men, the experience is commonly known as the indwelling of the Holy Spirit. It is believed by many orthodox scholars that God imparted to Adam, not only physical and mental life, but also the indwelling Spirit, which he lost because of sin, not only for himself but also for his descendants. This absence of the Spirit has left man in spiritual darkness and weakness. In relation to understanding, the unconverted cannot know the things of the Spirit of God (1 Cor. 2:14); in relation to the will, he cannot be subject to the law of God (Rom. 8:7); in relation to worship, he cannot call Jesus, Lord (1 Cor. 12:3); as regards practice, he cannot please God (Rom. 8:8); in regard to character, he cannot bear spiritual fruit (John 15:4); in regard to faith, he cannot receive the spirit of truth. John 14:17. All this is due to the absence of the Spirit, an absence which leaves man in spiritual death.

By faith and repentance man turns to God, and becomes regenerated. Regeneration by the Spirit involves a union with God and Christ (1 Cor. 6:17) which is known as indwelling. 1 Cor. 6:19. This indwelling of the Spirit or man's possession of the Spirit is the mark of a New Testament Christian. "But ye are not in the flesh, but in the Spirit, if so be that the Spirit of God dwell in you. Now if any man have not the Spirit of Christ, he is none of his." Rom. 8:9; compare Jude 19.

Writes Dr. Smeaton:

We must hold on the sure ground of Scripture that not only are the gifts of the Spirit poured into the heart of believers, but the personal Holy Ghost, who had left man's heart in ruins, and no longer His temple, returns to take up his abode in the redeemed, and occupies them with a personal, hidden, indwelling presence which our limited faculties in this transitory state do not permit us to measure or to comprehend. Enough that the fact is plainly taught us in the Holy Scriptures, however incapable we may be to grasp or explain it to ourselves or to other minds.

One of the most comprehensive definitions of a Christian is that he is a man in whom the Holy Spirit dwells. His body is a temple of the Holy Ghost, in virtue of which experience he is sanctified as the Tabernacle was consecrated by Jehovah's indwelling. He is then called a "saint" and it becomes his duty to guard the sanctity of the temple of his body. Compare 1 Cor. 6:19 and Rom. 12:1.

4. Sanctification.

In regeneration the Holy Spirit effects a radical change in the soul by imparting a new principle of life. But this does not imply that the child of God is at once perfect. There remain inherited and acquired weaknesses; there are still the world, the flesh and the devil to overcome.

Since the Spirit does not work magically, but in a vital and progressive manner, it is by degrees that the soul is renewed. Faith must be strengthened through many tests; love must be fortified to survive hardship and temptation. Allurements to sin must be overcome; tendencies and habits must be corrected.

If the Spirit of God did one work and then departed, the convert would indeed fall back into his old ways. But the Spirit continues the good work He has begun. The gospel, which was the means of our new birth, continues to be the means of growth in our Christian life. Those who have been born by the incorruptible seed of the Word of God (1 Peter 1:23), must, "as newborn babes, desire the sincere milk of the word, that ye may grow thereby." 1 Peter 2:2. Also, the Holy Spirit acts directly upon the soul producing those special virtues of Christian character known as the fruit of the Spirit. Gal. 5:22, 23. The operation of the Spirit is progressive, going "from the heart to the surface, from the interior to the exterior, from the seat of life to the manifestations of life, to the actions and to the words; at first allowing many things which are incompatible with His holy nature, then, little by little, attacking them one after another, one year these, another year those, going into all the details so thoroughly that, nothing being able to escape His influence, one day the entire man, glorified by the Spirit, will be resplendent with the life of God."

5. Enduement with power.

In this section we shall consider the following facts concerning the enduement of power: its general character, its special character, its initial evidence, its continuous aspect, the manner of its reception.

(a) Its General Nature. The foregoing sections have dealt with the regenerative and sanctifying work of the Holy Spirit; in this section we shall deal with another mode of operation, His energizing work. This last phase of the Spirit's work is set forth in Christ's promise: "But ye shall receive power, after that the Holy Ghost is come upon you: and ye shall be witnesses unto me." Acts 1:8.

(1) The main feature of this promise is power for service and not regeneration for eternal life. Whenever we read of the Spirit coming upon, resting upon, falling upon, or filling people, the reference is never to the saving work of the Spirit but always to power for service.

(2) The words were addressed to men already in intimate relationship with Christ. They had been sent out to preach, armed with spiritual power for that purpose (Matt. 10:1); to them it was said, "Your names are written in heaven" (Luke 10:20); their moral condition was described in the words, "Now ye are clean through the word which I have spoken unto you" (John 15:3); their relationship to Christ was illustrated by the figure, "I am the vine, ye are the branches" (John 15:5); they knew the presence of the Spirit with them (John 14:17); they had felt the breath of the risen Christ and heard Him say, "Receive ye the Holy Ghost." John 20:22.

The above facts show that one may be in touch with Christ and be a disciple of Christ and yet lack the special enduement of power mentioned in Acts 1:8. It may be objected that all this relates to the disciples before Pentecost; but in Acts 8:12-16 we have an instance of people baptized in water by Philip, yet receiving the Holy Spirit some days later.

(3) Accompanying the fulfillment of this promise (Acts 1:8) were supernatural manifestations (Acts 2:1-4), the most important and common of which was the miraculous utterance in other languages. That this supernatural utterance was an accompaniment of the receiving of spiritual power is stated in two other instances (Acts 10:44-46; 19:1-6) and implied in another. Acts 8:14-19.

(4) This impartation is described as a baptism. Acts 1:5. When Paul declares that there is but one baptism (Eph. 4:5) he refers to literal or water baptism. Both Jews and pagans practiced ceremonial washing, and John the Baptist had administered water baptism unto repentance, but Paul declares that there is now only one baptism valid in God's sight, namely that on the authority of Jesus and in the name of the Trinity—in other words, Christian baptism.

When the word "baptism" is applied to spiritual experience, it is used figuratively to describe immersion in the energizing power of the Divine Spirit. The word was used figuratively by Christ to describe His immersion in the floods of suffering. Matt. 20:22.

(5) This impartation of power is also described as a filling with the Spirit. Those who were baptized with the Holy Spirit on the day of Pentecost were also filled with the Spirit.

(b) Its Special Characteristic. The above facts lead us to this conclusion that in addition and subsequent to conversion, a believer may experience an enduement of power whose initial oncoming is signalized by a miraculous utterance in a language never learned by the speaker.

The above conclusion has been challenged. It is claimed that there are many Christians who know the Holy Spirit in regenerating and sanctifying power, and yet have not spoken in other tongues. Indeed, the New Testament teaches that one cannot be a Christian without having the Spirit, which is the same as being indwelt with the Spirit. "If any man have not the Spirit of Christ, he is none of his." Rom. 8:9. That the Spirit of Christ means the Holy Spirit is indicated by the context and proved by 1 Pet. 1:11 where "Spirit of Christ" can refer only to the Holy Spirit. Other references are cited as supporting the same truth. Rom. 5:5; 8:14, 16; 1 Cor. 6:19; Gal. 4:6; 1 John 3:24; 4:13. It is also affirmed that many Christian workers have experienced anointings of the Spirit by which they have been enabled to win people to Christ and to do other Christian work, and yet these have not spoken in other tongues.

It cannot be successfully denied that there is a real sense in which all truly regenerated persons have the Spirit. But the question naturally follows: What is there different and additional in the experience described as the Baptism with the Holy Spirit? We answer as follows:

There is one Holy Spirit, but many operations of that Spirit, just as there is one electricity but many operations of that electricity. The same electricity propels street cars, lights our houses, operates refrigerators, and performs many other tasks. In like manner, the one Spirit regenerates, sanctifies, energizes, illumines, and imparts special gifts.

The Spirit regenerates human nature in the crisis of conversion, and then, as the Spirit of holiness within, produces the "fruit of the Spirit," the distinctive features of Christian character. At times, believers make a special consecration, and receive that victory over sin, and consequent accession of joy and peace, which has sometimes been called "sanctification" or a "second definite work of grace."

But in addition to these operations of the Holy Spirit, there is another, having for its special purpose the energizing of human nature for special service for God, and issuing in an outward expression of a supernatural character. In a general way, Paul refers to this outward expression as "the manifestation of the Spirit" (1 Cor. 12:7), perhaps in contrast to the quiet and secret operations of the Spirit. In the New Testament this experience is designated by such expressions as falling upon, coming upon, being poured out, being filled with, which expressions convey the thought of suddenness and supernaturalness. All these terms are connected with the experience known as the Baptism with the Holy Spirit. Acts 1:5.

The operation of the Spirit described by these terms is so distinct from His quiet and ordinary manifestations that scholars have coined a word to describe it. That word is "charismatic," from a Greek word frequently used to designate a special impartation of spiritual power. Wrote A. B. Bruce, a Presbyterian scholar:

The Spirit's work was conceived of as transcendent, miraculous, and charismatic. The power of the Holy Ghost was a power coming from without, producing extraordinary effects that could arrest the attention of even a profane eye like that of Simon the sorcerer.

While acknowledging that the early Christians believed also in the sanctifying operations of the Spirit (he cites Acts 16:14), and His inspiring of faith, hope, and love within people, he concludes that

the gift of the Holy Spirit came to mean . . . the power to speak ecstatically, and to prophesy enthusiastically, and to heal the sick by a word of prayer.

The point we desire to emphasize is the following: the Baptism with the Holy Spirit, which is a baptism of power, is charismatic in character, judging from the descriptions of the results of the impartation.

Now while freely admitting that Christians have been born of the Spirit, and workers anointed with the Spirit, we maintain that not all Christians have experienced the charismatic operation of the Spirit, followed by a sudden, supernatural utterance.

(c) Its Initial Evidence. How do we know when a person receives the charismatic impartation of the Holy Spirit? In other words, what is the evidence that one has experienced the Baptism with the Holy Spirit? The question cannot be decided from the four Gospels, because they contain prophecies of the coming of the Spirit, and a prophecy is made perfectly clear only by fulfillment; neither can it be settled by the Epistles, for they are largely pastoral instructions addressed to established churches where the power of the Spirit with outward manifestations was considered the normal experience of every Christian. It is therefore evident that the matter must be settled by the book of Acts which records many instances of people's receiving the Baptism with the Spirit, and describes the results that followed.

We grant that in every case mentioned in the book of Acts, the results of the impartation are not recorded; but where the results are described there is always an immediate, supernatural, outward expression, convincing not only the receiver but the people listening to him, that a divine power is controlling the person; and in every case there is an ecstatic speaking in a language that the person has never learned.

Is the above statement merely the private interpretation of one religious group or is it recognized by others? Dr. Rees, an English theologian of liberal views, writes:

Glossolalia (speaking in tongues) was the most conspicuous and popular gift of the early years of the church. It seems to have been the regular accompaniment and evidence of the descent of the Spirit upon believers.

Writes Dr. G. B. Stevens of Yale, in his "Theology of the New Testament"

The Spirit was regarded as a special gift which did not always accompany baptism and faith. The Samaritans were not regarded as having the Holy Ghost when they believed the Word of God. They had believed and had been baptized, but it was only when Peter and John laid their hands upon them that the gift of the Spirit was bestowed. Evidently some special endowment or experience is here in view.

Commenting on Acts 19:1-7 he writes:

Not only did they not receive the Holy Ghost when they believed, but after they had been baptized in the name of Christ it was only when Paul had laid his hands upon them that the Holy Ghost came upon them and they spoke with tongues and prophesied. Here it is obvious that the gift of the Spirit is regarded as synonymous with the ecstatic charismata (spiritual impartation) of speaking with tongues and prophesying.

Writes Dr. A. B. Macdonald, a Scotch Presbyterian minister:

The church's belief in the Spirit sprang from her experience of a fact. Very early in her career the disciples became aware of a new power working within them. Its most striking manifestation at first was "speaking in tongues," the power of ecstatic utterance in an unintelligible speech; and both those seized by this power and those who saw and heard its manifestations were convinced that some Power from a higher world had broken into their lives, endowing them with capacities of utterance and with other gifts, which appeared to be something different from a mere heightening of endowments already theirs. People who hitherto had seemed to be nothing out of common suddenly became capable of impassioned prayer and speech, or of lofty moods in which they were manifestly holding converse with the Unseen.

He states that the speaking in tongues "appears to have been the most arresting and at first the most characteristic of the manifestations of the Spirit."

Is there any place in the New Testament where a distinction is made between those who have received the enduement of power and those who have not? A. B. Macdonald, the writer quoted above, answers in the affirmative. He points out that the word "unlearned" in 1 Cor. 14:16, 23 (which he translates, "private Christian") denotes persons who are differentiated from unbelievers by the fact that they take part in the worship to the extent of saying "Amen"; they also are distinguished from believers by the fact that they are unable to take active part in Spirit-manifestations. It seems that a special section in the meeting-house was reserved for the "unlearned ones." 1 Cor. 14:16.

Weymouth translates the word "unlearned" by the expression, "some who lack the gift." Thayer's lexicon renders it: "one who is destitute of the gift of tongues; a Christian who is not a prophet." Macdonald describes him as "one who waits, or is kept waiting, for the decisive moment when the Spirit will descend upon him."

Regardless of their denomination or school of theological thought, able scholars admit that the receiving of the Spirit in the early church was no formal ceremony or doctrinal theory, but a real experience. Canon Streeter says that Paul asks the Galatians whether it was by the law or by the hearing of faith that they received the gift of the Spirit, "as if the reception of the Spirit was something as definite and observable as, for example, an attack of influenza."

(d) Its Continuous Aspect. The experience

described as being "filled with the Spirit" is connected with the thought of power for service. Three phases of this experience are to be distinguished:

(1) The initial filling when a person is for the first time baptized with the Holy Spirit.

(2) A habitual condition is referred to in the words, "full of the Holy Ghost" (Acts 6:3; 7:55; 11:24), which words describe the daily life of a spiritual person, or one whose character reveals "the fruit of the Spirit." The habitual condition is referred to in the exhortation, "Be filled with the Spirit." Eph. 5:18.

(3) Fillings or anointings for special occasions. Paul was filled with the Holy Spirit after his conversion, but in Acts 13:9 we learn that God gave him a special enduement wherewith to resist the evil power of a sorcerer. Peter was filled with the Spirit on the day of Pentecost, but God granted a special anointing when he stood before the Jewish council. Acts 4:8. The disciples had received the infilling or Baptism with the Spirit on the day of Pentecost, but in answer to prayer God gave them a special enduement to fortify them against the opposition of the Jewish leaders. Acts 4:31. As the late F. B. Meyer once said:

You may be a man full of the Holy Ghost in your family, but, before entering the pulpit be sure that you are especially equipped by a new reception of the Holy Ghost.

(e) **The Manner of Its Reception.** How may one receive this baptism of power?

(1) A right attitude is essential. The first group who experienced the oncoming of the Spirit "continued with one accord in prayer and supplication." Acts 1:14. Ideally, one should receive the enduement of power immediately after

conversion, but, actually, there are certain circumstances of one kind or another which may make tarrying necessary.

(2) The receiving of the gift of the Holy Spirit subsequent to conversion is connected with the prayers of Christian workers. The writer of Acts thus describes the experiences of the Samaritan converts who had already believed and had been baptized: "Who, when they (Peter and John) were come down, prayed for them, that they might receive the Holy Ghost. . . . Then laid they their hands on them, and they received the Holy Ghost." Acts 8:15, 17.

Weinel, a German theologian, made a thorough study of the spiritual manifestations during the apostolic age. He says that "what might be called 'inspirational sessions' were held till well on into the second century, strange as they seem to outsiders." The Holy Ghost, he states, was communicated to converts by the laying on of hands and prayer and wrought signs and wonders. "Inspirational sessions" would seem to describe special services for those who desired to receive the Spirit's power.

(3) The receiving of spiritual power is connected with the united prayers of the church. After the Christians of the church at Jerusalem had prayed for boldness to preach the Word, "the place was shaken where they were assembled together; and they were all filled with the Holy Ghost." Acts 4:31.

The expression "place was shaken" implies something spectacular and supernatural which convinced the disciples that the power which descended on the day of Pentecost was still present in the church.

(4) A spontaneous outpouring may, in some cases, make prayer or effort unnecessary as was the case with those in the house of Cornelius,

whose hearts had already been "purified by faith." Acts 10:44; 15:9.

(5) Since the baptism of power is described as a gift (Acts 10:45) the believer may plead before the throne of grace the promise of Jesus: "If ye then, being evil, know how to give good gifts unto your children: how much more shall your heavenly Father give the Holy Spirit to them that ask him?" Luke 11:13.

A certain school of interpreters teach that one should not ask for the Spirit, for the following reason. At Pentecost the Holy Spirit came to dwell permanently in the church; since then, every one who is added to the church by the Lord, and baptized unto Christ, by that very fact becomes a partaker of the Spirit. 1 Cor. 12:13.

It is true that the Spirit abides in the church, yet that should not deter the believer from asking and seeking. As Dr. A. J. Gordon has pointed out, though the Spirit was given once and for all to the church on the day of Pentecost, it does not follow that every believer has received the Baptism. God's gift requires an appropriation. God gave (John 3:16), we must receive. John 1:12. As sinners we accept Christ; as saints we accept the Holy Spirit. As there is a faith toward Christ for salvation, so there is a faith toward the Spirit for power and consecration.

Pentecost is once for all; the baptism of believers is ever for all. The shutting up of certain great blessings of the Holy Ghost within the ideal realm called the "Apostolic Age," however convenient it may be as an escape from fancied difficulties, may be the means of robbing believers of some of their most precious covenant rights.

(6) Individual prayer. Saul of Tarsus fasted and prayed three days previously to his being filled with the Holy Spirit. Acts 9:9-17.

(7) Obedience. The Holy Ghost is He

"whom God hath given to them that obey him."
Acts 5:32.

6. Glorification.

Will the Holy Spirit be with the believer in
heaven or will the Spirit leave him? The answer
is that the Holy Spirit in the believer is as a well
of living water springing up into **everlasting life.**
John 4:14. The indwelling of the Spirit represents just the beginning of life eternal, which will
be consummated in the life to come. "Now is our
salvation nearer than when we believed," wrote
Paul, which words imply that we have only the
beginning of a salvation which is to be consummated in the life to come. The Holy Spirit represents the beginning or first part of this complete
salvation. This truth is expressed under three illustrations:

(a) **Commercial.** The Spirit is described as
"the earnest of our inheritance until the redemption of the purchased possession." Eph. 1:14; 2
Cor. 5:5. The Holy Spirit is a pledge that our
deliverance shall be complete. It is more than a
pledge; it is an installment handed over in advance
as a guarantee that the remainder will follow.

(b) **Agricultural.** The Holy Spirit is the
first-fruits of the future life. Rom. 8:23. When
the Israelite brought the first-fruits of his produce to God's temple, it was an acknowledgement
that all belonged to God, and the offering of a
part symbolized the offering of all. The Holy
Spirit in believers is the first-fruits of the glorious
harvest to come.

(c) **Domestic.** Just as children are given a
slight taste of some delicacy previous to a ban-
quet, so in the experience of the Spirit, Christians
have but "tasted . . . the powers of the world to
come." Heb. 6:5. In Rev. 7:17 we read that "the
Lamb which is in the midst of the throne shall

. . . lead them unto living fountains of waters." Notice the plural in these last words. In the life to come Christ will be the Giver of the Spirit, and He who imparted the foretaste will lead His followers to fresh supplies of the Spirit and to means of grace and spiritual enrichment unknown during their earthly pilgrimage.

7. Sins Against the Spirit.

The gracious operations of the Spirit bring great blessings but these involve corresponding responsibilities. Generally speaking, the believers may grieve, lie to the Person of the Spirit, and quench His power. Eph. 4:30; Acts 5:3, 4; 1 Thess. 5:19. Unbelievers may blaspheme the Person of the Spirit and resist His power. Acts 7:51; Matt. 12:31, 32. The context in each case will explain the nature of the sin. William Evans points out that "Resisting has to do with the regenerating work of the Spirit; grieving has to do with the indwelling Holy Spirit; quenching has to do with the enduement for service."

V. THE GIFTS OF THE SPIRIT.

1. The General Nature of the Gifts.

The **gifts** of the Spirit must be distinguished from the **gift** of the Spirit. The former describes the supernatural abilities imparted by the **Spirit** for special ministries; the latter refers to the impartation of the Spirit to believers as ministered by the ascended **Christ.** Acts 2:33.

Paul speaks of the gifts of the Spirit ("spirituals" in the original Greek) in a threefold aspect. They are "charismata," or a variety of gifts bestowed by the one Spirit (1 Cor. 12:4, 7); "diakonai," or varieties of service rendered in the cause of the one Lord; and "energemata" or varieties of the power of the one God who works all in all. All these aspects are referred to as "the manifestation of the Spirit," which is given to men for the profit of all.

What is the main purpose of the gifts of the Spirit? They are spiritual enablements for the purpose of building up the church of God through the instruction of believers and the winning of converts. Eph. 4:7-13. Paul enumerates nine of these gifts in 1 Cor. 12:8-10, which may be classified as follows:

1. Those that impart power to **know** supernaturally: the word of wisdom, the word of knowledge, discernment.

2. Those that impart power to **act** supernaturally: faith, miracles, healings.

3. Those that impart power to **speak** supernaturally: prophecy, tongues, interpretation.

These gifts are described as "the manifestation of the Spirit," "given to every man to profit withal" (that is, for the benefit of the church). Here we have the Scriptural definition of a "manifestation" of the Spirit—namely, the operation of any of the nine gifts of the Spirit.

2. The Variety of the Gifts.

(a) **The word of wisdom.** By this expression is meant the utterance of wisdom. What kind of wisdom? This will be best determined by noting in what senses the word "wisdom" is used in the New Testament. It is applied to the art of interpreting dreams and giving sage advice (Acts 7:10); the intelligence evinced in discovering the meaning of some mysterious number or vision (Rev. 13:18; 17:9); skill in the management of affairs (Acts 6:3); a devout prudence in dealings with those outside the church (Col. 4:5); skill and discretion in imparting Christian truth (Col. 1:28); the knowledge and practice of the requisites for godly and upright living (James 1:5; 3:13, 17); the knowledge and skill in affairs requisite for the successful defense of Christ's cause (Luke 21:15); an acquaintance of Divine things and human duties joined to a power of discoursing concerning them and of interpreting and applying sacred Scripture (Matt. 13:54; Mark 6:2; Acts 6:10); the wisdom and instruction with which John the Baptist and Jesus taught men the plan of salvation (Matt. 11:19). In Paul's writings "wisdom" is applied to: a knowledge of the Divine plan previously hidden, of providing men with salvation through the atonement of Christ (1 Cor. 1:30; Col. 2:3); hence all the treasures of wisdom are said to be hidden in Christ (Col. 2:3); the wisdom of God as evinced in forming and executing His counsels. Rom. 11:33.

The word of wisdom, then, would seem to signify supernatural ability to utter forth wisdom along the above mentioned lines.

(b) The Word of Knowledge is a supernaturally inspired utterance of facts. Along what lines? A study of the New Testament usage of the word "knowledge" will supply the answer. The word denotes: the knowledge of God, such as is offered in the Gospels (2 Cor. 2:14), especially in Paul's exposition of it (2 Cor. 10:5); the knowledge of things that belong to God (Rom. 11:33); intelligence and understanding (Eph. 3:19); the knowledge of the Christian faith (Rom. 15:14; 1 Cor. 1:5); the deeper, the more perfect, and enlarged knowledge of this religion, such as belongs to the more advanced (1 Cor. 12:8; 13:2, 8; 14:6; 2 Cor. 6:6; 8:7; 11:6); the higher knowledge of Christian and Divine things which false teachers boast of (1 Tim. 6:20); moral wisdom such as is seen in right living (2 Peter 1:5) and in relations with others (1 Peter 3:7); knowledge concerning things Divine and human duties. Rom. 2:20; Col. 2:3.

What is the difference between wisdom and knowledge? According to one scholar, knowledge is the insight into Divine things, and wisdom is the skill which regulates the Christian life according to its foundation principles. Thayer's Lexicon states that where "knowledge" and "wisdom" are used together, the former seems to be knowledge regarded by itself, the latter knowledge as exhibited in action.

(c) Faith. (Weymouth renders: "special faith.") This must be distinguished from saving faith, and that confidence in God without which it is impossible to please Him. Heb. 11:6. It is true that saving faith is described as a gift (Eph. 2:8), but in this passage "gift" is used as opposed to "works," while in 1 Cor. 12:9 the word used means a special endowment of the power of the Spirit. What is the gift of faith? Donald Gee describes it as follows:

. . . a quality of faith, sometimes called by our older theologians the "Faith of Miracles." It would seem to come upon certain of God's servants in times of special crisis or opportunity in such mighty power that they are lifted right out of the realm of even natural and ordinary faith in God, and have a Divine certainty put within their souls that triumphs over everything. . . . Possibly the same quality of faith is the thought of our Lord where He says in Mark 11:22, "Have the faith of God" (margin). It was faith of this peculiar quality of which He could say that a grain of it would remove a mountain. Matt. 17:20. A little of that Divine faith, which is an attribute of the Almighty, dropped into the soul of man—what miracles it can produce!

Examples of the operation of the gift: 1 Kings 18:33-35; Acts 3:4.

(d) Gifts of Healing. To say that a person has the gifts (note the plural, perhaps referring to a variety of healings) means that he is used of God in supernaturally ministering health to the sick, through prayer. It seems to be a sign-gift, especially valuable to the evangelist for attracting people's attention to the gospel. Acts 8:6, 7;

28:8-10. It is not to be understood that the possessor of this gift (or the person possessed by this gift) has the power to heal **everyone;** allowance must be made for the sovereignty of God and the sick person's attitude and spiritual condition. Even Christ was limited in His miracle-working ability by the unbelief of the people. Matt. 13:58.

The sick person is not absolutely dependent upon one possessing the gift. All believers in general, and elders of the church in particular, are empowered to pray for the sick. Mark 16:18; James 5:14.

(e) The Working of Miracles, literally, "works of power." The keynote is **power.** Compare John 14:12; Acts 1:8. The "special" miracles at Ephesus are an illustration of the operation of the gift. Acts 19:11, 12; 5:12-15.

(f) Prophecy.

Prophecy, generally speaking, is utterance inspired by the Spirit of God. Biblical prophecy may be by revelation, wherein the prophet proclaims a message previously received through a dream, a vision, or the Word of the Lord. Or it may be ecstatic, inspirational utterance on the spur of the moment. There are many Scriptural examples of both forms. Ecstatic, inspirational prophecy may take the form of exaltation and worship of Christ, or hortatory admonition, or inspirational comfort and encouragement to the saints.—J. R. F.

Prophecy is distinguished from ordinary preaching in that while the latter is generally the product of the study of existing revelation, prophecy is the result of a spontaneous spiritual inspiration. It was not intended to supplant preaching or teaching but to supplement it with the inspirational touch.

The possession of the gift constituted a person a "prophet." See Acts 15:32; 21:9, 10; 1 Cor. 14:29. The purpose of the New Testament gift of prophecy is stated in 1 Cor. 14:3—the prophet edifies, exhorts, and comforts believers.

The inspiration manifest in the gift of prophecy is not on a level with that of Scripture. This is implied by the fact that believers are instructed to test or judge prophetic messages. See 1 Cor. 14:29. Why judge them or test them? For one reason, because of the possibility of the human spirit (Jer. 23:16; Ezek. 13:2, 3) mingling its message with that of the Divine. 1 Thess. 5:19-20 deals with the operation of the gift of prophecy. The conservative Thessalonians had gone so far in their distrust of these messages (verse 20) that they were in danger of quenching the Spirit (verse 19); but Paul tells them to test each message (verse 21), hold on to what is good (verse 21), and reject what appears to be unsound. Verse 22.

Should prophecy or interpretation be given in the first person; for example, "It is I, the Lord, who am speaking to you, My people"? The question is an important one, for the quality of certain messages has caused people to wonder as to whether the Lord Himself could have thus spoken. The answer may depend on our view of the mode of inspiration.

Is it **mechanical;** that is, does God use the speaker as we would use a megaphone, the person being entirely passive and becoming simply a mouthpiece? Or, is the method **dynamical;** that is, does God supernaturally quicken the spiritual nature (note: "My spirit prayeth." 1 Cor. 14:14), enabling the person to speak the divine message in terms beyond the natural scope of the mental faculties.

If and when God inspires according to the first-named method, the first person would naturally be used; according to the second method the message would be given in the third person; for example, "The Lord would have His people look up and be encouraged," etc.

Many experienced workers believe that interpretations and prophetic messages should be given in the third person. See Luke 1:67-79; 1 Cor. 14:14, 15.

(g) Discerning of Spirits. We have seen that there can exist a false inspiration, the work of seducing spirits or of the human spirit. How shall people detect the difference? By the gift of discernment which enables the possessor to determine whether or not a prophet is speaking by the Spirit of God. This gift enables the possessor to "see through" all outward appearances and know the true nature of an inspiration. The gift of discernment may be checked by two other tests: the doctrinal (1 John 4:1-6) and the practical. Matt. 7:15-23.

For some illustrations of the working of this gift see John 1:47-50; John 3:1-3; John 2:25; 2 Kings 5:20-26; Acts 5:3; 8:23; 16:16-18. These references imply that the gift enables one to discern a person's spiritual character. Distinguish this gift from natural insight into human nature, and above all, from a fault-finding spirit.

(h) Tongues. "Divers kinds of tongues." "The gift of tongues is the power of speaking supernaturally in a language never learned by the speaker, that language being made intelligible to the listeners by means of the equally supernatural gift of interpretation." There seem to be two kinds of messages in tongues: first, ecstatic praise addressed to God alone (1 Cor. 14:2), and second, a definite message for the church (1 Cor. 14:5). Distinguish between tongues as a **Sign** and tongues as a **Gift.** The former is for all (Acts 2:4), the latter is not for all. 1 Cor. 12:30.

(i) Interpretation of Tongues. Writes Donald Gee:

The purpose of the gift of interpretation is to render the ecstatic and inspired utterances by the Spirit which have gone forth in a tongue unknown to the vast majority present, available to the general understanding of all, by repeating them distinctly in the ordinary language of the people assembled.

It is purely a spiritual operation. The same Holy Spirit who inspired the speaking in other tongues, whereby the words expressed flow from the spirit rather than through the intellect, is able to inspire the interpretation also. Interpretation is therefore inspirational, ecstatic, spontaneous. As the utterance, when speaking in tongues, is not conceived in the mind, so the utterance of interpretation emanates from the spirit rather than from the intellect of man.

Notice that tongues plus interpretation are equal to prophecy. (See 1 Cor. 14:5). Why not then be content with prophecy? Because tongues are a "sign" for the unbeliever. 1 Cor. 14:22.

Note.   It has been suggested that the ministries enumerated in Rom. 12:6-8 and 1 Cor. 12:28 should also be included under the classification of "charismata"—thus broadening the scope of spiritual gifts to include all Spirit-inspired ministrations.

3.   The Regulation of Gifts.

The lightning that rends trees, burns houses, and destroys people is of the same nature as the electricity that operates so smoothly through a power house. The difference lies in the matter of control. In 1 Corinthians 12 Paul has revealed the mighty spiritual resources of power available for the church; in the fourteenth chapter he exhibits the "controls" by which this power is to be regulated, so that it will build up rather than destroy the church. The instruction was needed, for a reading of this chapter will show that pandemonium had been reigning in some meetings due to a lack of knowledge of spiritual manifestations. Chapter fourteen lays down the following principles for such regulation:

(a) **Proportionate Value.** Verses 5-19. The Corinthians had become overbalanced on the gift of tongues, no doubt because of its spectacular nature; but Paul reminds them that interpretation and prophecy are needed so that the people might have an intelligent knowledge of what was being said.

(b) **Edification.** The purpose of the gifts is the building up of the church, by encouraging believers and converting the unsaved. But, says Paul, if an outsider enters the church and hears nothing but uninterpreted speaking in tongues, he will rightly conclude that the people are demented. Verses 12, 23.

(c) **Wisdom.** Verse 20. "Brethren, be not children in understanding." In other words, "Use your common sense."

(d) **Self-control.** Verse 32. Some Corinthians might protest: We cannot be silent; if God's Spirit comes upon us, we just **have** to speak out. Answers Paul, "The spirits of the prophets are subject to the prophets." That is, the one possessing the gift of tongues can control his utterance and speak to God alone, when such control is advisable.

(e) **Orderliness.** Verse 40. "Let all things be done decently and in order." The Holy Spirit, the great Designer of all the beauty of the universe, will certainly not inspire that which is disorderly, or disgraceful. When the Holy Spirit is working in power there will be a stirring and a moving, and those who have learned how to yield to Him, will not create unedifying scenes.

(f) Teachableness. One may infer from verses 36, 37 that some of the Corinthians had resented the criticism of some of their leaders.

Note 1. The fourteenth chapter of 1 Corinthians implies that there exists power to be controlled. Therefore the chapter would be meaningless to a church which does not experience the manifestations of the Spirit. It is quite true that the Corinthians had gotten off the track in the matter of spiritual gifts—but they had a track to be thrown off from! Had Paul acted like certain modern critics, he would have taken the track away, instead, he wisely put them back on the track.

When the church of the second and third centuries reacted against some extravagances, they went to the opposite extreme and left very little place for the Spirit's operations. But that is only part of the explanation for the cooling off of the church's enthusiasm and the general cessation of spiritual manifestations. Early in the history of the church there began a process of centralizing of organization and the formulating of hard and fast creeds. While all this was necessary as a defense against false cults, it tended to check the free moving of the Spirit and make Christianity a matter of orthodoxy rather than of spiritual vitality.

Writes Dr. T. Rees:

In the first century, the Spirit was known by His manifestations, but in the second century and afterwards, by the rule of the church, and any spiritual phenomenon that did not conform to that rule was attributed to evil spirits.

The same causes have, in modern times, resulted in a neglect of the doctrine and work of the Holy Spirit, a neglect recognized and deplored by many religious leaders.

Nevertheless, the flow of the Spirit has never failed to burst through all hindrances of indifference and formalism, and work in revival power.

Note 2. One should differentiate between **manifestations** and **reactions**. To illustrate: the light in the electric bulb is a **manifestation** of electricity; it is the nature of electricity to manifest itself as light. But when a person touches a live wire and lets out an ear-splitting scream, we cannot describe that scream as a manifestation of electricity; for it is not in the nature of electricity to manifest itself in a spoken voice. What occurred were the person's **reactions** to the electrical power. Naturally the reaction will be conditioned by the person's character and temperament. Some well-controlled individuals might simply gasp and say nothing.

Let us apply this rule to spiritual power. The operations of the gifts in 1 Cor. 12:7-10 are Scripturally described as manifestations of the Spirit. But many actions commonly called "manifestations" are really people's **reactions** to the moving of the Spirit. We refer to such actions as shouting, weeping, raising the hands, and others.

What practical value is there in the knowledge of this distinction? (1) It will enable us to honor and recognize the working of the Spirit without charging up to Him everything that may be done at a meeting. Critics, ignoring the distinction referred to, incorrectly conclude that because an individual's actions may not be elegant or "esthetic," that such a person is not under the inspiration of the Spirit. Such critics may be likened to a person, who, seeing the antics of an electrically shocked person, exclaims in disgust, "Electricity simply does not act that way!" The direct impact of the Holy Spirit is of so stirring a nature that frail human flesh may well be excused for not acting as calmly and indifferently as it would under the moving of a gentle breeze. (2) The knowledge of the distinction will naturally encourage one to react to the moving of the Spirit in a manner that will always glorify God. Certainly it would be just as unfair to criticize a young convert's extravagances as to criticize the stumblings and falls of a babe learning to walk. But at the same time, judging from 1 Corinthians 14, it is clear that God wants His people to react to the Spirit in an intelligent, edifying, and self-disciplined manner. "Seek that ye may **excel** to the edifying of the church." 14:12.

4. The Receiving of the Gifts.

God is sovereign in the matter of the bestowal of gifts; He is the One to decide as to the kind of gift that shall be imparted. He may impart a gift without human intervention at all, and even without the person's asking. But generally God works in co-operation with man, and there is something that man can do about the matter. What is required of those who would have the gifts?

(a) Submission to the Will of God. Not what I want, but what He wants, should be the attitude.. We may want some spectacular gift; He may decide otherwise.

(b) Holy Ambition. "Desire spiritual gifts." 1 Cor. 12:31; 14:1. Ambition has been often directed toward wrong and harmful ends, but that is no reason why we should not consecrate it to the service of God.

(c) Strong desire for gifts will naturally result in prayer, but always in submission to God. Compare 1 Kings 3:5-10; 2 Kings 2:9, 10.

(d) Faith. "Should we **tarry** for the gifts?" some have asked. Since spiritual gifts are "tools" for the upbuilding of the church, it seems more reasonable to go right to work for God and then trust Him to impart the gift necessary for the particular task. Thus the Sunday school teacher will trust God for the operation of the gifts necessary for a teacher; so will the pastor, the evangelist, and the lay member. A good way to secure a position is to go prepared to work; a good way to receive spiritual gifts is to be "on the job" for God, instead of sitting down with folded hands and waiting for the gift to drop from heaven.

(e) Yieldedness. The fire of inspiration may be quenched (1 Thess. 5:19) through negligence; hence the need of stirring up (literally, "kindling") the gift that is in us. 2 Tim. 1:6; 1 Tim. 4:14.

5. The Testing of the Gifts.

The Scriptures admit the possibility of demonic inspiration as well as supposedly prophetic messages originating in one's own spirit. The following tests are laid down whereby one may distinguish the true inspiration from the false.

(a) Loyalty to Christ. While in Ephesus, Paul received a letter from the Corinthian church containing certain enquiries, one of which was "concerning spiritual gifts." 1 Cor. 12 verse 3 suggests a probable reason for the enquiry. During one of their meetings, when the gift of prophecy was in operation, a voice was heard crying out, "Jesus is accursed!" It is possible that some heathen soothsayer or temple devotee had attended their meeting and when the power fell upon the Christians these pagans yielded to demonic control and opposed the confession, "Jesus is Lord," with the diabolic denial, "Jesus is accursed!" The records of modern missions in China and other countries could supply similar instances.

Paul immediately explains to the perplexed and distressed Corinthians that there are two kinds of inspiration, Divine and demonic, and explains the difference. He reminds them of the demonic impulses and ecstasies they had experienced or witnessed in some idol temples, and points out that this inspiration led to idol worship. See 1 Cor. 10:20. On the other hand, the Spirit of God inspires people to confess the Lordship of Jesus. "Wherefore I give you to understand, that no man speaking by the Spirit of God calleth Jesus accursed: and that no man can say that Jesus is the Lord, but by the Holy Ghost." Compare Rev. 19:10; Matt. 16:16, 17; 1 John 4:1, 2.

Of course, this does not mean that a person cannot say in parrot-like fashion that Jesus is Lord. The meaning is that no one can utter the **heart conviction** of the Deity of Jesus without the illumination of the Holy Spirit. Compare Rom. 10:9.

(b) The Practical Test. The Corinthians were spiritual in the sense that they displayed a keen interest in spiritual gifts (1 Cor. 12:1; 14:12). But while glorying in the Spirit's energizing power they seemed lacking in His sanctifying power. They were fostering factions; the church was tolerating a case of unspeakable immorality; brethren were going to law with one another; some were slipping back to pagan standards; others had partaken of the Lord's Supper in a drunken condition.

We may be sure that the apostle did not judge these converts too harshly, remembering the vile pit of heathenism from which they had been recently rescued and the temptations with which they were surrounded. But he felt that they must be impressed with the truth that, however important spiritual gifts might be, Christian character and right living must be the supreme aim of their endeavors. After encouraging them to "covet earnestly the best gifts" (1 Cor. 12:31), he adds, "and yet shew I unto you a more excellent way." Then follows his sublime discourse on Divine love, the crown of character.

But right here we must be careful to distinguish things that differ. Opponents of speaking in tongues (who, by the way, are un-Scriptural in their attitude, 1 Cor. 14:39), maintain that people would do better to seek love which is the supreme gift. They are guilty of confusion of thought. Love is not a gift but a fruit of the Spirit. The fruit of the Spirit is the progressive development of the Christ-life implanted at regeneration; while the gifts may be bestowed suddenly to any Spirit-filled believer at any point in the believer's experience. The first represents the sanctifying power of the Spirit, while the second involves His energizing power.

Nevertheless, one will make no mistake in

insisting upon the supremacy of Christian character. Perplexing as it may appear, it is a fact of experience that persons defective in holiness may exhibit manifestations of the gifts. But the following facts should be pondered: (1) The Baptism in the Holy Spirit does not make a person immediately perfect. Enduement of power is one thing. Maturity of Christian graces is another. Both the new birth and the Baptism with the Holy Spirit are gifts of God's grace and reveal His grace toward us. There may still remain a need for a personal sanctification which comes through an operation of the Holy Spirit, developing the grace of God within us. (2) The operation of the gifts does not have a sanctifying power. Balaam experienced the gift of prophecy while in the depths of his heart he wanted to betray God's people for money. (3) Paul tells us plainly of the possibility of possessing the gifts without possessing love.

Serious consequences may ensue for the one who exercises the gifts apart from love. First, he will be a constant stumblingblock to those who know his real character; second, the gifts profit him nothing. No amount of spiritual manifestations, no zeal in the ministry, no accomplishing of results, can make up for lack of personal holiness. Heb. 12:14.

(c) The Doctrinal Test. The Holy Spirit has come to operate in the sphere of truth relating to Christ's Deity and atoning work. It is unthinkable that He should contradict what had already been revealed by Christ to His apostles. Therefore, for example, any prophet who denies the incarnation of Christ can not be speaking by the Spirit of God. 1 John 4:2, 3.

VI. THE SPIRIT IN THE CHURCH.

1. The Advent of the Spirit.

The Saviour lived before His incarnation and continued to live after His ascension; but during the intervening period He exercised what we may call His dispensational or "temporal" mission, which He came into the world to fulfill, and having accomplished it, He returned to the Father. So the Spirit came into the world at an appointed time for a definite mission and will leave when His mission is accomplished. He came to earth not only for an appointed purpose but also for an appointed time.

There are three major dispensations in the Scriptures corresponding to the Three Persons of the Godhead. The Old Testament is the dispensation of the Father; Christ's earthly ministry is the dispensation of the Son; and the age between the ascension and the second coming of Christ is the dispensation of the Spirit. The Spirit's ministry will continue until Jesus comes, after which another dispensational ministry will succeed. The characteristic name for the Spirit during this dispensation is the Spirit of Christ.

The entire Trinity co-operates in the full manifestation of God during the great dispensations. Each exercises an earthly ministry: the Father descends at Sinai, the Son descends at the incarnation, the Spirit descends on the day of Pentecost. The Father commends the Son from heaven (Matt. 3:17), the Son commends the Spirit (Rev. 2:11), and the Spirit testifies to the Son. John 15:26. As God the Son fulfills to men the work of God the Father, so the Holy Ghost fulfills to men the work of God the Son.

John Owen, a theologian of the seventeenth century, points out, how, throughout the dispensations, there are certain tests of orthodoxy related to each of the three Persons. Before the advent of

Christ the great test was the oneness of God, Creator and Ruler of all. After the coming of Christ the great question was whether a church orthodox on the first point would now receive the Divine Son, incarnate, sacrificed, risen and ascended, according to the promise. And when the working of this test had gathered out the church of Christian believers, the Holy Spirit came into prominence as the touchstone of true faith. "The sin of despising His Person and rejecting His work now is of the same nature with the idolatry of old, and with the Jews' rejection of the Person of the Son."

As the eternal Son became incarnate in a human body at His birth, so the eternal Spirit became incarnate in the church which is His body. This occurred on the day of Pentecost, "the birthday of the Spirit." What the cradle was to the incarnate Christ so the upper room was to the Spirit. Note what occurred on that memorable day.

(a) The birth of the church. "And when the day of Pentecost was fully come." Pentecost was an Old Testament feast that occurred fifty days after the Passover, for which reason it is called "Pentecost," which means "fifty." See Lev. 23:15-21. Let us notice its position in the festal calendar. (1) First came the Passover feast, which commemorated the deliverance of Israel in Egypt in the night when the death angel slew the firstborn of Egypt while God's people ate the lamb in houses sealed with blood. This is typical of the death of Christ, the Lamb of God, whose blood shelters us from the judgment of God. (2) On the Sabbath after the Passover night a sheaf of barley which had already been marked out was reaped by the priests and offered before Jehovah as the first-fruits of the harvest. The principle was that the first part of the harvest must be offered to Jehovah in recognition of His rulership and ownership. After this, the remainder of the harvest could be reaped. This is a type of Christ "the first-fruits of them that slept." 1 Cor. 15:20. Christ was the first to be reaped from the field of death and to ascend to the Father never to die again; being the first-fruits, He is the guarantee that all who believe on Him shall follow Him in the resurrection to life everlasting. (3) Forty-nine days were to be counted from the offering of this wave sheaf, and on the fiftieth day—Pentecost—two loaves, the first loaves made from the wheat harvest, were waved before God. Before any loaves could be made and eaten the first two must be offered to Jehovah in acknowledgment of His rulership over the world. After that, other loaves could be baked and eaten. The following is the typical meaning: The hundred and twenty in the upper room were the "first loaves" of the Christian church, offered up before the Lord by the Holy Spirit fifty days after the resurrection of Christ. It was the first-born of the multiplied thousands of churches that have since been established during the last nineteen centuries.

(b) The Evidence of Christ's Glorification. The descent of the Holy Spirit was a supernatural "telegram" so to speak, announcing Christ's arrival at the right hand of the Father. See Acts 2:33.

"How do you know that your mother is upstairs?" asked a man of his nephews as they studied their Sunday school lesson.

"I saw her go," answered one.

"You mean that you saw her **start** upstairs," said the uncle. "Perhaps she did not get there, and she may not be there now even if she has been there."

"I know that she is there," replied the youngest child, "for I went to the foot of the steps and called her and she answered me."

The disciples knew that their Master had ascended because He answered them by the "sound from heaven."

(c) The Completion of Christ's Work. The Exodus was not complete until fifty days later when at Sinai Israel was organized as the people of God. In like manner the benefit of the atonement was not completed, in the fullest sense, until the day of Pentecost, when the outpouring of the Spirit was a sign that Christ's sacrifice was accepted in heaven, and that the time had therefore come to proclaim His finished work.

(d) The Anointing of the Church. As the Lord's baptism had been followed by His ministry in Galilee, so the baptism of the church was to be preparatory to a world-wide ministry: a ministry not like His own, creative of a new order, but one of simple testimony; yet only to be fulfilled in the power of the Spirit of God.

(e) The Indwelling of the Church. After Israel's organization at Sinai, Jehovah came down to dwell in their midst, His presence being localized in the Tabernacle. On the day of Pentecost the Holy Spirit came down to dwell in the church as in a temple, His presence being localized in the collective body and individual Christians. The Spirit came into His office to administer the affairs of Christ's kingdom. This fact is recognized throughout the book of Acts; for example, when Ananias and Sapphira lied to Peter they were really lying to the Holy Ghost who dwelt and ministered in the church.

(f) The Beginning of a Dispensation. The Pentecostal outpouring was not merely a miraculous display of power intended to arrest attention and invite inquiry into the new faith. It was the beginning of a new dispensation. It was an advent of the Spirit as the Incarnation was the advent of the Son. God sent forth His Son, and when the mission of the Son had been fulfilled, He sent forth the Spirit of His Son to take up the work under new conditions.

2. The Ministry of the Spirit.

The Holy Spirit is Christ's representative to whom has been committed the entire administration of the church until Jesus comes. Christ took His seat in heaven as "head over all things to the church," and the Spirit came down to begin the work of building up the body of Christ. The perfecting of the Body of Christ is the final purpose of the Comforter.

Belief in the Spirit's guidance was deeply rooted in the early church. There was no domain of life where His right to control was not recognized, and where the fact of His control was not experienced. The church committed her whole life to the Spirit's leading. She continued to reject set forms of worship until, towards the close of the century, the influence of the Spirit began to wane and ecclesiasticism took the place of the Spirit's control.

The Spirit's control is recognized in the following aspects of the life of the church.

(a) **Administration.** The great missionary movements of the early church were commanded and approved by the Spirit. Acts 8:29; 10:19, 44; 13:2, 4. Paul was conscious that his whole ministry was inspired by the Holy Ghost. Rom. 15: 18, 19. On all his journeys he recognized the Spirit's leading. Acts 16:6, 7. The Spirit guided the church in her organization. Acts 6:3; 20:28.

(b) **Preaching.** The first Christians were accustomed to hearing the gospel preached "with the Holy Ghost sent down from heaven" (1 Peter 1:12), which they received "with joy of the Holy

Ghost." 1 Thess. 1:6. "For our gospel came not unto you in word only, but also in power, and in the Holy Ghost, and in much assurance." 1 Thess. 1:5. A. J. Gordon many years ago made the remark: "Our age is losing its grip on the supernatural—the pulpit is descending to the level of the platform."

(c) **Prayer.** Jesus, following John, taught His disciples a model of prayer as a guide for their petitions. But before leaving He spoke of a new kind of prayer, prayer "in my name" (John 16:23), not repeating His name as a kind of a charm, but the approaching of God spiritually united to Christ by the Spirit. Thus we pray as though Jesus Himself stood in God's presence. Paul speaks of "praying always with all prayer and supplication in the Spirit" (Eph. 6:18); Jude describes true Christians as "praying in the Holy Ghost" (v. 20); and in Rom. 8:26, 27 we are told that the Spirit is doing the same thing in us that Christ is doing for us in heaven—that is, interceding for us. Heb. 7:25. As Christ on earth taught His disciples how to pray, so today He teaches the same lesson by means of the Comforter or Helper. Then, it was by an outward form; now it is by an inward guidance.

(d) **Singing.** As a result of being filled with the Spirit believers will be found "speaking to yourselves in psalms and hymns and spiritual songs, singing and making melody in your heart to the Lord." Eph. 5:18, 19. "Speaking to yourselves" implies congregational singing. "Psalms" may refer to the Old Testament Psalms, which were sung or chanted; "spiritual songs" denotes spontaneous outbursts of melody and praise directly inspired by the Holy Spirit.

(e) **Testimony.** There did not exist in the primitive church that line of separation between ministry and laity observed in Christendom today.

The church was governed by a group or council of elders but the ministry of public utterance was not rigidly confined to them. Whoever was endowed with a gift of the Spirit—whether prophecy, teaching, knowledge, tongues or interpretation—was permitted to contribute his portion to the service.

The metaphor "body of Christ" well describes the functioning of collective worship under the control of the Spirit. It brings to our mind a scene of members one after another performing their separate functions in the complete act of worship and all alike controlled by the same animating Power.

3. The Ascension of the Spirit.

What is true of Christ is true of the Spirit. After accomplishing His dispensational mission He will return to heaven in a body which He has fashioned for Himself—that "new man" (Eph. 2:15), which is the church, which is His body. The distinctive work of the Spirit is "to gather out a people for his (Christ's) name" (Acts 15:14), and when this is accomplished and the "fullness of the Gentiles be come in" (Rom. 11:25), there will take place the rapture, which, in the words of A. J. Gordon, is "the earthly Christ (1 Cor. 12:12, 27) rising to meet the heavenly Christ." As Christ shall ultimately give up His kingdom to the Father, so the Holy Ghost shall give up His administration to the Son.

Some have concluded that the Spirit will no longer be in the world after the taking away of the church. This cannot be, for the Holy Spirit, as Deity, is omnipresent. What will take place is the conclusion of the Spirit's dispensational mission as the Spirit of Christ, after which He will still be in the world in another and different relationship.

10

THE CHURCH

"Plainly Jesus designed that there should be a society of His followers to give to mankind His gospel and minister to mankind in His spirit, to labor as He did for the increase of the kingdom of God. He fashioned no organization or plan of government for this society. . . . He did a greater thing than give organization—He gave life. Jesus formed the society of His followers by calling them together about Himself. He communicated to it as far as He could while He was on earth His own life, His spirit, and purpose. He promised to continue to the end of the world to impart His life to His society, His church. His great gift to the church, we may say, was Himself."—Robert Hastings Nichols.

OUTLINE

I. THE NATURE OF THE CHURCH.
1. Words Describing the Church.
2. Words Describing Christians.
   a. Brethren. b. Believers. c. Saints. d. The elect. e. Disciples. f. Christians. g. Those of the Way.
3. Illustrations of the Church.
   a. The body of Christ.
   b. The temple of God.
   c. The bride of Christ.

II. THE FOUNDING OF THE CHURCH.
1. Prophetically Considered.
2. Historically Considered.

III. THE MEMBERSHIP OF THE CHURCH.

IV. THE WORK OF THE CHURCH.
1. To Preach Salvation.
2. To Provide Means of Worship.
3. To Provide Religious Fellowship.
4. To Hold Up a Moral Standard.

V. THE ORDINANCES OF THE CHURCH.
1. Baptism.
   a. Mode.
   b. The formula.
   c. The recipient.
   d. The efficacy.
   e. The meaning.
2. The Lord's Supper. Keynotes:
   a. Commemoration.
   b. Instruction.
   c. Inspiration.
   d. Assurance.
   e. Responsibility.

VI. THE WORSHIP OF THE CHURCH.
1. The Public Service.
2. The Private Service.

VII. THE ORGANIZATION OF THE CHURCH.
1. The Government of the Church.
2. The Ministry of the Church.
   a. The general and prophetic ministry.
   b. The local and practical ministry.

I. THE NATURE OF THE CHURCH

What is the Church? The question may be answered by considering: (1) The words describing that institution. (2) Words describing Christians. (3) Illustrations describing the church.

1. Words Describing the Church.

The New Testament Greek word for church is "ecclesia," meaning "an assembly of called-out ones." The term is applied to (1) The whole body of Christians in one city. Acts 11:22; 13:1. (2) A congregation. 1 Cor. 14:19, 35; Rom. 16:5. (3) The whole body of believers on earth. Eph. 5:32.

Our English word "church" is derived from the Greek "kuriake," meaning "that which belongs to the Lord." The church, then, is a company of people called out from the world, who profess and tender allegiance to the Lord Jesus Christ.

2. Words Describing Christians.

(a) Brethren. The church is a spiritual brotherhood or fellowship, in which all divisions that separate mankind have been abolished. "There is neither Jew nor Gentile"—the deepest of all divisions based on religious isolation is overcome; "there is neither Greek nor barbarian"—the deepest of cultural divisions is overcome; "there is neither bond nor free"—the deepest of social and economic divisions is overcome; "there is neither male nor female"—the deepest of all human divisions is overcome.

(b) Believers. Christians are called "believers" because their characteristic doctrine is faith in the Lord Jesus.

(c) Saints. They are called "saints" (literally "consecrated or holy ones") because they are separated from the world and dedicated to God.

(d) The Elect. They are referred to as "the elect," or "the chosen," because God has chosen them for an important ministry and a glorious destiny.

(e) Disciples. They are "disciples" (literally, "learners") because under spiritual training with Christ-inspired instructors.

(f) Christians. They are "Christians" because their religion centers around the Person of Christ.

(g) Those of the Way. In the early days they were often known as "those of this way" (Acts 9:2) because they lived according to a special way of life.

3. Illustrations of the Church.

(a) The Body of Christ. The Lord Jesus Christ left this earth more than nineteen hundred years ago; but He is still in the world. By this we mean that His presence is manifested through the church, which is His body. As He lived His natural life on earth in an individual human body, so He lives His mystical life in a body drawn from the human race in general. At the conclusion of the Gospels we do not write, "The End," but rather, "To Be Continued," because the life of Christ continues to be expressed through His disciples as evidenced by the Book of Acts and by subsequent Church History. "As my Father hath sent me, even so send I you." "He that receiveth you receiveth me."

Before He left this earth, Christ promised to assume this new body. However, He used another illustration, "I am the vine, ye are the branches." The vine is incomplete without the branches, and the branches are nothing apart from the life which flows from the vine. If Christ is to be known to the world, it must be through those who bear His name and share His life. And to the extent that the church has kept in touch with Christ her Head, has she shared His life and experiences.

As Christ was anointed at the Jordan, so the Church was anointed at Pentecost. Jesus went about preaching the gospel to the poor, healing the broken-hearted, and preaching deliverance to the captives; and the true Church has ever followed in His footsteps. "As He is, so are we in this world." 1 John 4:17. As Christ was denounced as a political menace and finally crucified, so His church has, in many instances, been crucified (figuratively speaking) by persecuting rulers. But, like her Lord, she has risen again! The life of Christ within her renders her indestructible. This thought of the Church's indentification with Christ must have been in the mind of Paul when he spoke about completing "that which is behind (remains) of the afflictions of Christ in my flesh for his body's sake, which is the church."

The use of the above illustration reminds us that the church is an organism not merely an organization. An organization is a group of individuals voluntarily associated together for a certain purpose, such as a fraternal organization or trade union. An organism is any living thing, which develops by inherent life. Used figuratively it means the sum total of related parts, in which the relationship of each part to part involves a relationship to the whole. Thus, an automobile could be called an "organization" of certain mechanical parts; a human body is an organism because composed of many members and organs animated by a common life.

The human body is one, yet it is made up of millions of living cells; in like manner the body of Christ is one, though composed of millions of born again souls. As the human body is vitalized by the soul, so the body of Christ is vitalized by the Holy Spirit. "For by one Spirit are we all baptized into one body."

The above facts point to a unique feature of Christ's religion. Writes W. H. Dunphy:

He—and He alone—of the founders of religion—brought to life a permanent organism, a permanent union of minds and souls, centering in Himself. Christians are not merely followers of Christ, but members of Christ, and of one another. Buddha developed his society of the awakened ones, but the relation between them is merely external—the relation of teacher and pupil. It is his doctrine which unites them, not his life. The same may be said of Zoroaster, of Socrates, of Mohammed and the other religious geniuses of the race. But Christ is not only the Teacher, He is the Life of Christians. What He founded was not a society which studied and propagated His ideas, but an organism which lived by His life, a Body indwelt and guided by His Spirit.

(b) The Temple of God. 1 Pet. 2:5, 6. A temple is a place in which God, who dwells everywhere, localizes Himself in one particular place where His people may always find Him "at home." Ex. 25:8; 1 Kings 8:27. As God dwelt in the Tabernacle and Temple, so He now lives, by His Spirit, in the church. Eph. 2:21, 22; 1 Cor. 3:16, 17. In this spiritual temple Christians, as priests, offer up spiritual sacrifices—sacrifices of prayer, praise and good works.

(c) The Bride of Christ. This is an illustration used in both Old and New Testaments to picture the union and communion of God and His people. 2 Cor. 11:2; Eph. 5:25-27; Rev. 19:7; 22:17; 21:2. But it should be remembered that it is just one illustration, and should not be pressed too far. The purpose of a symbol is to illuminate one particular side of truth and not to provide the foundation for any doctrine.

II. THE FOUNDING OF THE CHURCH

1. Considered Prophetically.

Israel is described as a church in that it was a nation called out from other nations to be the servant of God. Acts 7:38. When the Old Testament was translated into Greek the word "congregation" (of Israel) was rendered "ekklesia" or "church." Israel, then, was the congregation or church of Jehovah. After His rejection by the Jewish church, Christ predicted the founding of a new congregation or church, a Divine institution that should continue His work on earth. Matt. 16:18. This is the church of Christ, which came into existence on the Day of Pentecost.

2. Considered Historically.

The church of Christ came into existence as such on the day of Pentecost, when it was consecrated by the anointing of the Spirit. Just as the Tabernacle was built and then consecrated by the descent of the Divine glory (Ex. 40:34), so the first members of the church were assembled in the upper room and consecrated as the church by the descent of the Holy Spirit. It is likely that the first Christians saw in this event the return of the Shekinah, which had long departed from the Temple, and whose absence was lamented by some of the Rabbis.

David gathered the materials for the building of the temple but the work was done by his successor, Solomon. In like manner Jesus had gathered the materials, so to speak, of His church, during His earthly ministry, but the edifice itself was reared by His successor, the Holy Spirit. Actually, this work was done by the Spirit working through the apostles, who laid the foundations and built the church by their preaching, teaching and organizing. Therefore the church is described as being "built upon the foundation of the apostles." Eph. 2:20.

III. THE MEMBERSHIP OF THE CHURCH.

The New Testament lays down the following conditions for membership: implicit faith in the gospel and a heart-felt trust in Christ as the only Divine Saviour. Acts 16:31; submission to water baptism as a symbolic testimony to faith in Christ, and verbal confession of faith. Rom. 10:9, 10. (Perhaps it would be more correct to describe submission to water baptism as a characteristic of church membership.)

In the beginning practically the entire membership of the church was truly regenerate. "And the Lord added to the church daily such as should be saved." Acts 2:47. Entering the church was not a matter of joining an organization but of becoming members of Christ, as a branch is grafted to a tree. In course of time, however, as the church increased in numbers and popularity, water baptism and catechizing took the place of conversion; the result was the influx into the church of large numbers of people who were not Christian at heart. And this has been, more or less the condition of Christendom ever since. As, in Old Testament times, there was an Israel within an Israel—Israelites indeed as well as Israelites in creed—so in the course of church history we see a church within the church—possessing Christians in the midst of professing Christians.

We must therefore distinguish between the church invisible, which is composed of real Christians from all denominations, and the church visible, consisting of all who profess to be Christians —the first being composed of those whose names are written in heaven, the second comprising all those who have their names on the church books. This distinction is implied in Matthew 13, where the Lord speaks of "the mysteries of the kingdom of heaven"—which expression corresponds to the general designation, "Christendom." The parables in this chapter trace the spiritual history of Christendom between the first and second advents of Christ, and in them we learn that there will be a mixture of good and bad in the church until the Lord's coming when the church will be puri-

fied and a separation made between the genuine
and the false. Matt. 13:36-43, 47-49. Paul the
apostle expresses the same truth by comparing
the church to a house in which there are many
vessels, some unto honor, and others unto dishonor. 2 Tim. 2:19-21.

Is the church synonymous with the kingdom
of God? That the church age is a phase of the
kingdom is implied in Matt. 16:18, 19, by the parables in Matt. 13, and by Paul's description of Christian work as being in the sphere of God's kingdom. Col. 4:11. Inasmuch as "kingdom of heav-
en" is a comprehensive term we may also describe
the church as a part of the kingdom. "The Church
may be looked upon as a part of the kingdom of
God just as Illinois is part of the United States,"
writes William Evans. The church preaches the
message dealing with man's birth into the kingdom of God. John 3:3-5; 1 Peter 1:23.

IV. THE WORK OF THE CHURCH.
1. To Preach Salvation.
It is the work of the church to preach the
gospel to every creature (Matt. 28:19, 20), and to
expound the plan of salvation as taught in the
Scriptures. Christ has made salvation possible by
providing it; the church must make it actual by
proclaiming it.

2. To Provide a Means of Worship.
Israel possessed a divinely appointed system
of worship by which they approached God in all
the needs and crises of life. The church likewise
must be a house of prayer for all people where God
is honored in worship, prayer, and testimony.

3. To Provide Religious Fellowship.
Man is a social being; he craves fellowship
and an exchange of friendship. He naturally as-
sembles with those who share the same interests.

The church provides a fellowship based on the Fatherhood of God, and the Lordship of Christ. It is a brotherhood of those who share a common spiritual experience.

The warmth of fellowship was one of the outstanding characteristics of the early church. In a world governed by the machine-like Roman empire, where the individual was practically ignored, men longed for a fellowship where they might lose the feeling of loneliness and helplessness. In such a world one of the strongest drawing features of the church was the warmth and solidarity of fellowship—a fellowship where all earthly distinctions were obliterated and where men and women became brothers and sisters in Christ.

4. To Hold Up the Moral Standard.

The church is "the light of the world," to banish moral ignorance; it is "the salt of the earth" to preserve it from moral corruption. The church must teach men how to live as well as how to die. It must hold forth God's plan for the regulation of all spheres of life and activity. Against the downward trends of society it must lift a warning voice; at all danger points it must plant a beacon light.

V. THE ORDINANCES OF THE CHURCH.

New Testament Christianity is not a ritualistic religion; at the heart of it is man's direct contact with God through the Spirit. Therefore it does not lay down a hard and fast order of worship but leaves the church in every age and land to adapt the method best suited for the expression of its life. There are, however, two ceremonies which are essential because divinely ordained, namely, water baptism and the Lord's Supper. Because of their sacred character they are sometimes described as sacraments—literally, "sacred things" or "oaths consecrated by a sacred rite";

they are also referred to as ordinances because
they are ceremonies "ordained" by the Lord Himself.

Water baptism is the rite of entrance into
the Christian church, and symbolizes spiritual life
begun; the Lord's Supper is the rite of communion
and signifies spiritual life continued. The first
pictures faith in Christ, the second pictures fellowship with Christ. The first is administered
only once, for there can be but one beginning of
the spiritual life; the second is administered frequently, teaching that spiritual life must be nourished.

1. Baptism.

(a) **The Mode.** The word "baptize" used in
the formula means literally to dip or to immerse.
This interpretation is confirmed by Greek scholars
and church historians; even scholars belonging to
churches which baptize by sprinkling admit that
immersion was the earliest mode. Moreover, there
is good reason for believing that to the Jews of
apostolic times the command to be "baptized"
would suggest immersion. They were acquaint-
ed with "proselyte's baptism" which signified a
heathen's conversion to Judaism. The convert
stood up to his neck in water while the law was
read to him, after which he plunged himself beneath the water as a sign that he was cleansed
from the defilements of heathenism and had begun
to live a new life as a member of God's covenant
people.

Whence, then, came the practice of sprinkling
and pouring? When the church forsook the sim-
plicity of the New Testament and became influenced by pagan ideas, it attached an un-Scriptural importance to water baptism, which came to
be considered fully essential to regeneration. It
was therefore administered to the sick and dying. Since immersion was out of the question

in such cases, baptism was administered by sprinkling. Later because of the convenience of the method it was made general. Also, because of the importance of the ordinance, pouring was permitted when there was insufficient water for immersion. Witness the following quotation from an ancient writing of the second century:

Now concerning baptism, baptize thus: Having taught all of these things, baptize ye into the name of the Father, and of the Son, and of the Holy Ghost, in living (running) water. And if thou hast not living water, baptize into other water: and if thou canst not in cold, then in warm. But if thou hast neither, pour water thrice upon the head in the name of the Father, and of the Son, and of the Holy Ghost.

However, the Scriptural, original mode is by immersion, which is true to the symbolical meaning of baptism, namely death, burial, and resurrection. Rom. 6:1-4.

(b) The Formula. "Baptizing them in the name of the Father, and of the Son, and of the Holy Ghost." How reconcile this with Peter's command, "Be baptized every one of you in the name of Jesus Christ"? Acts 2:38. These latter words do not represent a baptismal formula, but were simply a statement that such persons were baptized as acknowledged Jesus to be Lord and Christ. For example the "Didache," a Christian document of A. D. 100, speaks of Christian baptism being in the name of the Lord Jesus, but when it comes to describe the rite in detail the Trinitarian formula is prescribed. When Paul speaks of Israel's being baptized in the Red Sea "unto Moses," he is not referring to a formula that was pronounced at the time; he simply means that because of the miraculous passage through the Red Sea the Israelites accepted Moses as their heaven-sent guide and teacher. In like manner, to be baptized in the name of Jesus means to commit oneself wholly and eternally to Him as a heaven-sent Saviour, and acceptance of His leadership dictates the acceptance of the formula given by Jesus Himself in Matthew 28.

The literal rendering of Acts 2:38 is, "be baptized **on** the name of Jesus Christ." This means, according to Thayer's Lexicon, that the Jews were to "repose their hope and confidence in His Messianic authority."

Notice that the Trinitarian formula is descriptive of an experience. Those who are baptized in the name of the triune God are thereby testifying that they have been plunged into spiritual communion with the Trinity; so that to them it may be said, "The grace of the Lord Jesus Christ, and the love of God, and the communion of the Holy Ghost, is with you." 2 Cor. 13:14.

(c) The Recipient. All who sincerely repent of their sins and exercise a living faith in the Lord Jesus are eligible for baptism. In the apostolic church the rite was accompanied by the following outward expressions: (1) Profession of faith. Acts 8:37. (2) Prayer. Acts 22:16. (3) Vow of consecration. 1 Peter 3:21.

Since infants have no sins to repent of and cannot exercise faith they are logically excluded from water baptism. We are not thereby forbidding them to come to Christ (Matt. 19:13, 14) for they may be dedicated to Him in a public service.

(d) The Efficacy. Water baptism in itself has no saving power; people are baptized not in order to be saved but because they are saved. Therefore we cannot say that the rite is absolutely essential to salvation. But we may insist that it is essential to full obedience. As the election of the president of our land is made complete by his inauguration, so the convert's election to God's grace and glory is made complete by his public inauguration as a member of the church of Christ.

(e) The Meaning. Baptism pictures the following ideas: (1) Salvation. Water baptism is a sacred drama (if we may so speak), portraying the fundamentals of the gospel. The lowering of the convert pictures Christ's death accomplished; the submersion of the convert speaks of death ratified, or His burial; the raising of the convert signifies death conquered, or Christ's resurrection. (2) Experience. The fact that the acts are performed with the convert shows that he has been spiritually identified with Christ. The immersion proclaims the message: "Christ died for sin in order that this man might die to sin." The raising of the convert conveys the following message: "Christ rose from the dead in order that this man might live a new life of righteousness." (3) Regeneration. The experience of the new birth has been described as a "washing" (literally "bath" Tit. 3:5), because thereby the sins and defilements of the old life are washed away. As washing with water cleanses the body, so God, in connection with the death of Christ and through the Holy Spirit, cleanses the soul. Water baptism pictures this cleansing. "Arise, and be baptized, and wash away thy sins (that is, as a sign of what has already been done)." Acts 22:16. (4) Testimony. "For as many of you as have been baptized into Christ have put on Christ." Gal. 3:27. Water baptism signifies that the convert has by faith "put on" Christ—the character of Christ—so that men may see Christ in him as they see the uniform upon the soldier. By the rite of baptism the convert, figuratively speaking, publicly dons the uniform of the kingdom of Christ.

2. The Lord's Supper.

The Lord's Supper or Holy Communion may be defined as the distinctive rite of Christian worship, instituted by the Lord Jesus on the eve of His atoning death. It consists of a religious partaking of bread and wine which, having been presented to the Father in memorial of Christ's inexhaustible sacrifice, becomes a means of grace whereby we are inspired to increased faith and faithfulness toward Him.

The following are the keynotes of this ordinance:

(a) Commemoration. "This do in remembrance of me." Every year, on July 4, the American people remember in a special manner that event which made them a free people. Every time a group of Christians gather to celebrate the Lord's Supper they are remembering in a special manner the atoning death of Christ which freed them from their sins.

Why remember His death above every other event in His life? Because it was the crowning event in His ministry and because we are saved not merely by His life and teachings—Divine though these are—but by His atoning sacrifice.

(b) Instruction. The Lord's Supper is a sacred object lesson setting forth the two fundamentals of the gospel: (1) The incarnation. As we take the bread we hear John the apostle saying, "And the Word was made flesh, and dwelt among us" (John 1:14); we hear the Lord Himself declaring, "For the bread of God is he which cometh down from heaven, and giveth life unto the world." John 6:33. (2) The atonement. But the blessings included in the incarnation are imparted to us through the death of Christ. Bread and wine are a picture of death—the separation of body and life, the separation of flesh and blood. The bread tells us that the Bread of life must be broken in death in order to be distributed among the spiritually hungry; the poured-out wine tells us that His blood, which is His life, must be shed in death in order that its cleansing and quickening power may be supplied to needy souls.

(c) Inspiration. The elements, especially the wine, remind us that by faith we may become partakers of Christ's nature, that is, have "communion" with Him. As we partake of the bread and wine of the Communion, we are reminded and assured that, by faith, we may truly receive His Spirit and reflect His character.

(d) Assurance. "This cup is the new testament (covenant) in my blood."

In ancient times the most solemn form of agreement was the blood-covenant, which was sealed or signed with sacrificial blood. The covenant made with Israel at Mount Sinai was a blood covenant. After God had laid down His conditions and the people had accepted them, Moses took a basin filled with sacrificial blood and sprinkled half of it upon the altar of sacrifice, signifying that God had bound Himself to His part of the agreement; he then sprinkled the rest of the blood upon the people, thus binding them to keep their part of the contract. Ex. 24:3-8.

The new covenant instituted by Christ is a blood covenant. God has accepted the blood of Christ (Heb. 9:14-24) and has therefore bound Himself, for Christ's sake, to pardon and save all who come to Him. The blood of Christ is the Divine guarantee that He will be gracious and merciful to the penitent. Our part in this contract is to believe in the atoning death of Christ. Rom. 3:25, 26. Then we can testify to being sprinkled with the blood of the new covenant. 1 Pet. 1:2.

(e) Responsibility. Who shall be admitted to or excluded from the Lord's Table? Paul deals with the question of sacramental worthiness in 1 Cor. 11:20-34. "Whosoever shall eat this bread, and drink this cup of the Lord, unworthily, shall be guilty of (an offence or sin against) the body and blood of the Lord."

Does this mean that only those who are worthy may approach the Lord's Table? Then every one of us is excluded! for who among the children of men is worthy of the least of God's mercies? No, the apostle is not speaking about the unworthiness of **persons,** but the unworthiness of **actions.** Thus, strange as it may sound, it is possible for an unworthy person to partake worthily. And in a sense, only those who sincerely feel their unworthiness are in a right state to approach the table; the self-righteous are never fit. Further, it has been noticed that it is the deeply spiritual people who feel their unworthiness the most. Paul described himself as "chief of sinners."

The apostle warns us against unworthy acts and an unworthy attitude in partaking of the sacrament. How may one partake unworthily? By doing anything that hinders us from clearly appreciating the meaning of the elements, and from approaching in a solemn, thoughtful and reverent attitude. In the case of the Corinthians the hindrance was a serious one, namely, drunkenness.

VI. THE WORSHIP OF THE CHURCH.

From Paul's epistles we gather that there were two kinds of meetings for worship: one was in the nature of a prayer, praise, and preaching service; the other was a worship service, known as the Love Feast ("Agape"). The first was a public service; the second was a private service to which only Christians were admitted.

1. The Public Service.

The public meeting "was carried on by people as the Spirit moved them," writes Robert Hastings Nichols, and continues:

Prayers were offered and testimony and instruction given. There was singing of the Psalms and also of Christian hymns which began to be written in the first century. The Old Testament Scriptures were read and expounded, and there was reading or recitation from memory of accounts of the words and deeds of Jesus. When apostles sent to churches letters such as we have in the Epistles of the New Testament, these were also read.

At any time this simple service might be broken into and superseded by the manifestation of the Spirit in the form of prophecy, tongues and interpretations or some inspired insight into the Scriptures. This feature of primitive worship is recognized by all careful students of church history regardless of their church affiliation or school of thought.

That this Spirit-inspired worship was a powerful means of touching the unconverted may be gathered from 1 Cor. 14:24, 25.

2. The Private Service.

We read that the first Christians continued in "breaking of bread." Acts 2:42. Do these words describe an ordinary meal or the celebration of the Lord's Supper? Perhaps both. This is what may have occurred: at first the fellowship of the early disciples was so close and vital that they had their meals in common. As they surrounded the table to ask God's blessing upon the food the memory of Christ's last Passover meal would come to their minds, and the blessing over the food would spontaneously enlarge itself into a service of worship, so that in many cases it would be difficult to determine whether the disciples were having a common meal, or partaking of the Communion. Life and worship were closely related in those days!

But very early the two acts—breaking of bread and the Lord's Supper were distinguished, so that the following was the order of service. On a stated day the Christians would assemble for a sacred fellowship meal known as the Love Feast, which was a joyful and sacred meal symbolizing brotherly love. Everyone brought provisions for the meal and these were to be shared by all alike. In 1 Cor. 11:21, 22 Paul rebukes the selfishness of those who ate their food without sharing with the poor. At the close of the Love Feast the Lord's Supper was celebrated. In the Corinthian church some of the people became drunk at the "Agape" and partook of the sacrament in that unworthy condition.

Later in the first century the Lord's Supper was separated from the Agape and celebrated on the Lord's Day morning.

VII. THE ORGANIZATION OF THE CHURCH.

1. The Government of the Church.

It is clear that the Lord Jesus purposed that there should be a society of His followers to give mankind His gospel and to represent Him in the world. But He fashioned no organization or plan of government, gave no detailed rule of faith and practice. He did, however, ordain the two simple rites of baptism and communion. Yet He did not ignore organization, for His promise of the coming Comforter implied that the apostles should be led into all truth concerning these matters.

What He did for the church was something higher than organization—He imparted to it His very life, making it a living organism. As a living body adapts itself to its environment so the living body of Christ was left free to select its own forms of organization according to its needs and circumstances. Of course the church was not free to follow any development contrary either to the teachings of Christ or apostolic doctrine. Any development contrary to Scriptural principles is a **corruption.**

During the days following Pentecost the believers had practically no organization and for a time worshiped privately in their homes and kept the prayer times of the temple. Acts 2:46. This was supplemented by apostolic teaching and fellowship. As the church grew in numbers, organization developed from the following sources: first, church officers were added to meet arising emergencies, as for example in Acts 6:1-5; second, the possession of spiritual gifts singled out certain individuals for the work of the ministry.

The first churches were democratic in government—a circumstance natural in a community where the gift of the Spirit was available to all and where any and all could be divinely endowed with gifts for a special ministry. It is true that the apostles and elders presided at business meetings and at the appointing of officers; but these things were done in cooperation with the congregation. Acts 6:3-6; 15:22; 1 Cor. 16:3; 2 Cor. 8:19; Phil. 2:25.

From Acts 14:23 and Tit. 1:5 it might seem that Paul and Barnabas and Titus appointed elders without consulting the congregation; but reliable church historians state that they "appointed" them in the usual way, by the vote of the members of the church concerned.

We see plainly that there is no warrant in the New Testament for the merging of the churches into an ecclesiastical machine governed by a hierarchy.

In the early days there was no centralized government of the whole church. Each local church was self-governing and managed its own affairs in freedom. Naturally the "Twelve" were regarded with deference because of their relation to Christ and they exercised a certain authority.

See Acts 15. Paul kept general oversight over the Gentile churches; however this authority was purely spiritual, and not an official authority such as that granted by an organization.

While each local church was independent of the other as far as jurisdiction was concerned, the New Testament churches did enter into cooperative relationships with one another. Rom. 15:26, 27; 2 Cor. 8:19; Gal. 2:10; Rom. 15:1; 3 John 8.

In the early centuries the local churches, while they never lacked the sense that they all belonged to one body, were independent, self-governing communities, preserving relations with each other, not by any political organization embracing them all, but by fraternal fellowship through visits of deputies, interchange of letters, and some indefinite giving and receiving assistance in the election and setting apart of pastors.

2. The Ministry of the Church.

Two kinds of ministry are recognized in the New Testament: (1) The general and prophetic ministry—general because exercised in relation to the churches in general rather than to one church in particular, and prophetic in that it was created by the possession of spiritual gifts. (2) The local and practical ministry—local because confined to one church, and practical because dealing with the administration of the church.

(a) The General and Prophetic Ministry.

1. Apostles. These were men who received their commission from the living Christ Himself (Matt. 10:5; Gal. 1:1), who had seen Christ after His resurrection (Acts 1:22; 1 Cor. 9:1), enjoyed a special inspiration (Gal. 1:11, 12; 1 Thess. 2:13), exercised administrative power over the churches (1 Cor. 5:3-6; 2 Cor. 10:8; John 20:22, 23), carried supernatural credentials (2 Cor. 12:12) and whose chief work was the establishing of churches in new fields. 2 Cor. 10:16. They were Christ-

called, Spirit-filled, church executives and missionary organizers. The twelve apostles of Jesus and Paul (who stood in a class by himself) were the apostles by pre-eminence, but the title was also given to others who engaged in missionary work. The word "apostle" itself simply means "missionary." Acts 14:14; Rom. 16:7. Have there been apostles since? The relationship of the Twelve to Christ was a unique one which none have occupied since. However the work of such men as John Wesley may be justly described as apostolic.

2. Prophets were those endowed with the gift of inspired utterance. From the earliest time down to the close of the second century an uninterrupted stream of prophets and prophetesses appeared in the Christian churches. While the apostle and evangelist carried his message to the unbelieving (Gal. 2:7, 8), the prophet's ministry was particularly to Christians. Prophets traveled from church to church much as evangelists do today, although every church had prophets who were regular members of the church.

3. Teachers were those gifted in the exposition of the Word. Like the prophets many of them traveled from church to church.

2. The Local and Practical Ministry.

The local ministry which was appointed by the church, on the basis of certain qualifications (1 Tim. 3) included—

1. Presbyters, or elders, to whom was given also the title "bishop," meaning overseer, or superintendent. These had general oversight of the local assembly, especially in relation to pastoral care and discipline. Their duties were chiefly of a spiritual nature. They are sometimes called "pastors" or "shepherds" Eph. 4:11, compare Acts 20:28.

During the first century every Christian community was governed by a group of elders or bishops, so that there was no one officer doing for the church what a modern pastor does. At the beginning of the third century one man was placed at the head of each community with the title of pastor or bishop.

2. Associated with the presbyters were a number of assistant rulers called deacons (Acts 6:1-4; 1 Tim. 3:8-13; Phil. 1:1) and deaconesses (Rom. 16:1; Phil. 4:3), whose work appears to have been largely house-to-house visitation and practical ministry to the poor and needy. 1 Tim. 5:8-11. The deacons also assisted the elders in the celebration of the Lord's Supper.

11

THE LAST THINGS

"Thus saith the Lord, . . . I am the first, and I am the last." Isa. 44:6. God has written both the first and the last chapter in the history of all things. In the book of Genesis we read of the beginnings of all things—the universe, life, man, sin, death, society. In the prophetic Scriptures, climaxed by the Revelation, we learn how all things will find their goal and consummation. Many, like Daniel, ask, "What shall be the end of these things?" Dan. 12:8. Only God can answer that question, and He has done so in the Scriptures.

OUTLINE

I. DEATH.

II. THE INTERMEDIATE STATE.
1. The Scriptural View.
2. False Views.
   a. Purgatory. b. Spiritism. c. Soul-Sleeping.

III. THE RESURRECTION.
1. The Importance of the Resurrection.
2. The Nature of the Resurrection. The resurrection body will be characterized by:
   a. Relationship. b. Reality. c. Incorruption. d. Glory. e. Agility. f. Subtlety.

IV. THE FUTURE LIFE.
1. Old Testament Teaching.
2. New Testament Teaching.

V. THE DESTINY OF THE RIGHTEOUS.
1. The Nature of Heaven.
2. The Necessity for Heaven.
3. The Blessings of Heaven.
   a. Light and beauty. b. Fullness of knowledge. c. Rest. d. Service. e. Joy. f. Stability. g. Social joys. h. Fellowship with Christ.

VI. THE DESTINY OF THE WICKED.
1. The Scriptural View.
2. False Views.
   a. Universalism.
   b. Restorationism.
   c. Second probationism.
   d. Annihilationism.

VII. THE SECOND COMING OF CHRIST.
1. The Fact of His Coming.
2. The Manner of His Coming.
3. The Time of His Coming.
4. The Signs of His Coming.
5. The Purpose of His Coming.
   a. In relation to the church.
   b. In relation to Israel.
   c. In relation to Antichrist.
   d. In relation to the nations.

I. DEATH.

Death is the separation of soul and body and the introduction of man to the unseen world. It is described as sleep (John 11:11; Deut. 31:16), the earthly house of this tabernacle being dissolved (2 Cor. 5:1), putting off this tabernacle (2 Peter 1:14), God requiring the soul (Luke 12:20), going the way whence there is no return (Job 16:22), being gathered to one's people (Gen. 49:33), going down into silence (Psalm 115:17), yielding up the ghost (Acts 5:10), returning to the dust (Gen. 3:19), being cut down (Job 14:2), departing. Phil. 1:23.

Death is the first outward and visible effect or manifestation of sin, and it will be the last effect of sin from which we shall be saved. Rom. 5:12; 1 Cor. 15:26. The Saviour has abolished death and brought life and immortality ("incorruption") to light through the gospel. 2 Tim. 1:10. The word "abolish" means to annul, or make negative. Death is made void as a sentence of condemnation, and life is offered to all. Meanwhile, though death continues, it becomes a door to life in the case of those who accept Christ.

How is death connected with the doctrine of immortality? There are two terms, "immortality" and "incorruption," which are both used with reference to the resurrection of the body. 1 Cor. 15:53, 54. Immortality means not subject to death, and in the Scriptures it is applied to the **body** and not to the soul (although the immortality of the soul is implied). Even Christians are mortal because their bodies are subject to death. After the resurrection and the rapture they will attain to immortality; that is, they will have glorified bodies not subject to death.

The wicked, too, have a resurrection; but does this mean that they have immortality? No; their entire condition is one of death, separation from

God. They have existence, but not the fellowship with God and the glorification of the body which constitute real immortality. They exist consciously in a condition of subjection to death. Theirs is not "the resurrection of life" but the "resurrection of damnation." John 5:29.

If "immortality" in the Scriptures applies to the body, what justification is there for speaking of the immortality of the **soul?** In both Old and New Testaments death is the separation of body and soul; the body dies and goes to the dust, the soul or spirit continues to exist consciously in the unseen world of spirits. Thus man is mortal, his body being subject to death, yet his soul is immortal, surviving the death of the body.

What is the distinction between immortality and eternal life? Immortality is **future** (Rom. 2:7; 1 Cor. 15:53, 54), and refers to the glorification of our mortal bodies at the resurrection. Eternal life concerns mainly man's spirit, is a **present** possession, and is unaffected by the death of the body.

Eternal life will reach its perfection at the coming of Christ, and will be lived in a glorified, deathless body. All Christians, both living and deceased, already have eternal life, but will not have immortality until the resurrection.

II. THE INTERMEDIATE STATE.

By the intermediate state we mean the state of the dead between death and the resurrection.

1. The Scriptural View.

It should be carefully noted that the righteous do not enter into their final reward, nor the wicked into their final punishment, until after their respective resurrections. Both classes are in an intermediate state, awaiting that event. Departed Christians go to be "with the Lord," but do not receive their **final reward.**

The intermediate state of the righteous is one of rest (Rev. 14:13), waiting (Rev. 6:10, 11), activity (Rev. 7:15), and holiness. Rev. 7:14. The wicked, too, pass into an intermediate state, where they await their final punishment, which takes place after the White Throne judgment, when Death and Hades are emptied (literal translation) into the lake of fire. Rev. 20:14.

2. False Views.

(a) Purgatory. The Roman Catholic church teaches that even the faithful need a process of purification before becoming fit to enter God's presence. This view is held by certain Protestants, who, believing in "once in grace always in grace," and yet knowing that "without holiness no man shall see God," have concluded that there is a "purgatory" where carnal and imperfect Christians are purged of their dross. This process they say will take place during the Millennium while the overcomers are reigning with Christ. However, there is no evidence for this view in Scripture, and there is much against it.

Writes John S. Banks, a Methodist scholar:

Scripture speaks of the immediate happiness of the dead in Christ. Luke 16:22; 23:43; 2 Cor. 5:6, 8. Surely ordinary Christians after a long time of growth in grace are as fit for heaven as the penitent thief or as Lazarus in the parable. Besides, unlimited efficacy is ascribed in the Scriptures to the blood of Christ. If, indeed, the existence of such a middle state were taught in the Scripture, we might say that its cleansing power is derived from the atonement, as we say of the means of grace in the present state; but when no such doctrine is taught, we can only regard the state as a work of supererogation (more than required, extra). It undertakes to do what there is already ample provision for.

The New Testament knows of but two classes, the saved and the unsaved. The destiny of each class is determined in this life, which is the only probationary period mentioned. Death closes the period of probation, and then follows judgment according to the deeds done **in the body.** Heb. 9:27; 2 Cor. 5:10.

(b) Spiritism teaches that we may communicate with departed spirits, these communications being mediated through a "medium." But note: (1) The Bible expressly forbids consulting such spiritists, the very prohibition indicating that there is evil and danger in the practice. Lev. 19:31; 20:6,7; Isa. 8:19. It is vain for spiritists to quote the example of Saul, because that unfortunate man perished for consulting a witch. 1 Chron. 10:13. (2) The dead are under the control of God, the Lord of life and death, and cannot therefore be subject to mediums. See for example Rev. 1:18; Rom 14:9. Spiritists cite the case of the witch bringing up Samuel and the account of the appearing of Moses and Elijah at the Transfiguration. But even **if** Samuel did actually appear to Saul, it was by Divine permission, and the same can be said of Moses and Elijah. The account of the rich man and Lazarus proves that the departed are not permitted to communicate with the living. Luke 16. (3) Though much of the phenomena of spiritism has been proved to be deception, there is some reality to it. Since the departed are under God's control and cannot communicate with the living, we must conclude that spiritistic manifestations are due to the operations of strange psychic forces, of which we are ignorant, or that the messages originate from lying and seducing spirits. 1 Kings 22:22; 1 Tim. 4:1.

Many people who embrace spiritism or consult mediums are those who have cast off faith in Christianity. Those who believe the Scriptures have sufficient light to illuminate that mysterious land beyond the grave.

(c) Soul-sleeping. Some groups, such as the Seventh-day Adventists, believe that the soul exists in an unconscious state until the resurrection. This belief, known as "soul-sleeping," is shared by individuals in other groups. It is true that the Bible describes death as a sleep, but that is because the believer loses consciousness of a world of weariness and sufferings and awakes to a realm of peace and bliss. The Old Testament teaches that while the body enters the grave, the departed spirit enters Sheol (translated "hell" in our version), where it lives a conscious existence. Compare Isa. 14:9-11; Psalm 16:10; Luke 16:23; 23:43; 2 Cor. 5:8; Phil. 1:23; Rev. 6:9.

III. THE RESURRECTION.

1. The Importance of the Resurrection.

The Corinthians, like other Greeks, were people of keen, restless minds, fond of philosophic speculation. That some of the members of the Corinthian church partook of that spirit will be seen from a reading of the first two chapters of the epistle, where Paul declares the immeasurable superiority of Divine revelation over human speculation. With keen insight he foresaw that under the influence of the Greek spirit the gospel might evaporate into a beautiful but powerless system of philosophy and ethics. In fact, that tendency was already apparent. Some of the members of the church were influenced by an old Greek doctrine of immortality which taught that at death the body perished forever but that the soul continued to live. Indeed, so ran this teaching, it was good that the body perish for it was a clog and hindrance to the soul. It was being taught in the Corinthian assembly that, while soul or spirit lived after death, the body was gone forever and would know no resurrection; that the only resurrection was the spiritual resurrection of the soul from its death in trespasses and sins. See Eph. 2:1; compare 2 Tim. 2:17, 18. The apostle challenges the truth of the teaching. "Now if Christ be preached that he rose from the dead, how say some among you that there is no resurrection of the dead?" 1 Cor. 15:12. Taking this error as the starting point, Paul expounds the true doctrine and gives us the great Resurrection chapter of the Bible, 1 Corinthians 15.

As a basis for his argument Paul takes the Biblical doctrine of man, which in contradiction to the pagan doctrine, declares that the body is sanctifiable (1 Cor. 6:13-20), redeemable, and included in man's salvation. In the beginning God created man both spirit and body, and when spirit and body came together as a living unit, man became "a living soul." Man was created immortal in the sense that he need not die, but mortal in the sense that he could die if he disobeyed God. Had man continued faithful, he would have developed to the fullest extent possible on earth and then might have been translated, for translation seems to be God's perfect way of taking human beings from the earth. But man sinned, lost the right to the tree of life, and as a result began to die, the process culminating in the separation of spirit and body. And the physical death was the outward expression of that spiritual death which is the consequence of sin.

Since man is both soul and body, redemption must include the quickening of both soul and body; hence the need of resurrection. And while man may become right with God and live spiritually (Eph. 2:1), yet his body dies as a result of his racial inheritance from Adam. But since the body is inherently part of his personality, his salvation and his immortality are not complete until the body is raised and glorified. Such is the teaching of the New Testament. See Rom. 13:11; 1 Cor. 15:53, 54; Phil. 3:20, 21.

Paul's argument in verses 13-19 is as follows: To teach that there is no resurrection of the body is to strike a blow at the reality of salvation and the hope of immortality. He develops his argument as follows: If there is no resurrection of the body, then Christ, who took a human body, did not rise from the dead. If Christ did not rise from the dead then Paul's preaching is empty talk; worse, it is false and misleading. And if the preaching is vain, so also is the faith and hope of those who accept it. If Christ did not actually rise from the dead, then there is no salvation for sin; for how do we know that His death was an atoning one—different from ordinary death—unless He rose from the dead? And if the body of the Master did not rise, what hope is there for those who trust in Him? And if all this be true, then sacrifice, self-denial, and suffering for the sake of Christ have been in vain. Verses 19, 30-32.

2. The Nature of the Resurrection.

It is easy enough to state the **fact** of the resurrection, but when we attempt to explain the **how** of the matter we find ourselves in deep waters, because we are dealing with mysterious supernatural laws beyond the grasp of our minds. We do know, however, that the resurrection of the body will be characterized by—

(a) Relationship. It will bear some relation to the old body—which fact Paul illustrates by the grain of wheat. 1 Cor. 15:36, 37. The grain is cast into the ground, dies, and the act of dissolution fertilizes the living germ within it, so that it develops into a beautiful new green plant. "Only by the dissolution of the material particles in the seed is the germ of life (which no microscope can detect) made to operate."

Who vitalizes the human body, making it capable of the glorious transformation into the **resurrection body? The Holy Spirit! See 1 Cor.**

6:19. Speaking of the resurrection, Paul utters the words in 2 Cor. 5:5, which one Greek scholar has translated as follows: "I am prepared for this change by God, who has given me the Spirit as its pledge and installment."

(b) Reality. There are certain people who have no desire to go to heaven because they have the idea that life there will be an unsubstantial, vague kind of existence. On the contrary, the life to come will be just as real as this present one—in fact, more so. Glorified bodies will be real and tangible, and we shall know each other, converse with one another, and engage freely in heavenly activities. Jesus in His resurrection body was real indeed to His disciples; though glorified, He was the very same Jesus.

(c) Incorruption. "Raised in incorruption and in power," the resurrection body will be free from sickness, pain, weakness, and death. Rev. 21:4.

(d) Glory. Our old bodies are perishable, subject to decay and weariness because they are "natural" ("soulish") bodies, fitted to an imperfect existence in a very imperfect world; but the resurrection body will be adapted to a glorious, immortal life in heaven. When Peter the Great of Russia worked as a mechanic in Holland in order to learn shipbuilding, he wore the humble garments of a mechanic; but on returning to his palace, he was clothed in the resplendent bejeweled robes of royalty. Man's spirit, originally inbreathed by God, now lives a humble existence in a perishable body (Phil. 3:21); but in the resurrection it will be clothed with a glorious body, fitting it to see God face to face.

(e) Agility. It will pass through space with lightning speed, due to the mighty energy quickening it.

(f) Subtlety, that is, the power of penetrating solid substances. In walking the earth in a glorified body we shall not be deterred by such a trifle as a wall or a mountain—we shall simply walk through it! Compare John 20:26.

There are many things we do not, and cannot yet, know about the future life; "it doth not yet appear what we shall be." However, this we do know: "Now are we the sons of God," and "when he shall appear, we shall be like him; for we shall see him as he is." 1 John 3:1, 2.

IV. THE FUTURE LIFE.

1. Old Testament Teaching.

In studying Old Testament teaching concerning the future life, it should be remembered that the redemptive work of Christ has exerted a mighty effect in relation to death and life. He "hath abolished death, and hath brought life and immortality to light through the gospel." 2 Tim. 1:10. Christ brought fullness of light and assurance concerning the life to come. He also effected a certain deliverance for Old Testament saints in the intermediate state, which resulted in an increase of blessedness for them.

But though the Old Testament revelation concerning life after death is not so full as that of the New Testament, the doctrine is undoubtedly taught.

The Old Testament doctrine of immortality is based on man's relation to God. Man, made in the image of God, is fitted for the knowledge of God, and for fellowship with Him. This implies that man is more than an animal; that he has a life which transcends time. He was created for life, not mortality. But sin brought death into the world and so frustrated man's destiny. Death in its physical aspect, is the separation of body and soul. Death, however, does not imply the extinction of the soul. The Old Testament consistently teaches that man's personality survives death.

Man's body was laid in the grave while the soul passed into Sheol (translated "hell," "the pit," "the grave"), the abode of departed spirits. That Sheol was not heaven is shown by the fact that it is described as being beneath (Prov. 15:24), downward (Ezek. 32:21), in the nether parts of the earth. Ezek. 32:18. That it was not a place of bliss is evident from its description as a place of thanklessness (Psalm 6:5), cruelty (S. of S. 8:6), place of pain (Job 24:19), place of sorrow (Psalm 18:5), a place from which none seemed to return. Job 7:9.

Sheol, unillumined by the radiance of the risen Christ, was a gloomy and forbidding place, and for this reason some of the Old Testament saints "shrank back from Sheol as a child shrinks from a darkened room." See for example Psalm 88 and Isaiah 38.

Sheol was inhabited by both the righteous (Job 14:13; Psalm 88:3; Gen. 37:34, 35) and the wicked. Prov. 5:3-5; 7:27; Job 24:19; Psalm 31:17. From the incident of the Rich Man and Lazarus we learn that there were two parts in Sheol—a place of suffering for the wicked (Luke 16:23, 24) and another part for the righteous, a place of rest and comfort. Luke 16:25.

However, Old Testament believers were not without hope. God's Holy One, the Messiah, would descend into Sheol; God's people would be redeemed from Sheol. Psalm 16:10; 49:15. This was fulfilled when Christ, after His death, descended into the world of departed spirits (Matt. 12:40; Luke 23:42, 43), and delivered the Old Testament saints from Sheol to the upper paradise. Eph. 4:9, 10, 8. This last scripture seems to indicate that a change took place in the world

of spirits, and that the place where the righteous
await their resurrection is now located in the
heavenlies. Eph. 4:8; 2 Cor. 12:2. Since then, the
spirits of the righteous go up to glory and the
spirits of the wicked go down to condemnation.
Rev. 20:13, 14.

Other evidences of the teaching of a future
life in the Old Testament are the following: (1)
The phrase "gathered to his fathers" or "people,"
used of Abraham, Moses, Aaron and David, must
refer to conscious existence after death and not
to burial, for these men were not buried in their
ancestral burying places. (2) The translations of
Enoch and Elijah prove certainly the existence
of a future life of bliss in the presence of God.
(3) Christ's words in Matt. 22:32 represent a very
a strong statement of Jewish belief. Otherwise
it would have had no force for the hearers. (4) The
doctrine of the resurrection from the dead is
plainly taught in the Old Testament. Job 19:26;
Dan. 12:1, 2. (5) When Jacob said, "I will go
down into the grave (literally, "Sheol") unto my
son mourning" (Gen. 37:35), he certainly could
not have meant the literal grave, because the body
of Joseph was supposed to have been devoured
by a wild beast.

2. The New Testament Teaching.

The New Testament recognizes a state beyond
death in which the spiritual life is continued under
new and better conditions. To enter into this
life is the highest aim of man. Mark 9:43. By having Christ Himself the believer has already in this
life made the transition from death to life. John
3:36. However, this is only the beginning; its
fullness belongs to another state of existence
which commences with the "resurrection of life."
John 5:29. There is a life to come (1 Tim. 4:8);
it is hidden now, but will be manifested when
Christ our life appears (Col. 3:4), who will award

the crown of life promised to those that love Him. James 1:12. Even the state of the dead members of Christ holds something better than the present life in Him. Phil. 1:21. But their fuller life, their land of Promise, their birthright as the sons of God, will be disclosed at His coming. Rom. 8:17; Gal. 4:7.

Physical death cannot interrupt the fellowship between the Christian and his Lord. "I am the resurrection, and the life: he that believeth in me, though he were dead, yet shall he live: and whosoever liveth and believeth in me shall never die." John 11:25, 26. With these words Jesus assured Martha and Mary that their brother had not really perished, but was safe. He as much as said: "I loved your brother and had sweet fellowship with him; realizing who I am, remembering My power, do you imagine for a moment that I will allow death to interrupt the fellowship which has been a delight to both of us?"

There are many formal arguments for immortality, but more reassuring than cold logic is the knowledge that we are in fellowship with God and His Christ. Here is a saint who for years has had delightful fellowship with the Son of God—has heard His voice and felt His presence. As he now lies upon his death bed shall the Son of God say to him, "We have walked together and held sweet converse, but now we must part and say an eternal farewell"? Unthinkable! Those who are "in Christ" (1 Thess. 4:14-17) cannot be separated from Him either by life or by death. Rom. 8:38. For one who has consciously lived in the presence of Christ, to be separated from Christ by death is impossible. For those bound by God's love to drop out of that love into nothingness or desolation is inconceivable.

Christ says to all believers: "Is Lazarus, is any one, joined to Me? Has he attached himself

trustfully to my Person? Then whatever I am,
whatever power is in Me, will be operative in his
life. Your brother is joined to Me by confidence
and affection; and since I am the Resurrection and
the Life, that power must operate in him."

V. THE DESTINY OF THE RIGHTEOUS.

1. The Nature of Heaven.

The righteous are destined to eternal life in
the presence of God. God created man to know,
love, and serve Him in this present world and to
enjoy Him forever in the world to come.

The Christian during his earthly life, experiences by faith the presence of the invisible
God, but in the life to come this experience of
faith will become an actual reality. He will see
God face to face—a blessing described by some
theologians as the Beatific Vision.

Heaven is described by various names: (1)
Paradise (literally, a garden), reminding us of the
happiness and blessedness of our first parents
as they walked and talked with the Lord God.
Rev. 2:7; 2 Cor. 12:4. (2) "Father's house," with
its many mansions (John 14:2), conveying the
thought of home, rest and fellowship. (3) A
heavenly country to which we are traveling as
Israel of old traveled to Canaan, the earthly Promised Land. Heb. 11:13-16. (4) A city, suggesting
the idea of an organized society. Heb. 11:10;
Rev. 21:2.

The following three phases in the condition
of the departed Christians should be distinguished:
first, there is the intermediate state of rest while
awaiting the resurrection; second, after the resurrection follows judgment for works (2 Cor. 5:10;
1 Cor. 3:10-15); third, at the close of the Millennium there descends from heaven the New Jerusalem, the final home of the blessed. Rev. 21. The
New Jerusalem comes down from heaven, is a part

of heaven, and is therefore heaven in a real sense. Wherever God reveals Himself in personal presence and unveiled glory is heaven; and such is true of the New Jerusalem. Rev. 22:3, 4.

Why does this city come down out of heaven? God's ultimate purpose is to bring heaven to earth. Compare Deut. 11:21. In the dispensation of the fullness of time He will "gather together in one all things in Christ, both which are in heaven, and which are on earth" (Eph. 1:10), and then God shall be "all in all." 1 Cor. 15:28. While the New Jerusalem will not actually descend to earth, yet it will be within sight of earth, for the "nations of them which are saved shall walk in the light of it."

2. The Necessity for Heaven.

The history of religions discloses the fact that the human soul instinctively believes that there is such a place. This instinct for heaven has been implanted within the soul of man by God Himself, the Creator of human instincts. Arguments proving the existence of a future life are not formulated primarily that men may believe in it, but because of the fact that they do believe in it, and are desirous of bringing the mind into subjection to the deepest intuitions of the heart.

Then, too, such a place is essential to fulfill the demands of justice. The sufferings of the righteous upon earth and the prosperity of the wicked demand a future state where full justice is done. And the Bible teaches that such a place does exist. Plato, the wisest of the Greeks, discussed the future life as a probability, and advised men to gather the best opinions on the subject, and embark upon them as a raft, and sail perilously through life, "unless one could more securely and less perilously sail on a stronger vessel or some Divine word." The Divine word of

certainty which wise men have desired is found
in the Scriptures, where the existence of a future
life is taught, not as an opinion or theory, but as
an absolute fact.

3. The Blessings or Heaven.

(a) Light and Beauty. Rev. 21:23; 22:5.
Human language at its best is inadequate to por-
tray the realities of the life to come. In Revelation 21 and 22 the Spirit employs language which
helps us to gain a slight conception of the beauties
of the other world.

A mole burrowing in the ground cannot imagine the
life of an eagle soaring above the mountain tops; a miner,
if there be any such, born, living, working and dying a
thousand feet below the surface of the earth is only bewildered if you expatiate to him upon green trees, flowers
in the meadows, running brooks, orchards, mountain peaks,
and starlit sky; he knows not what you say, for his eye
hath not seen, his ear hath not heard, and it hath not
entered his mind to conceive it.

(b) Fullness of Knowledge. 1 Cor. 13:12. The
sentiment expressed by the wise Socrates when
he said, "One thing I know and that is that I
know nothing," has been echoed by wise men ever
since. Man is surrounded by mystery and hungers
for knowledge. In heaven this thirst for knowledge will be perfectly satisfied; the mysteries of
the universe will be made plain; perplexing theological problems will shine as clear as day. The
brightest kind of knowledge shall then be ours—
the knowledge of God.

(c) Rest. Rev. 14:13; 21:4. A conception of
heaven may be formed by contrasting it with the
disadvantages of this present life. Think of all in
this world that makes for weariness, pain, strife
and grief, and consider that heaven is a place
where such may not enter.

(d) Service. There are people of active life who are apparently uninterested in heaven because they conceive it as a place of inactivity, where ethereal figures spend their time strumming harps. However, this is a misconception. The redeemed will indeed play on harps, for music will be one of the joys of heaven. But there will be work to be done as well. They "serve him day and night in his temple. . . . And his servants shall serve him." Rev. 7:15; 22:3. He who placed man in the first paradise with instructions to keep and dress it will certainly not leave him inactive in the second paradise.

(e) Joy. Rev. 21:4. The greatest conceivable earthly happiness, increased a millionfold but feebly expresses the enjoyment awaiting God's children in the realm of the blessed. If a powerful king, with limited means wished to build a palace for his bride, it would be everything that art, skill and resources could provide. God loves His children infinitely more than could any human lover. Having exhaustless resources and infinite skill, He can build a home whose beauty is beyond the power or knowledge of human art or imagination. "I go to prepare a place for you."

(f) Stability. Heaven's happiness will be forever. Indeed, permanence is necessary to complete happiness. Regardless of the wonderful beauty and blessedness of heaven, the realization that it would come to an end would cause its joy to lose its perfection. For the mind would be continually weighed down by the knowledge that the end was inevitable, and such a frame of mind would prove a constant bar to perfect enjoyment. Everyone craves permanence—permanent health, permanent peace, permanent prosperity. Instability and insecurity are feared by all. But the happiness of heaven carries with it the Divine assurance that its joy will never end or diminish in intensity.

(g) Social joys. Heb. 12:22, 23; 1 Thess. 4:13-18. Man is by nature a social being. A solitary man is abnormal and exceptional. If in this life social joys afford pleasure, how great must be the rapture of companionship in heaven with those whom we love! In human relationships even those dearest to us have faults or objectionable traits which detract from their attractiveness. In heaven friends and relatives will be faultless. Social joys in this present life are accompanied by disappointments. Loved ones often become a cause of sorrow to us, friendships are broken, affections are blighted. But in heaven there will be no misunderstandings, no strife—everyone will be good and beautiful, without shadow or defect, filled with heavenly wisdom and resplendent with a heavenly personality.

(h) Fellowship with Christ. John 14:3; 2 Cor. 5:8; Phil. 1:23. "Whom having not seen, ye love; in whom, though now ye see him not, yet believing, ye rejoice with joy unspeakable and full of glory." 1 Peter 1:8. In that day we shall be like Him, for we shall see Him as He is; our bodies will be fashioned like unto His glorious body; we shall see His face; and He who shepherded His people through the vale of tears, will in heaven lead them from joy to joy, from glory to glory, from revelation to revelation.

VI. THE DESTINY OF THE WICKED.

1. The Scriptural View.

The destiny of the wicked is eternal separation from God, and that eternal suffering of His wrath, known as the second death. Because of its terrible nature, it is a subject from which one naturally shrinks; yet it is one which must be faced, because it is a positive truth of Divine revelation. Hence the Christ of gentleness and love warned men against the sufferings of hell.

What He said concerning the hope of heaven might well be applied to His teaching in regard to the existence of hell—"If it were not so, I would have told you." John 14:2.

Hell is a place of: extreme suffering (Rev. 20:10), memory and remorse (Luke 16:19-31), unsatisfied desire (Luke 16:24), contempt (Dan. 12:2), vile companionship (Rev. 21:8), hopelessness. Prov. 11:7; Matt. 25:41.

2. False Views.

(a) Universalism teaches that everybody will finally be saved. That God is too loving to exclude anyone from heaven seems to be their argument. The theory is disputed by such scriptures as Rom. 6:23; Luke 16:19-31; John 3:36 and others. It is, in reality, a mercy that God excludes the sinful from heaven for a defiled sinner would be just as miserable in heaven as a saint of God would be in hell.

(b) Restorationism teaches that punishment in hell is not eternal, but a temporary experience for the purpose of purifying the sinner to fit him for heaven. If this were the case the fires of hell would have more power than the blood of Christ. Besides, experience teaches that punishment in itself is not regenerative; it can restrain but cannot transform.

Teachers of this school contend that the word "eternal" in the Greek means "age-long" and not endless duration. But according to Matt. 25:41, if the punishment of the wicked has an end, so has the bliss of the righteous. Comments Dr. Maclaren:

Reverently accepting Christ's words as those of perfect love and infallible wisdom, the present writer . . . dreads lest, in the eagerness of discussing the duration the solemn fact of the reality of future retribution should be dimmed and men should argue about the "terror of the Lord" till they cease to feel about it.

Habit tends to fixedness. Character tends to final permanence. God will no more force a man to be saved in the future than He does in the present.

(c) **Second Probationism** holds that all will have a second chance, or opportunity, to accept salvation between death and the resurrection. The Scriptures, however, teach that at death man's destiny is fixed. Heb. 9:27. Moreover, if people think that they will have a second chance, how many will accept the first chance? And if they neglect the first chance, according to the laws of human nature, they will be weaker to accept the second.

(d) **Annihilationism** teaches that God will annihilate the wicked. Annihilationists point to 2 Thess. 1:9 and other passages which state that the wicked shall be destroyed. However, in Scriptural usage the word does not mean annihilation but ruin. And if the word "destruction" in this verse really means annihilation, then the word "eternal" would be superfluous, for annihilation would be forever.

They cite also scriptures which set forth death as the penalty of sin. But in these cases the reference is to spiritual not physical death, and spiritual death means separation from God. God's promise of life to the obedient does not mean the gift of existence—for all men already have that. And if life as a reward does not mean the gift of bare existence then death as a penalty does not mean the mere loss of existence.

VII. THE SECOND COMING OF CHRIST.
1. The Fact of His Coming.

The second coming is mentioned more than 300 times in the New Testament. Paul refers to it in his Epistles at least fifty times. It is claimed that the Second Coming is mentioned eight times as often as the first coming. Whole books (1 and 2 Thessalonians) and chapters (Matthew 24; Mark 13) are devoted to it. It is without doubt one of the most important doctrines of the New Testament.

2. The Manner of His Coming.

It will be personal (John 14:3; Acts 1:10, 11; 1 Thess. 4:16; Rev. 1:7; 22:7), literal (Acts 1:10; 1 Thess. 4:16, 17; Rev. 1:7; Zech. 14:4), visible (Heb. 9:28; Phil. 3:20; Zech. 12:10) and glorious. Matt. 16:27; 2 Thess. 1:7-9; Col. 3:4; Matt. 25:31.

Interpretations are held which seek to avoid the literal and personal view of Christ's coming. Some teach that death is the second coming of Christ. But the Second Coming is set forth as the opposite of death, for the dead in Christ shall rise when Christ comes again. At death we go to Him, but at the coming He comes for us. Certain verses (Matt. 16:28; Phil. 3:20) become meaningless if we substitute death for second coming. Finally, death is an enemy, while the Second Coming is a glorious hope.

Some hold that the second coming was the descent of the Spirit on the day of Pentecost. Others teach that Christ came at the destruction of Jerusalem in A. D. 70, but in each case there did not occur the resurrection of the dead, the rapture of the living, and other events which are to accompany the second Advent.

3. The Time of His Coming.

Attempts have been made to calculate the time of Christ's coming, but each time the Lord has failed to keep the appointment! He has declared that the exact time of His coming is hidden in the counsels of God. Matt. 24:36-42; Mark 13:21, 22. The arrangement is wise. Who would care, for instance, to know in advance the exact time of his death? Such knowledge would tend to disturb and unfit a person for the duties of life. It is sufficient to know that death may come at any time and therefore one must work while it is day "for the night cometh when no man can work." And the same reasoning may be applied to the "death day" of this present age. That day has not been revealed to us. But we know that it will be sudden (1 Cor. 15:52; Matt. 24:27) and unexpected. 2 Peter 3:4; Matt. 24:48-51; Rev. 16:15. The Lord's word for His waiting servants is— "Occupy till I come."

The following is a general view of Christ's teaching relative to the time of His coming: After the destruction of Jerusalem the Jews shall be wanderers among all nations, driven from their land which shall come under Gentile control until the end of the age, when God shall judge the Gentile nations. Luke 21:24. During this period Christ's servants will carry on His work (Luke 19:11-27) by preaching the gospel to all nations. Matt. 24:14. It will be a time of delay when the church will sometimes wonder why the Lord does not appear (Luke 18:1-8)— when some will prepare themselves and others will be negligent, while the Bridegroom tarries (Matt. 25:1-11)—when unfaithful ministers will fall away, saying within themselves, "My Lord delayeth his coming." Luke 12:45. "After a long time (Matt. 25:19, "at midnight" (Matt. 25:6), at a time the day and the hour of which not one of His disciples knows (Matt. 24:36, 42, 50), the Lord will appear suddenly to gather His servants and to judge them according to their works. Matt. 25:19 and 2 Cor. 5:10. Later, after the gospel has been universally preached and wilfully rejected—when the people of the world shall be living in utter oblivion of the coming catastrophe, as in the days of Noah (Matt. 24:37-39) and as in the days of the destruction of Sodom (Luke 17:28, 29)—the Son of man will appear in outward glory and power to judge and rule over all the nations of the world. Matt. 25:31-46.

4. The Signs of His Coming.

The Scriptures teach that the appearing of Christ ushering in the Millennial Age will be preceded by a troublous transition (crossing over) period characterized by physical disturbances, wars, economic difficulties, moral declension, religious apostasy, infidelity, and general panic and perplexity. The latter part of this transition period is known as the "Great Tribulation," a period during which the entire world shall be under the sway of an Anti-God and Anti-Christian government. Believers in God will be brutally persecuted, and the Jewish nation in particular will pass through the furnace of affliction.

5. The Purpose of His Coming.

(a) In Relation to the Church. Writes Dr. Pardington:

Just as the first coming of the Lord extended over a period of thirty years, so the second coming includes different events. At the first coming He was revealed as a Babe in Bethlehem, later as the Lamb of God at His baptism, and as the Redeemer at Calvary. At the Second Coming, He will first appear to His own secretly and suddenly to catch them away to be present at the Marriage Supper of the Lamb. Matt. 24:40 41.

The appearance is called the Rapture, or the Parousia (Greek for "appearing" or "presence" or "arrival"). At this time believers will be judged to determine rewards for service. Matt 25:14-30.

After the Rapture, follows a period of terrible tribulation ending in the revelation, or open manifestation of Christ from heaven for the purpose of establishing the Messianic kingdom on earth.

(b) In Relation to Israel. He who is the Head and Saviour of the Church, the heavenly people, is also the promised Messiah of Israel, the earthly people. As Messiah He will deliver them from tribulation, gather them from the four corners of the earth, restore them to their ancient land and rule over them as their long promised King of the House of David.

(c) In Relation to the Antichrist. The spirit of Antichrist is already in the world (1 John 4:3; 2:18; 2:22), but there is a final Antichrist who is yet to come. 2 Thess. 2:3. In the last days he will arise from the old world (Rev. 13:1) and become ruler over a resurrected Roman empire achieving world dominion. He will assume great power politically (Dan. 7:8, 25), commercially (Dan. 8:25; Rev. 13:16, 17), and religiously. Rev. 17:1-15. He will be anti-God and anti-Christ, and will persecute all believers in an attempt to completely destroy Christianity. Dan. 7:25; 8:24; Rev. 13: 7, 15. Knowing that man must have a religion of some kind, he will establish one based on the divinity of man and the supremacy of the State. As the embodiment of the State, he will demand worship, and will appoint a priesthood to enforce and foster this worship. 2 Thess. 2:9, 10; Rev. 13:12-15.

Antichrist will carry to its extreme the doctrine of the supremacy of the State—which teaches that the government is the supreme power to which everything—even man's conscience—must be subordinated. Since there is no higher power or law than that of the State, God and His law must be abolished and the State worshiped.

The first attempt to establish State-worship is recorded in Daniel 3. Nebuchadnezzar was proud of the mighty empire he had built. "Is not this great Babylon that I have built?" Dan. 4:30. So dazzled was he by human might and governmental power that the State became as a god in his eyes. What better way of impressing men with its glory than by commanding that its symbol be venerated! He therefore set up a great golden image and commanded all people to bow before it under penalty of death. The image was not of any local deity but represented the State itself. To refuse worship was considered atheism or treason. In instituting this new devotion Nebuchadnezzar as much as said to the people: "Who gives you beautiful cities, good roads, magnificent gardens? The State! Who sees that you are fed and given work, who builds your schools and supports your temples? The State! Who defends you when enemies attack? The State! Is not, then the State a mighty power, yea, even a god? Indeed, what greater god do you need, other than your exalted government? Bow before the symbol of the great Babylon!" And if God had not cast him down from his blasphemous pride (Dan. 4:28-37) Nebuchadnezzar might have claimed worship as the head of the State.

As the three Hebrew Children (Daniel 3) were persecuted for refusing to bow before Nebuchadnezzar's image, so the Christians of the first century suffered because of their refusal to render Divine honors to Caesar's image. There was tolerance for all religions in the Roman empire, but on condition that Caesar's image be venerated as the symbol of the State. The Christians were persecuted not primarily because thy acknowledged Jesus Christ but because they refused to worship Caesar and say, "Caesar is Lord." They would not worship the State as god.

The French Revolution offers another example of this policy. God and Christ were cast out and a god, or goddess, was made of "La Patrie" (the State). Said one of the leaders: "The State is supreme in all things. When the State has spoken, the Church has nothing to say." Loyalty to the State was elevated to the place of a religion. The legislature decreed the erection in all villages of altars inscribed with the words, "The citizen is born, lives and dies for 'La Patrie.'" There was prepared a ritual for civic baptism, civic marriage, and civic burial. The religion of the State had its hymns and prayers, fasts and festivals.

The New Testament regards human government as divinely ordained for the maintenance of order and justice. The Christian therefore owes loyalty to his country. Both Church and State have a part in God's program, and each is to work in its own sphere. God is to receive the things that are God's, and Cæsar is to receive the things that are Cæsar's.

But very often Cæsar has demanded the things that are God's, with the result that the Church has, against her desire, found herself in conflict with the government.

The Scriptures predict that this conflict will one day reach its culmination. The last civilization will be anti-God, and Antichrist its head, the world-dictator, will make the law of the world-State supreme above every law, and will claim worship as the embodiment of the State. The same Scriptures assure us that God will triumph and that upon the ruins of the anti-Christian world-empire He will establish a rule where God is supreme—the Kingdom of God. Dan. 2:34, 35, 44; Rev. 11:15; 19:11-21.

(d) **In Relation to the Nations.** The nations will be judged, the kingdoms of earth overthrown, and all peoples will be subject to the King of kings. Dan. 2:44; Mic. 4:1; Isa. 49:22, 23; Jer. 23:5; Luke 1:32; Zech. 14:9; Isa. 24:23; Rev. 11:15. Christ will rule the nations with a rod of iron, sweep all oppression and injustice from the earth,

394 KNOWING THE DOCTRINES OF THE BIBLE

and usher in the Golden Age of a thousand years. Psa. 2:7-9; Psa. 72; Isa. 11:1-9; Rev. 20:6.

"Then cometh the end, when he shall have delivered up the kingdom to God, even the Father." 1 Cor. 15:24. There are three stages to Christ's work as Mediator: His work as Prophet, accomplished during His earthly ministry; His work as Priest begun at the cross and continued during this age; His work as King beginning at His coming and continuing throughout the Millennium. After the Millennium He shall have completed His work of uniting mankind to God, so that the inhabitants of heaven and earth shall form one great family where God shall be all and in all. Eph. 1:10; 3:14, 15. However, Christ will still reign as the God-man, and share in the Divine Government, for "of his kingdom there shall be no end." Luke 1:33.

Index of Subjects